SAVE YOUR DRAMA FOR YOUR MAMA

CHARLIE SHEPPARD

Charlie Sheppard
www.charliesheppard.com
www.sheppardpartners.com

aChoice Publishing
www.achoice.com

Printed in the United States of America

First Printing: March 2013

ISBN-978-0-9881720-0-5

More Praise for
Save Your Drama For Your Mama

"This book should be part of Leadership 101 at every company and organization…the health of our entire nation would substantially improve. I choose Drama free."

Shawn Tomasello, VP and General Manager, Celgene Corporation

"This book is not just for leaders. Anyone from any part of your organization will benefit from the clear concepts and the clear choices presented in Sheppard's book. I highly recommend."

David Dibble, Executive Vice President, Yahoo!

"Charlie Sheppard shows very clearly the power that we all possess to lead and inspire others and to make positive and constructive change. He very eloquently demonstrates that it all comes down to one simple, personal choice."

Steve Reid, COO, Goldcorp Inc.

"This is a genuinely significant book for anyone who works in a team environment, whether at work, in the community, at home, etc. Of all the business books I have read on leadership, this one stands at the top of the pack. The strength of this book lies in the fact that it gets at the heart of the behaviors that disrupt and erode company culture. The principles presented in Save Your Drama for Your Mama are solid and will get real results in creating a leadership culture."

Kara Goldin, CEO, Hint Water

"Sheppard is bursting with wisdom, and that means all 360+ pages are overflowing with great ideas for how to run a company. It's refreshing for an author to just come right out and say it, and what he has to say is both brilliant and practical. The book teaches the three roles of leadership in great detail and in a way that is usable in your organization. Read the book as a group and get started making your company healthy."

Richard Carr, Vice Chairman of the Board, Vistage International

"Embracing the concepts that Charlie Sheppard teaches in this book—the destructiveness of drama, the importance of accountability, the power of positive intent, and that ultimately, leadership is a choice—has helped me immensely in my journey to become a better leader. Keep this book close and you will change your organization and your life."

Rick Fair, Vice President, Oral Oncolytics Sales & Marketing, Genentech

"I'm an angry man. Why wasn't this available when I first had a leadership role? It would have saved me much heartache: I had to learn all this stuff from scratch. If you have a child or a friend in their twenties, buy this for them now! And if you're from the UK/Europe and wondering if this is a soppy American text, have no fear—it reads well across the Atlantic—as befits an author who has inspired and learned from audiences throughout the world."

Ted Smith, Group HR Director at Medical Research Council

"Practical, timely, and effective. This book is a must-have guide to the vision, support and ability to act that will be the driving force for the success of your company and your team. If I had to pick one book to keep as my leadership "how to," this would be the one. Buy it, read it, and then read it again."

Al Babbington, CEO of PrescribeWellness

"For anyone involved in any type of leadership role, whether it's at work, home, school, community, etc., this is an invaluable resource."

Scott Garland, Chief Commercial Officer, Exelixis, Inc.

"I'm delighted to see that the work Charlie has been doing so successfully in corporate America is now accessible to all! Charlie challenges the reader to embrace their personal power and leadership, sharing scientific research and personal stories that create "ah ha" moments of self-reflection and discovery. Be prepared to be entertained, humbled and enlightened! A must read."

Wendy Miller, Senior Director, Global Learning and Development, Yahoo! Inc.

"Sheppard's book achieves a critical first by showing how drama kills organizational culture. Then he makes clear how to change it in your life, your team, and your organization."

John Chendo, President, Access Information Management

"Read this book, now! The principles and framework outlined in Save Your Drama for Your Mama will have a profound impact on those you lead, those you work with, and those you live with. The stuff in here is actionable tomorrow. You don't need twenty steps or a PhD in leadership, you just need to choose your triangle."

Tom Civik, Vice President, Genentech

"Sheppard's book will provide anyone with the ability to take their own skills to the next level, and unleash the full potential of any team. This is an excellent book for all levels of any organization—perfect for both current and future leaders."

Rex Jackson, Senior Vice President, Business Services at JDS Uniphase

"After reading this book you may see yourself and your team from a much different perspective than in the past. I believe this is best new theory for developing people I have seen in the last ten years. Sheppard has created a book that business executives and leaders at all levels will read and keep handy for reference."

Don Serva, Senior Director of Learning & Development for Allianz of America

"I have been friends with and worked with Charlie for over 20 years. I invited Charlie to work with every one of my teams over this time. While I still use some of the first concepts that Charlie taught me, I find that his work in leadership vs. drama is his most powerful work to date. Sheppard is one of the best in the business on this subject. This is an absolutely critical book for all levels of leadership—perfect for both current and future leaders as well as personal and business relationships."

Michael Polenske, Chairman of Blackbird Vineyards and Ma(i)sonry Napa Valley

"Sheppard brilliantly tackles the issues of culture that everyone struggles with today. Using engaging stories, new thinking about creating a responsive leader-driven organization, and case studies that drive the point home, Sheppard lays out a game plan for creating a drama-free culture."

Brandon Kotaniemi, Director - HIV Marketing, Gilead Sciences

"Outstanding and original leadership material. Focused on making leaders whole people and authentic leaders. The material is comprehensive but not overwhelming and gives practical steps to developing your leadership capacity and performance."

Mark J. Ahn, President & CEO, Galena Biopharma

"A must-read on Leadership and Organizational Health: you'll be inspired to think differently, see differently, act differently, work differently."

Bill DeWitt, Senior Vice President, Wells Fargo Bank

"This book connects dots from the past, present, and future, simplifying complex issues that can appear daunting to today's leaders. Sheppard's model for navigating today's drama-filled business environment reveals the principles and practices leaders should keep and those they should leave behind to create highly competitive organizations where people fully engage their hearts and minds. Compelling stories and pragmatic tools in every chapter help readers apply those insights immediately."

Tash Elwyn, President, Private Client Group at Raymond James & Associates

"Practical. Useful. Inspiring. Managers and leaders who want to engage the hearts and minds of every employee will find all the tools they need in Save your Drama for Your Mama. If you choose, this book will change who you are as a leader."

Sherry Allred, Senior Vice President, InterAct

"This book will give managers the ability to draw out a higher level of commitment from their workers, and ensure that all are working at their highest level of performance. An excellent resource for any business leader!"

Jeff Taylor, Executive Vice President Operations & CIO, Cost Plus World Market

"Sheppard does an excellent job laying out the basic elements of developing a successful vision and catalyzing change in an organization. Most importantly, his book leads you through a self-evaluation of your personal traits, strengths, and leadership style and how they support or encumber the process of achieving your goals. Save Your Drama for Your Mama is a must-read for those of us in leadership positions or who desire to be high-performance contributors."

William Annett, Partner at Accenture

"Charlie Sheppard has an incredibly distinctive point of view about leadership and organizations which has taught me and my clients a great deal. We continue to turn to his fresh insights and timeless wisdom to help guide us through the complex and changing landscape of global business. This book is a terrific encapsulation of his decades of work and is full of practical ideas for leaders at all levels."

Gordon Rudow, CEO, Bonfire Communications

"Drama" plays the role of antagonist in Mr. Sheppard's excellent book about becoming more aware of our own unproductive behaviors while understanding the opposing behaviors for creating better results. As a professional in the field of leadership development, I can say that his practical advice is very clear and will be easy to put into action."

Duke Holliday, Manager Organizational Effectiveness, McKesson Corporation

"Accessible to all, the principles described in Save your Drama for Your Mama will not only help you be more successful at work but in every dimension of your life. It is a practical reminder of the power inherent in every one of us to control our own destiny and be a positive influence in the world. If you are a leader who is serious about getting the best from your team members, make this the next book you read. Managing others is never simple, but with the techniques taught here, you are sure to see incredible changes in your company's culture."

Jenn Bonilla, Ph.D., Vice President, Genomic Health

"Charlie has been an inspiration in both my work and personal life. He has proved to me that one is never too old to learn more about themselves and adjust for effectiveness even in the sunset of one's career. This book brings together all his wisdoms and should be a must-read for anyone interested in real leadership and how to provide it."

Peter Busse, Chief Operating Officer, Platinum Group Metals Ltd

"Charlie makes it clear that we are in charge, we make a choice in every moment of every day, leadership or drama, Visionary or Victim. It's not just a way to lead, it's the way to live."

Gary Friedman, Chairman Emeritus, Restoration Hardware

"One part therapist and one part leadership coach, Sheppard shows that in understanding the roots of drama, we can conquer it. For leaders, parents and students of business, this book will help us get what we want. A must-read if you must succeed."

Steven K. Galson, Acting Surgeon General of the United States, 2007-2009

"Save Your Drama for Your Mama is the blueprint for effective leadership. Charlie Sheppard provides the best guidance for resolving problems and conflicts quickly and honestly. His methodologies will help you facilitate and maintain the open communication channels required for building and sustaining high-performance teams. He practically teaches you how to cultivate a motivational work environment. This is the one leadership book that I routinely reference."

Erik Harris, VP Sales & Marketing, Crescendo Bioscience

"Reading Sheppard's book made me chuckle as I saw so many of the characters and character traits we deal with daily. As I got deeper into it the book opened up some powerful new thinking for me as a leader and team builder. In Save Your Drama for Your Mama, Charlie Sheppard has achieved the brilliant task of adding meaningful dialogue and new thinking to the subject of Leadership. I'm planning to give a copy of Charlie's book to each of my managers."

John Dannerbeck, President & COO, Anchor Brewing Company

Contents

Introduction

I HAD JUST FINISHED delivering a two-week leadership retreat as an extension of Rockhurst University's School of Business in Kansas City. At the end of this program my colleagues and I sat around saying it was the best leadership curriculum we had delivered. It was leading edge, it was transformational and it had a profound impact on the participants, yet I was still troubled. The individual leaders who needed the program the most, embraced it the least. And the individual leaders who needed it the least, embraced it the most. They had transformational insights and took their leadership to the next level. What bothered me is we didn't have the same kind of impact we wanted on those individuals who needed it the most. Additionally, we observed limiting patterns back in their respective organizations. We saw organizational cultures that limited individual leadership and the full engagement of teams. This observation started me down the path to develop new ways of making leadership development more impactful and to dive deeper into what traps prevent people from leading more. The questions I started to explore were:

- What is the opposite of leadership?
- What is holding people back?
- What makes authentic leadership such a rare experience?

This led me to my research into the patterns of behavior and thinking that leads to drama in people's lives, teams and organizations. I explored the damage that drama brings with it, in limiting a team's full potential to execute effectively. The basic premise of this book is that you really need to understand the patterns of drama that limit your full expression of leadership and with that understanding you can make a new choice. The insight I took from teaching this program was to contrast the patterns of leadership with the patterns of drama.

Save Your Drama for Your Mama is designed to remind us that the behaviors we learned as children don't provide us with the best leadership competencies as adults. Leadership is a choice. You can make that choice at any time in your life. At any age, you can choose to live either in the Drama Triangle or in the Leadership Triangle.

The Drama Triangle demonstrates external dependency or an external locus of control. A person is living inside the Drama Triangle when he or she allows their control of life to be held externally, or by someone else. When your mindset follows drama, you abdicate control of your life to those you perceive to be more powerful.

A person who lives in the Leadership Triangle demonstrates trust in their own point of view; their locus of control is internal. If you have this leadership mindset, you take control of your life, your choices, and the outcomes.

At its most basic, leadership must be seen as the ability to make a choice. This ability to choose is the behavior that will guide you to mastering the skills of leadership.

Being able to choose to be the leader in your life is the foundation for this book. To be able to lead others effectively, you must first become a leader in your own life. Leading does not necessarily mean managing others. We contribute more when we act as leaders, regardless of job title or the number of people reporting to us. There are leaders on Little League teams. In the history of business, to say nothing of the history of the world, there are numerous examples of great leaders, each of whom made a difference because they chose to lead.

My goal in writing this book is to provide a roadmap for people to understand their own leadership and to be able to choose more leadership more often. I also want to provide a roadmap for people who get stuck in the Drama Triangle—stuck being Adversarial, stuck being Rescuers, or stuck at the bottom of the triangle as a Victim—so they can have a means to recognize what is happening and some methods for getting out.

Drama in all of its forms is becoming epidemic in corporate settings, on work teams, and in government organizations. (Families, of course, also experience drama. This book, although its message and methods can be translated into the family, is targeted more toward institutions and teams.) *Save Your Drama for Your Mama* is designed to get these patterns of drama behavior up on the table, out of the shadows. When people identify which of their behaviors are ineffective, they are less likely to behave in those ways. Isolating, naming, and understanding the behavior makes it impossible to continue doing it unconsciously. Once conscious of the behavior, you're more likely to "see" yourself acting in drama, and choose to stop.

The easiest way to learn something is to contrast it. By engaging the power of opposites, we can shake the foundation of long-held, limiting perspectives and paradigms. I especially feel that you can learn more about leadership by learning about drama and you can learn about drama by learning about leadership. So I wrote this book in such a way as to expose you to new concepts that can lead to more freedom in your life and more control over what you want to experience. You get to choose. All I am doing is laying out a clear map of the options available to you.

This book does come with a warning: Once you have been exposed to this way of thinking, your life will never be the same. Be thoughtful and reflective as you go through this book. Examine your own behaviors and your own choices. Decide whether you're living a life filled with drama and devoid of choice, or if you are fundamentally a leader, making your own independent choices for your life.

Expanding your ability to lead will bring more leadership opportunities into your life. Your example will empower people around you. Being more of a leader will reduce the amount of drama you allow into your world.

I mention many examples of leadership throughout this book, and many of the leaders are in positions of authority and power at high levels. However, leadership is first about leading yourself. In truly successful organizations, everyone is a leader, regardless of their official title or role.

Leadership, however, begins with making the choice to be a leader—a choice that can be made in sixth grade, graduate school, your first year on your first job, or when you're the CEO. For most of us, it's not a choice we make once: even leaders can stumble into drama, then make the choice to lead once again. *Save Your Drama for Your Mama* and the Leadership is a Choice® model will help you and any organization you're involved with create more leadership.

The tools I'm making available to you in this book are tools that have helped our clients to resolve conflicts, build powerful teams, and realize visions. Every person is unique, of course, so no model can give you the perfect, step-by-step sequence, and *voila!*, you're a more effective leader. What we do provide is a model that, once you learn it, you'll find to be a powerful tool for leading yourself and helping others develop their own leadership abilities.

We've honed these ideas in our work with many individuals and companies, and they have proven to be easily learned and simple to understand. In the pages ahead you will find:

- An in-depth explanation of the elements of our drama and leadership model.
- Advice on how to avoid creating and participating in drama.
- The tools necessary to more effectively lead yourself, your team, and your organization.

My wish is that these ideas will be a catalyst for your own leadership development. As always, though, it is your choice.

CHAPTER 1

How Drama Was Born

T O LEARN ABOUT LEADERSHIP, we first have to learn about drama. One of the primary ways to create drama is through the abdication of choice. In drama, you are dependent on others and you let them limit you. This isn't the same as choosing to follow a leader. When you're in drama, you resent that others are exercising what you perceive as control over your life. Your resentment and frustration might be passive or aggressive or both in tandem—and you might be oblivious to it. In drama, you react against that assumed, externally-located control, and most often you do so without being aware of it.

Leadership is, first and foremost, the choice to lead yourself. When you choose to lead yourself, you can then develop the ability to lead others. In leadership, a person motivates or assists others into action toward a goal or objective. As a leader, you can do this from any level inside an organization, even as an individual contributor.

Your job title doesn't make you a leader. If you're a manager or executive, you have authority over others. That does not mean you are a leader. It just means you're the boss and you have a type of power. You may manage dozens of people and still not be a leader (or be immune from drama). You might manage no one, yet

7

demonstrate outstanding leadership traits which your peers and managers appreciate. Leaders aim for great heights and amazing goals instead of just wanting to order people around. Leaders choose to control the actions of their lives.

HIDDEN IN THE MIND

Evolutionary psychologists John Tooby and Leda Cosmides have studied how the brain works through a broad field of research. Two of their core tenets are:

- "Our neural circuits were designed by natural selection to solve problems that our ancestors faced during our species' evolutionary history."
- "Consciousness is just the tip of the iceberg; most of what goes on in our minds is hidden from us."

In other words, we take lots of actions without being aware of why we do so. They become automatic, unconscious habits. We grew up learning to make certain choices and follow certain behaviors. Part of who you are is a set of habits that run so deeply and automatically that they are outside of your conscious awareness.

Throughout *Save Your Drama for Your Mama*, I'll offer you ways to better understand your own automatic patterns and how they are limiting you. With understanding, you can create a new set of patterns to serve your intentions that have much greater utility.

How the Dependent Ensure Their Survival

When you were born you were completely dependent on others for your survival. Baby humans are the most dependent species on the planet.

Let's take a look at other infants:

- A mountain goat is born weighing 7 pounds, about the same as a human baby, except it can stand within 30 minutes, walk in 60 minutes and in a few hours, the kid skips along 45-degree rocky inclines, chasing the herd. Weaned at one month, he is completely independent from his parents in less than a year.
- Bear cubs spend two years with their mother, and then are capable of fending for themselves.
- Most perching birds are ready to fly during the first two weeks. Some birds literally push their babies out of the nest!

How do humans compare? There is no other species as reliant or dependent upon external resources, and for such a long period of time, as the human child. Your first month of life, you could barely move. It takes weeks for us to develop the strength and dexterity to lift our heads or roll over. We can't even crawl for months or walk until almost a year. It takes perhaps a dozen years before a human child has sufficient coordination, knowledge and judgment to be left unsupervised for any length of time.

We generally believe that it takes 18-20 years for a child to become an adult, and even then not a mature adult. The human child is intensely, critically dependent.

Babies quickly learn to develop behaviors that get them what they need. Luckily for you, nature provided you with powerful phero-mones designed to make your parents and siblings fall in love with you. If you have ever smelled the top of a child's head, you have experienced the effect of these biological advantages provided to an infant to survive. When your parents or caregivers smelled the top of your head, your scent also released pheromones designed to bond them to you. Nature didn't leave it to chance that you would be cared for. Once bonded, you learned quickly that if you changed your behavior, you could get others to do things for you, things that would allow you to survive:

- I cry = They give me warm milk.
- I fuss = They hold and rock me, so I feel comforted and safe.
- I point = They hand me my toy, blanket, bottle…

Although this cause-and-effect and complex biology was beyond your infant comprehension, you took advantage of it. These dependent behaviors are lodged in your long-term memory, and because they were learned at a pre-verbal age, they became an unconscious set of behaviors that you enact even to this day.

You grew to understand that an external source would meet your needs.

Wired for Drama

From day one, your baby brain was creating and cultivating the significant neuron growth found in modern human brain development. In our early brain development, we create neurological patterns of dependency. This provides us with a bit of insight into how this dependency became imprinted and patterned, and how it can continue on into later life.

Parents, the most common external source of control, can and often do keep this pattern of dependence alive. On the one hand, a parent must provide what's best for a dependent child (and most do so with love). When you're a baby and a toddler and even in grade school, you need to depend on others for your survival.

On the other hand, when adults provide too much and do too much for the child, they instill a level of dependency that can last a lifetime. If the child (as he becomes a teen, then a young adult) never learns to develop an internal sense of control and choice, he cannot make his own decisions and develop self-reliance. Instead, he becomes a co-dependent adult who feels "OK" only if others validate his sense of self. Unconscious habits of non self-reliance will continue to "run the show" throughout life if left unchallenged.

Can you see the potential damage this pattern might have on both child and parent?

Educated for Dependence

What's more, these behaviors were not just enabled in the home when you were a baby: you went to school. Who among us hasn't wanted to please a teacher?

In our current educational system, preparing a student for the future of his or her choice isn't the priority. Instead, all students are being prepared to join the work force. At school, teachers are the external source of control. They teach courses aimed to prepare each student to get a job where he or she will report to a boss who will be the external source of control.

To teach students the basic reading, writing, and arithmetic they need for industrial jobs, most schools follow a standard, traditional pattern:

- Students sit in neat rows.
- The teacher stands in front of the class, facing them.
- Students recite the required material as laid out in the state's or nation's curriculum.

The uninspired teacher's job is not to stimulate curiosity and original thought among her students, it is to follow the curriculum. When a teacher does create curiosity and original thought, we remember that teacher for a lifetime.

Grades provide more external validation. As a baby, you cried and got a bottle. In school, you performed and got a grade. Grades reinforce the lesson that you are only successful if the external source says you are successful. (Babyhood was at least "pass/fail"— the bottle did or did not show up—but school grades tell you not just if you measure up, but how well.)

Children and schools are clearly not as mechanistic as this generalization implies, and schools are moving in the direction of helping children make good choices, because most people, children included, do not respond well to being treated as parts of an assembly line. But let me stress again my point: In school, we become further conditioned to accept the external rewards of teacher approval and good grades more than we're helped to develop self-reliance and the internal desire to grow.

Think of your own education. Were you moved by an innate desire to learn, or were you more concerned with getting good grades? Even if your answer is "both," didn't you ever try to figure out "what do I have to do in this course to get an A?"

Our school years are a time of thorough indoctrination during which other people know what you need better than you do. These are years in which young people not only seek external approval; they are encouraged to seek it. Well before graduation, you have learned to accept the opinions and follow the advice of others. Such behavior and attitude has the associated risks of not serving you later in life.

We spend years learning to be dependent:

- Our pattern of dependence is embedded in long-term memory before we learn how to speak.
- Being slow-developing humans, we are reliant or dependent upon external resources for years.

That's why it's difficult to get out of dependency later in life. Both at home and in school, we spend years following a complex set of externally enforced rules, which we realize helps us to gain approval.

Others Have the Power

Most of the skills you learned early in life were based on the core presupposition that the power is external to you. Think of the amount of time you have spent measuring yourself by other people's standards.

- You measured yourself by what your parents thought of you.
- You measured yourself by what the other kids thought of you.
- You measured yourself by your teachers' opinions of you.

No wonder it's difficult for personal, internal rules and values to develop naturally. No wonder much of our own drama is driven by childish urges.

In essence, as a child you went out of your way to make sure that you were not forgotten. So it makes sense that children learn where the power is in their environment. You knew what Mom could provide for you, what Dad could provide (and what they couldn't provide), as well as how much power your siblings and your teachers had over you. You developed certain aspects of your personality in order to interact with these powerful people, to ensure your own comfort and well-being. What did you do as a child in order to please others? The behaviors you learned might have helped you handle tricky conversations, calculate how to fit in, develop techniques for emotional blackmail, and charm your parents out of resources.

Put plainly, many of the methods you learned gave you the tools to survive childhood.

DRAMA REARS ITS HEAD

When a child learns that power comes from those in control, he decides that the opposite must be true: power does not come from him.

Think of a time, as a kid, when you felt like you were not in control of a particular situation, or when you wanted to save someone from a difficulty, or when you tried to assert control over others. In such situations, you were learning the patterns of drama. With drama, you were trying to control an environment that you felt was fundamentally out of your control.

This struggle for control can be called "human nature" or an acquiring of "survival techniques." It becomes questionable or detrimental when you don't grow out of it. If you don't leave childhood tactics behind and become an independent, internally-validated and accountable adult, then your way of life becomes about creating drama.

I am not saying that your problems with drama are due to your parents and your schooling. You are responsible for your behavior, whether you choose ineffective drama or empowering leadership.

Our society as a whole is becoming less self-sufficient and more dependent. We are shockingly quick to point a finger and assume it is someone else's fault. This world-wide reluctance to accept responsibility has become an epidemic.

Drama Is Epidemic...and Expensive

We need to hold people accountable for their own choices and actions. In drama, people deflect and diffuse any responsibility. It's pervasive. It's expensive in terms of time lost at work, lawsuits clogging the courts, and the emotional toll on all parties involved.

Here are just two examples of how drama is shaping the thinking of our culture:

Tardiness is not my fault

A data processor for the Philadelphia School District was always late to his job. Finally, his superiors dismissed him. Instead of accepting the consequences of his actions, he sued, claiming that his lateness was a disease over which he had no control. Doctors diagnosed him as suffering from a compulsion to be late due to a problem he had with his parents. The Court agreed with his claim.

What's the message in this kind of drama? That it's OK to be a Victim and you are in no way responsible for your own behavior. There must be some reasons, out of your control, that make you behave in a particular way: it's someone else's fault.

It's not the tardy employee's fault: his parents are to blame. (While there is no denying that many of us have psychological scars from childhood, I know many such people who have used those life experiences to motivate themselves to create a better environment in their life now and some who haven't. It is always a choice.)

I am Powerless

> A worker at Stroh Brewery claimed that he became addicted to alcohol because he worked in a brewery that made beer available for free to the workers (as part of the union contract). The court agreed with the worker's argument that the nature of the job made him succumb to the "uncontrolled addiction." Therefore, he was awarded worker's compensation.

> The brewery worker received monetary compensation and kept his job, without taking any responsibility for his decision to drink, his decision to stay in a job that was hard on his health, or his decision not to seek treatment to control his addiction.

What's the message in this kind of drama? If we endorse "playing the victim," we can move through our lives without accepting any consequences of our missteps while leaving the responsibility of our choices, behaviors, and outcomes in the hands of others. How often do you enact such "victim blame" patterns? How often do you support such patterns?

A World of Wimps

Have we created a society that refuses to accept personal accountability? I can't back up my car without it beeping at me as a warning to me that I am backing up. I know I am backing up. Since I was the one who put it in reverse, this seems a bit redundant.

The abandonment of responsibility isn't just happening with individuals; it is becoming a legal requirement, making our systems much more complex and removing personal awareness and accountability for one's actions.

People keep passing the buck, and after doing that long enough, you wind up with:

The Recession of 2008

You can hide in the short run by making something complex. The hard part about the 2008 recession is finding one culprit to hold responsible, whether it is a poorly applied risk formula, the government providing cheap interest rates, or a lack of leadership in a division of AIG (more about them in Chapter 10). Untangling the mess is a challenge. Even today, it's complicated to figure out who owns which mortgages. With a system so convoluted, accountability is hard to create. Blaming the other guy is easy. Finding someone to blame is hard.

Firestone Tires

When their tires began to fail in 2000, executives at Bridgestone (who owned Firestone) repeatedly denied any problems. Yet, during a period in which 250 people died in SUVs equipped with Firestone tires, SUVs outfitted with Goodyear tires reported no fatalities. Bridgestone then decided to blame the drivers, stating "...we estimate that driving in high temperature, at high speeds, and under-inflated tires are factors in these accidents." Fearing to lose money and market share, they failed to accept responsibility— so they instead lost the trust of the marketplace.

"Weapons of Mass Destruction"

If you want to find examples of avoiding accountability, just look to the federal government. We went into Iraq to eradicate their weapons of mass destruction—only to find out there were none. This is a mistake that may cost many trillions of dollars. It was an intelligence failure of epic proportions, but George W. Bush seemed incapable of taking responsibility. He allowed CIA director George Tenet to retire with honors. He then backpedaled from his original certainty to a weak "we all thought there were weapons of mass destruction." A leader would say "the buck stops here." A president who says "I didn't know" and "mistakes were made" isn't leading.

Shift to Independence

Our society, our businesses, our schools, and our families all need internally driven, accountable leaders. And there are ways we can foster self-reliance in adults and children.

I ask parents and leaders to not provide a dependent environment for too long. Phase out dependence. Let your kids make decisions, even decisions that lead to unfortunate consequences. I don't mean give your 12-year-old the car keys because she's decided to drive. But if she chooses to spend her allowance on a sixth pair of jeans, don't give her some extra cash because she really needs a new computer game. And let her do her science project herself. Too bad it's not finished on time.

If your parents didn't provide you with this phased-out approach of lessening your dependency, you need to do it for yourself. You can replace your dependency with independence. The more responsibility you take on, the more internal and independent you will be. Yes, it might be painful at first, but less painful than the alternative: staying lost in pleasing others externally and being dependent on others to meet your needs.

Consider this aspect of animal behavioral research: It takes less time for the current generation to learn something if the previous generation learned it beforehand. The elder generation might have needed a certain amount of time and experiences to master a pattern. Their offspring will master it faster. These patterns can either be useful patterns or ineffective ones.

Does this hold true in human behavior? We now have a generation of those who are taught to be overly dependent on others. The danger is we may be starting down a path to "teach" this behavior to the next generation.

Rituals Are Missing

Many societies have manhood and womanhood rituals designed to signal the end of childhood, the entrance of the young person into self-reliant adult thinking, behavior and responsibility whereby the person can lead his or her own life. These rituals help young adults internally generate their ability to connect directly with their own existence without the need of support from their parents or caregivers. Tribal societies have mastered this transition very well, and if you look at multiple cultures you will find a common pattern.

Such rituals helped demonstrate to the child and to her parents that the child was maturing. The young adult was going to make her own choices, and accept new levels of personal responsibility. It's sad to see such rituals diffused or abandoned: they were truly significant in breaking the pattern of children's dependence upon their elders—and the parents' continued control of the children. Without them, the "child" struggles on the slippery slope of external dependence, creating the kinds of drama you should only be saving for your Mama—and she won't thank you for it!

In America today, the shift from dependency to independence sometimes occurs with a college or first job experience. It's the young person's first experience with freedom, without reliance on hovering parents. More often than not, young adults are not equipped for such independence. Rituals in our society include getting drunk for the first time or getting the keys to the car. What we need are quality rites of passage to help make the shift into being an adult. Yet at this age most young people are heavily influenced by their peer groups. These peer groups are also going through a massive hormonal imbalance that affects decision-making and quality choices. So here you have a situation where young adults are looking for answers, so they go to their peer group—and their peers are just as messed up as they are. Because we miss these rituals to help young adults make the shift necessary to lead their own lives, mental suffering, anxiety, and depression are widespread throughout college campuses. These young people, if they feel disconnected, will behave in many detrimental ways, including abusing substances, binge drinking and eating, and various other damaging behaviors to reduce the pain.

Go It Alone

As children—well into our teens, even college years—we had safety nets called parents, teachers, coaches, and older siblings. Even into adulthood, some of us keep the safety net, adding the spouse, boss, and even our own children.

Get rid of the net! Keep the people. Remove the reliance. Break away from anyone's support but your own for at least some period of time. It's important that you create a strong internal foundation for yourself. Without it, you'll find it impossible to create something great in your life. Each person has many gifts they can use to benefit this world. If you want to learn how to develop your gifts and how to trust in them, you'll find it immensely difficult if you allow the outside world to judge whether you're doing well or not.

Ask yourself:

- Am I a leader, at least in my own life?
- Am I willing to be a leader?
- What is my purpose?

- If I were absolutely fearless, what would I be doing right now?

As you answer these questions, think of the values that are underpinning your responses. Make sure you connect to your internally driven values and let yourself express those personal values in your work and in your relationships.

WE CAN CHANGE

Why am I talking about developmental psychology when this book is about being a leader? Because first you must:

- Know the reasons why you behave in a certain way, so you'll be able to make effective changes.
- Understand what leadership is as well as what it isn't. Being able to notice the opposite of leadership will help you create more leadership in your own life.
- Realize why others are behaving in a certain way, or you will have trouble leading them.

The aim of this book is to make you aware of the trap of drama, which keeps you from being a true and effective leader. Drama is born when you let others control you through their choices. Leadership starts when you make choices for yourself. Then, as a leader, you can begin to affect those around you—not through control, but by helping others choose also.

CHAPTER 2

Your Brain on Drama

T O UNDERSTAND LEADERSHIP, you first need to understand drama.

John apparently doesn't understand one or the other.

John, creative designer for an advertisement agency, is the senior member of a team about to launch a new children's game. Near the deadline, Sam, one of the team members, was given the task of collecting the prototype from the manufacturer so the team could then deliver it to the customer. However, Sam did not go over to the manufacturer's warehouse that day, which left the team in a pretty serious bind.

John started to stress out. As the senior member, he felt that he was going to be blamed for the delay. How did he handle the situation?

John, realizing that the client would not get their prototype on time, chose to tell anyone who would listen that:

- Sam didn't pick up the prototype.
- It wasn't his, John's, fault—although now everyone will think it is.
- He is always made the scapegoat when things fall apart.

John was, understandably, apprehensive when his supervisor called him into her office. When she asked why the work was not progressing as scheduled, John started to blame Sam. Sam was supposed to have picked up the prototype, so Sam ruined the client meeting, and Sam delayed the launch. His supervisor listened patiently and was quiet for a few minutes. She then simply asked, "How come you didn't go pick it up, then?"

John left her office dejected, without reflecting on her pertinent question. When his team asked what happened, he said, "The boss has always been after me. No one appreciates all the hard work I do around here."

We all make mistakes and no one is perfect. John, however—like all people who embrace drama—found someone else to blame. Contrast him with a leader who is not afraid to admit that he is wrong and who creates a different kind of environment. That honesty helps him to rectify errors and steer himself and others in the right direction. But poor leaders have no trouble seeing the faults in others while not looking to themselves for answers. Hence, they continue to make the same mistakes, time and time again.

We could all be like John: we all came hardwired for drama. It's part of our neurological processes. We do not come hardwired for leadership, but we can make the choice to be a leader at any time in our lives. Whichever path you follow, be it drama or leadership, your repeated behaviors establish a pattern—a brain circuitry—that helps you quickly access and repeat the behavior. Obviously, this can work to a leader's advantage, but is a great disadvantage if you are prone to drama.

CELEBRITY ANTICS

Like a play, drama has action and performances, but the difference lies in this: drama doesn't add value to the lives of the individuals involved in it.

There are three specific roles of drama that I'll discuss in the next chapter. But let's look at "Hollywood" drama as a useful cautionary tale. What do performers need more than anything in order to feel successful? Not talent and not a lucky break. Performers need, above all else, praise and acceptance.

If you've ever watched a child performer grow up, the pattern is so predictable that it is almost sad. The child star gets so much external validation as a youngster that his neurology establishes itself to feel good only by receiving external validation. When the external validation isn't there, he will seek out another source, and any validation will do. The result is the drama lifestyle of the star and starlet in his or her teens and early twenties (and, for some, their 30s and 40s). So many performers are "acting out," headline seeking, overdosing—and why? Do they hope that creating drama in their own lives will fill the need for external validation? The idea that "any press is good press" supports their conviction that their behavior doesn't matter so long as they are getting some response from others. Internally, when they empty themselves to take on a movie role, they exacerbate an inability to be themselves when off-camera and without stimulus from the outside. Combine this with wealth and sycophantic support systems, and it's a recipe for disaster that we see played out over and over again.

THE BRAIN'S AMYGDALA

So why do people embrace drama for that external "feel good" response? Turning to neuroscience, the scientific study of the nervous system, we can better understand how the brain functions.

- Your frontal cortex controls the executive functions, through which you display your personality, consciously make decisions, determine appropriate social responses, and grasp similarities and differences between events, things, and people.
- Your limbic system operates the endocrine system and the autonomic nervous system. It is highly interconnected with the brain's pleasure center (where you experience "highs" and "lows" from experiences and stimulants). Part of the limbic system is the amygdala.

I'm sure you've had the experience of feeling locked into an emotional state, when a flood of fight-or-flight hormones leaves you feeling trapped and overwhelmed. These hormones come from the amygdala. When the amygdala fires up, the effect can lead you to make an inappropriate response that you later regret.

Amygdala Overdrive

The amygdala assesses any situation that might be threatening to survival. "Does it eat me, or do I eat it?" Whenever you face a stressful situation, the amygdala triggers messages to go on the offensive—retaliate by fighting back—or go on the defensive and run like a rabbit, literally or figuratively. These "messages" are relayed as chemical and hormonal output, which rev up your body to respond. And do we ever respond, based on those chemicals. We follow the "message" until the threat subsides, the associated chemicals subside, and our behavior returns to normal.

We humans are still looking for the saber-tooth tiger hiding in the grass. The amygdala is your brain's first and most powerful radar, so when you sense danger, the amygdala rushes to your aid to help you survive. Most of us don't encounter true life-and-death danger each day, but our brain interprets some of our deep fears as intensely dangerous: fear of failing, fear of exclusion, fear of uncertain situations.

Take exclusion for example: We are wired to feel separation as a threat. For millennia, humans lived near those saber-tooth tigers and other predators. Our roots are social. Danger is best survived as a group. The worst punishment a family, tribe, or village could inflict was banishment. We currently live in a more independent social system, but we're still intensely social animals, so we still respond to exclusion as a danger.

When the danger is a sense of exclusion at work—perhaps you heard some news today that everyone else already knew, or you didn't get invited to Bill's retirement lunch—the amygdala releases powerful hormones that arouse you to fear and anger. Your heart speeds up, your blood pressure rises, and your IQ might drop by 20-30 points. You become more judgmental and more reactive. The normally integrated hemispheres of the brain separate: the higher centers are cut off, causing your thoughts to bypass the standard pathways for integrated functioning. This flood of hormones can stay in the system for up to four hours. The physical reactions they generate are designed to help you see things through your fight or flight lens. Unfortunately, in most situations, our lives are not threatened, and the "help" isn't very helpful.

When you misapply these survival systems, you create the potential for drama. After a "danger"-fueled incident, you might ask yourself, "why did I do that?" Well, the answer is that the fear-based emotion triggered the amygdala to heighten the fear and generate anger as a means to help you avoid danger. The amygdala fires and fosters the potential for drama, and drama's function is to create more drama.

Amygdala Triggers

Other perceived dangers can trigger the amygdala and lead you to create drama:

Experience. We more easily remember bad experiences than we do good ones. To help us survive, the brain typically stores and processes negative information faster than positive information. The difficulty with our primitive-based neurology in modern times is the amount of negative information we receive: Having our survival instincts fire all day long when we are not at real risk is a poor use of our brain and nervous system.

Our perceptions of others. With priority given to memories of negative experiences, we project expectations onto a person in the present. This is why an individual with whom you have a long negative history is able to provoke you with less effort than is another person.

Perceived lack of choice. When you think that you have no good options, the "overdriving" aspect of the amygdala kicks in, separating you from the higher centers of the brain and moving you from a logical to an instinctual mode. When you respond impulsively, full of anger, fear, and anxiety to a challenging situation, you even further limit the choices available to you. You strip yourself of your ability to deal with the unknown.

Overrule the Amygdala

So should we detach from our emotions? No. Without using our emotions in decision-making, we will not make good choices.

Our prefrontal cortex is the brain region from which we govern, by rational thinking, our impulsive behavior. However, we have but a short window of time to choose to override the impact of an overactive amygdala response. The more hormones that course through you, the harder it is to resist their chemical effect. But resistance is not futile. You can change. You want to change, because drama is in no way beneficial in building productive relationships.

Change the Neural Pathway

That being said, making any change is hard. We are designed for homeostasis, for equilibrium: we want balance in most of our systems. We have a built-in resistance to change.

Imagine if your doctor said you had to change your behavior or you would die. Do you think you would make the change? Heart bypass surgery patients are constantly told that, as a matter of life or death, they need to stop smoking, lose weight, and exercise more. They rationally know they should make the changes, but research proves that only 1 person out of 10 makes these changes and sticks to them. Neuroscience explains why people find change so difficult: doing any behavior over and over develops neural pathways, and our brain is designed to preserve those neural pathways. Whether it's drama, leadership, or a high-fat diet, the more often you enact a behavior, the more unconsciously and habitually your brain circuits will fire to launch that behavior.

By repeatedly acting out in drama, you turn a neural pathway into a four-lane freeway in your head, driving you straight into yet more drama.

UNDERSTAND DRAMA TO UNDERSTAND LEADERSHIP

These patterns of behavior have been around since the first records of history, and drama has been the default orientation for most of it. These patterns have also been around you for your whole life. As children, we often view the world as outside of our control. As adults, we view the world as potentially dangerous. These ways of viewing our environment are basic survival instincts.

Today, literal survival is not in question in most circumstances, but we've honed the fight-or-flight reactions partly through personal experience and partly through brain chemistry. Some people even find a subtle and powerful seduction in being powerless and not responsible. It saddens me to watch people become resigned to (even addicted to) creating more and more drama.

The more you understand drama, the better you can learn to lessen its impact and develop your leadership skills.

Understand the unconscious behaviors associated with drama. This is the first step in understanding the drama pattern. By recognizing these patterns you render them conscious, not unconscious. That helps you slow down your automatic response and take time to be intentional about making a different choice. (We'll discuss roles and behaviors in more detail in the next chapter.)

Build alternate choices ahead of time. We have little time to use our prefrontal cortex to make a rational response to a situation before a habitual pattern takes hold. You need to build patterns for leadership that run opposite to the behaviors of drama that are already seeded in your mind. As you build up those muscles associated with leadership behaviors, they become more readily activated in stressful situations. You can consciously build productive neural pathways and make choices for more helpful habitual patterns.

Root out fear. People who adopt a drama mindset have an attitude rooted in fear. This fear-based thinking is amplified especially when the fears of what might happen supersede the awareness of what is happening. Fear kills the impetus for insightful actions that propel things forward. Our government and news outlets feed us a daily dose of fear, and as we mentioned before, our neurology is not wired for this onslaught of negative impulses.

Leadership Is Not A Title

Regardless of where your job fits on the organizational chart, it is important that you both reduce the amount of drama you create and increase the amount of leadership you demonstrate.

Leadership is not about your position or job title. People follow leaders, not titles.

Usually when we think "leader," we equate that with "authority"—the CEO, the boss, our particular manager or team leader. However, a true leader first leads himself. In truly successful organizations, all participants are leaders, regardless of their official title or role. (And there are plenty of CEOs and company presidents who create drama rather than provide leadership. They fail to realize that by perpetuating the behaviors of drama, they are encouraging their subordinates to create their own drama.)

You become a leader through your relationships with other people. You are not a leader because of the resources you are given. You are a leader because others respect you. You are a leader if you have a better idea. One person, at any time, can make a difference as a leader, if they choose to act.

YOU CAN CHANGE

Life is too short for drama, for excuses, resignation, blaming, or abandoning your dreams. The way out of drama is by making choices. Martin Luther King, Jr., who was a great advocate for change, was opposed to slow reforms. "Either we risk or we don't," he said.

There's no middle ground with leadership and drama: you are either becoming more of a leader or you are resigning yourself to the status quo. It really is that simple.

CHAPTER 3

OPPOSING TRIANGLES

LET'S NOW LOOK at the distinct characteristics of the roles of drama and leadership. The model I use to represent these roles is in the form of triangles, as are used by many therapeutic modalities. A triangle is a representation of an effective web of interlocking relationships.

The Drama and Leadership Triangles, and their contrasting roles, are only a model; they are not absolute truth. Yet, models provide us with paths for developing skills and creating understanding. A useful model should be predictable enough to provide you, as a leader, with new insights and ways of understanding both for yourself and for others.

COMPARE AND CONTRAST

As you study the Drama and Leadership Triangles, you'll see the contrasts between the various elements.

Using contrast—comparing opposites—to transfer knowledge is not new. The Chinese philosophy of the *I Ching*, written during the early Han dynasty to identify the principal workings of the universe, put forth the concept of the yin and yang. Much more recently, twentieth century French anthropologist Claude Lévi-

Strauss, in his influential book, *The Raw and the Cooked*, discussed how people best understand concepts presented in opposite pairs. Lévi-Strauss looked at the power of metaphor and saw that the basic patterns were the same: the contrast of life and death, hard and soft, loud and quiet. He showed that myths are the same stories across all cultures, and all have structures based on opposites, which allow us to understand the fundamental lesson more easily. Our myths shape our social, national, and corporate cultures and the way we think about ourselves.

The higher the contrast of these opposites, the more obvious the distinction. For instance, a traffic light uses red and green because they are opposites on the color wheel. What if traffic signals used red for stop and pink for go? Red and pink represent such a low contrast, and they would be so difficult to distinguish from one another that they'd be dangerous.

In other leadership training courses, leadership is often contrasted with management. Management is not the opposite of leadership: drama is. Management is in many ways a poor contrast to leadership, like contrasting red and pink stop lights. The distinction between the two is difficult to identify and understand. We've all known managers who are also good leaders.

Leadership creates a high contrast to drama—it is completely opposite. The unmistakable blue and red lights on the top of a police car are one example; emergency vehicles have selected this combination because of the wavelengths of light. Red is easier to see during the day and blue is easier to see at night and in snow. The colors selected were by design to create contrast within the environment.

That's why I strongly believe that as you begin to really understand drama, you will be on the quickest and most productive road to learning about leadership.

Genuine Change

In my work, I have watched teams, individuals, and whole organizations use the Leadership Triangle/Drama Triangle distinction to create genuine change.

For example, Restoration Hardware shifted the manager role by creating Store Leaders in place of Store Managers. By emphasizing the leadership role, Restoration Hardware motivates every individual in the company to achieve a higher level of the leadership competency. By actively creating a team of leaders, Restoration Hardware has developed a foundation in human leadership capital that makes the organization stronger. Building their leadership competency goes beyond just the executives who have others reporting to them. Restoration Hardware has trained each individual contributor to have a leadership mindset. Everyone is asked to embrace the role of being a leader. With this foundation in place, the company built a level of immunity from the drama that might have resulted when the retail marketplace went soft in 2008.

When you really adopt a leadership mindset, it will of course be helpful in your work but also transferable to your family and community relationships as well. In fact, when you develop your leadership roles, you'll naturally carry them into every part of your life.

LEADERSHIP IS A CHOICE ®

A person choosing leadership	A person stuck in drama
• Assumes Positive Intent	• Assumes Negative Intent
• Chooses to be a · Catalyst · Coach · Visionary	• Succumbs to being a · Adversary · Rescuer · Victim
• Is Accountable	• Avoids Accountability
• Controlled Internally, by the self	• Controlled Externally, by others
• Is energetic, engaged, and focused	• Is resigned, angry, and confused

OUR ROLES IN LIFE

I'll be explaining, in detail, both the Drama Triangle and Leadership Triangle throughout the following chapters. In this chapter, we'll look at the three major roles within each Triangle. First, let's consider roles in general.

Roles help us define ourselves and express ourselves. We all take on roles in life: son or daughter, sibling, friend, husband or wife, sales associate, manager, dancer, parent, athlete, employee. With different people we inhabit different roles at different times. We can shift roles to be more productive. We can choose roles with more utility.

Some roles come with positive descriptive labels—responsible, smart, trustworthy. If we are less productive, we may be labeled with other roles such as arrogant, domineering, a pushover, insensitive, or always the scapegoat.

I wrote this book to help you determine the roles you want to create in your life. We each have the power to define, by choice, those roles. This power enhances our capacity to learn and affects our attitude toward learning. The learning potential you have within expresses itself by the choices you make for yourself. These choices are reflected in your behaviors from the roles you adopt in life.

When you fully embrace a role, you embrace its power—or its lack of power. You embrace its potential—or its limitation. You eventually embody the role. Roles become more and more fixed through habituation. When you adopt a role, you take on its inherent behaviors.

ARCHETYPICAL DRAMA ROLES

Take a close look at the Drama Triangle. It shows that drama adopts an external locus of control, which means that a person allows control of their life to be held by others. When your mindset follows drama, you avoid accountability and abdicate control of your life to those you perceive to be more powerful.

Drama has three archetypical roles: **Victim, Adversary**, and **Rescuer.**

The specific behavioral patterns associated with each of these are already active in our neurological memory as archetypes. If you are trapped in creating drama in your life, you tend to communicate reactively and will move systematically between each of the three drama roles, forming a Drama Triangle. When these roles interact with each other, they create even more drama. If you think visiting the Drama Triangle only happens to other people, read on. Low self-awareness virtually guarantees longer stays in the Drama Triangle. Learning about it will help you recognize it and mitigate its negative efforts more easily. You may not always be in the Drama Triangle, but when you are, increased self-awareness about it will help you to not visit as often or for as long.

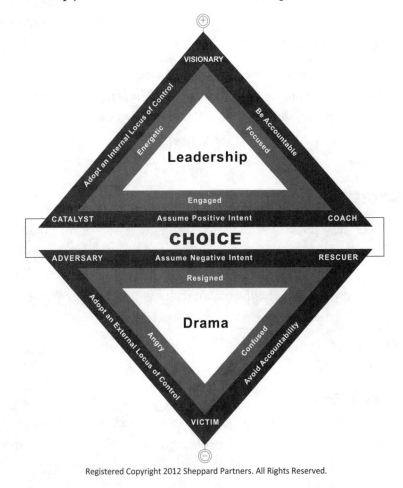

Let's consider each role briefly. I'll go into more detail about them in later chapters, when we look more closely at their characteristics of anger, resignation, and confusion.

Victim

A person in the Victim role is a master manipulator who persuades others to sympathize with his or her supposed helplessness. Victims use a variety of subtle, deceptive tactics such as playing nice, a willingness to listen, and an apparent capacity for understanding.

The Victim deals with issues indirectly. For them, passive-aggressive communication is the norm, displayed so subtly that people are rarely able to detect it.

- They pretend to be powerless and work to get others to agree with their powerless point of view.
- They do not accept responsibility for their behavior. Instead, they blame others for the negative outcomes in their lives.
- Victims refrain from expressing themselves directly, but talk behind others' backs and express displeasure with body language, such as rolling their eyes.
- Dishonesty and disingenuousness are fundamental traits of the Victim role.

Adversary

Someone in the Adversary role creates drama using criticism, blame, and other antagonizing tactics. The Adversary seeks to control others and to make them less productive by withdrawing from the relationship at any moment.

An Adversary can freeze an organization with their use of fear and emotional attacks. People walk on eggshells around them. The unpredictability of when and where they will lash out keeps others guessing their true intentions.

- Adversaries exert authority through threats, orders, and rigidity, which makes them hard to be around. They are always critical and find fault with others.
- They are blind to the impact of their communication style.
- Whether loud or quiet in nature, they have a coercive, pushy, and pressuring tendency and look to reign supreme by engaging in a top dog vs. underdog approach.
- They blame others directly and "show off" whenever possible.

Rescuer

When in the Rescuer role, a person surreptitiously seeks recognition by attempting to "save" others. It's not from kindliness: The Rescuer sees others as flawed, incapable of handling honest feedback, and unable to help themselves. Rescuers give resources, favors, and time but always with secret terms attached: the expectation that the receiving party will reciprocate. Rescuers are surprised and disappointed when this does not occur.

- The most pervasive trait of the Rescuer is to save others from feedback. Because they do not believe in the strengths of others, they withhold feedback for fear of hurting someone's feelings.
- The Rescuer needs significant amounts of external approval and recognition. The recognition is their reward. It's

their motivation for "helping"—but their "help" is really judging others and protecting their own feelings.

- Because Rescuers will help others without being asked, they are often perceived as meddlesome.

They Are Us

We have all witnessed these roles in others and have acted them out ourselves at some point. When we are in the Drama Triangle, our current external environment influences which of these roles we choose, whether consciously or unconsciously, to activate.

We usually end up playing a Drama Triangle role when we are not fully conscious of what we are doing and why we are doing it. We let resignation creep into a relationship or situation. We start to feel powerless to make a difference, or we think it would be too difficult to have a challenging conversation. When living unaware of our behaviors, we are resigned to the consequences of the roles of the Drama Triangle, without even recognizing that we abdicated our choice to do something differently.

When an individual shifts his or her role from, for example, Victim to Adversary, this causes even more drama. You've seen movies in which the scriptwriter cleverly heightened the drama by having the hero turn out to be the villain, or the victim becomes the hero. This creation of more drama is fine up on the big screen, but is not productive if it is created in your team or in your life.

Notice that the Drama Triangle is pointed downwards. It is balanced precariously on its point. In that position, a triangle point cannot support its own weight. Imagine the Great Pyramids standing upside down: they would fall over. The same is true of an individual stuck in drama. Their lives feel very unstable to them. Often, they do not know why. Drama becomes their way of life.

Drama As a Way of Life

I was leading a team integration process for the twelve top managers in a division of an organization of about 200 people. As I was facilitating the team through a number of experiences, it was obvious that the Director of HR had problems with her team leader. (I came to discover that she had accused the team leader of misusing funds. However, there had been a thorough, formal investigation, in which his record was found to be impeccable.)

During the first morning of this seminar, she made a flurry of vicious attacks. She was sucking all the oxygen out of the room. I felt that, if I had a camera, I could have captured on film the black cloud of negativity around her head.

During the lunch break, I sat down to talk with her. She made the trip through each role in the Drama Triangle, over and over. She continued attacking her manager (Adversary) and then, when I asked more questions, she replied, "Well, I am only doing this to save the other team members" (Rescuer). Upon further enquiry, she relayed to me all of her health issues (Victim). Then she attacked the parent corporation, vaguely hinted about her retirement package (needing rescue), and complained about how she had not been paid well over the years (Victim).

Of course, it was simply a matter of time before she attacked me for asking all these questions (Adversary), challenged if I was going to do this to all the other participants (Rescuer), and complained about how I was making her feel uncomfortable (Victim).

I tried to get her to discover her motives for herself. She was only six months away from retirement. I attempted to have her make a choice. My questions were designed to have her make a definitive statement about what she wanted—and she couldn't do it.

What she wanted (but was not able to verbalize) was to no longer work for this company—but quitting would have required her to make a choice, which she was no longer able to do. She was so caught by the Drama Triangle that she had moved in permanently. It was no wonder she had created so many issues around health, finances, and her relationships.

During this whole conversation, the VP of Corporate HR and the president were present. They understood, by watching the pattern play out over and over again, that only something from the external environment was going to move this person to an action. Within days, they made her a generous offer of early retirement, which kept her salary intact, her medical benefits intact, and her full retirement intact. She basically was being paid to not show up for work if she resigned. Any guesses as to how she responded to this generous offer? She attacked it as not being fair (Adversary), she would be letting down all of her coworkers (Rescuer) if she accepted, and she was being forced to leave (Victim). In the end, they gave her the package with the request that she retire immediately, making the choice for her to leave. Perversely, this allowed her to play the Victim by being fired.

To this day, I believe she wanted, however subconsciously, to be fired so she didn't have to make a choice. She wanted someone else to take control so she could complain about it.

ARCHETYPICAL LEADERSHIP ROLES

Let's look now at the Leadership Triangle. It rests firmly on its base and all of its elements are the opposite of drama. The Leadership Triangle has three roles that characterize a true leader as someone who adopts an internal locus of control, which means the person looks to themselves as the reason something happens or not. When you are a leader, you accept accountability and take responsibility for your actions. You locate the control of your behaviors and the results are internal or with yourself.

Let's consider each role briefly. (We'll look at each role more closely in later chapters, and at their characteristics of energy, engagement, and focus). When you look at a leader, you'll see:

The Visionary, who cultivates and communicates a compelling vision with passion. The Visionary sees real possibilities even in the absence of evidence. Visionaries can speak things into existence. They use their influence to create a future for themselves and others.

The Catalyst, who is able to accelerate collective action on the vision because of his or her deep belief in the right course of action. The Catalyst uses thorough, open and honest communication; everyone appreciates his trustworthiness. Within the team or organization in which he works, the Catalyst understands the system and relationships; he can leverage his resources to create the best result.

The Coach, who is committed to continuous personal and professional growth, from which she works to support others in realizing their potential. The Coach embraces honest feedback; she listens to it and provides it as the best means to share her point of view successfully. The Coach not only coaches others, she is receptive to being coached. The Coach has the courage to be candid and works to create a culture where candidness is the norm.

Leaders Develop

A Leader will display all three characteristics to one degree or another. A Leader makes the choice to continually improve in all of these areas, because excellent leaders are not just born; they develop themselves over the years. Your journey to effective leadership is a continuous process involving the study of yourself, the study of the principles of leadership, and the study of other leaders, along with determination, persistence, and experience. Good leaders are continually training to improve their leadership skills.

As a Leader, you must actively adopt the roles in the Leadership Triangle. To inspire you into the next level of leadership, incorporate these leadership roles into your thinking and behavior. Such roles do not always come naturally, and have to be acquired through practice and study.

Dan West: All the Attributes of Leadership

In Dan West, you'll meet a Visionary, Catalyst, and Coach, whose life's work demonstrates the interrelation of all the leadership roles.

In 1937, Dan West left his ranch in the Midwest and headed for Spain to help the civilians suffering from the impact of the Spanish Civil War. Dan's commitment to be a relief worker meant leaving his wife, children, and ranch for many months. But he felt needed, and indeed it was on this trip that Dan developed a vision to change the world.

In Spain, Dan's job was to provide nourishment in the form of powdered milk to families in need. He saw firsthand the loss of dignity in each person standing in line for food. Then supplies ran low and Dan didn't have enough supplies for the children. He was forced to decide who would receive milk, and who wouldn't. He was making life or death choices for others. I have no idea how Dan had the courage to make these decisions. If any situation could trap someone into the Drama Triangle, this one could.

Instead of resigning to the situation, instead of giving up, Dan thought of his own children and how well they ate and how well-nourished they were by the land. War-torn Spain, although without money to import enough food, was agriculturally a land similar to Dan's home state. As he considered ideas about how he could bring the same level of wellness to the children of Spain, he developed a vision: give them a cow. Dan's idea was to provide cows to families so they could produce the milk, right at home, to feed their own children.

And that idea generated a crucial concept that drove the success of Dan's vision: being self-sufficient was a better solution, long-term, than giving handouts to fight hunger. His vision was to move from relief efforts to local sustainability.

On his return to the United States, Dan planted the seeds of this idea within his community and enthusiasm started building. Dan was gifted at getting others involved. His inherent authenticity was a powerful influence. His ideas were infectious and he soon had others contributing solutions. He not only had the vision, but he was a Catalyst for action.

But there was one problem: how was Dan going to get the first donated cows from one location to another with limited resources? Dan himself was learning the best ways to be successful. A local professor coached Dan on how to ship pregnant heifers. They wouldn't need to be milked during transportation and would soon produce calves. The families receiving them would get two cows for the price of shipping one.

Dan West talked everywhere, summing it up with the words, "These children don't need a cup, they need a cow." Like any great vision, it soon belonged to many people who were invested in its success, who contributed to the second big vision: have the recipients of the cows "pay them forward." When a family received a heifer, they would donate the first calf to another family and also provide coaching on how to care for the calf, repeating the coaching they had received. Then, the process would be repeated by the new recipient family. This vision created an ever-expanding network of self-reliance, coaching people and coaching them to coach.

That's what a Catalyst does: they generate more from each situation to unleash maximum value. Dan's concept resulted in animals helping families and children across the world, and as the cows continued to produce calves, each heifer grew to produce her own calves—and the families got nourishing milk.

This "pay it forward" vision addressed another human need: each recipient would also become a donor. Families felt better about receiving their cow when they could also provide a cow, which gave each family a sense of pride.

As you look at Dan's life, you can see the overriding vision that guided all of his actions. In his own words, "in giving, we are blessed even more than in receiving." Each family was able to share in this vision. He created a context where he not only filled bellies, he nourished spirits, too.

Dan's vision was the beginning of a worldwide program known today as Heifer International, which has helped over seven million families in 125 countries and is still growing, providing cows and other sustainable livestock and plants to the financially-disadvantaged.

One man's vision became a vision for many. As a Catalyst, Dan leveraged the impact of his idea, which lead to coaching people who coach people throughout the world. Thanks to Dan's well-honed roles in the Leadership Triangle, people are learning and teaching and supporting each other, one family at a time. You can see the interlocking relationship of the three basic roles that are essential to becoming a leader.

THE FLIP SIDE

You've probably noticed the high contrast of the roles of drama to the roles of leadership. They are the flip side of each other:

- A Rescuer helps others because he thinks they are incompetent or can't handle feedback.
- A Coach helps others because he believes in the innate abilities of others to learn and to grow.

- A Victim sees no possibilities and believes himself to always be at the mercy of everyone else.
- A Visionary sees the possibilities and potential he can take in any situation.
- An Adversary uses threats to get people motivated.
- A Catalyst knows how to unlock the full potential of people and organizations.

Knowing these differences between drama and leadership will help you guide yourself, your team and your organization, and your family and community toward success.

The predisposition for drama comes as standard equipment with every human being: you must choose to engage in leadership, as it is an optional feature you have to select. Either mindset, and the behaviors it produces, has a fundamental impact on your leadership capacity. Your thoughts and actions create, over time, neurological patterns that impact future thoughts and actions. Habits develop. If the habit is drama, then drama becomes a way of life. That neuro-logical path becomes so well-traveled that a person treads it blindly, thinking drama is the only path available. Most people follow these paths because they are the paths of least resistance.

YOU CAN CHANGE

Every person has the power to lead their own lives and the ability to be the author of their own story. If you don't choose the roles you want, you'll get the roles that are shoved onto you, which may or may not serve you.

If you really adopt a leadership mindset, you will find it to be helpful in your work environment and transferable to other family and community situations as well.

Think about your own life and the roles you adopt. Are the roles you take on contributing to drama or to leadership? Are you being a Victim or a Visionary? An Adversary or a Catalyst? A Rescuer or a Coach?

CHAPTER 4

Perceptions and Intentions

HOW YOU THINK and what you think is what drives you either into the Drama Triangle or into the Leadership Triangle.

All through life, from infancy on, you store thoughts and memories of various experiences. You then begin to restrict your thinking by developing filters and perceptions. You create such perceptions as a useful way to reduce complexities so you can label and understand your world better. But, over time, your perceptual filters can start to limit what you can experience and, in some cases, these perceptual filters create obstacles. These are obstacles of your own making that do not need to be in your way. Your limiting perceptions of yourself and of others have the potential to limit your thinking and limit your leadership potential.

Classic limiting perceptions include thoughts about race, gender, nationality and religion. You're probably aware of some of your perceptions. If I were to name sports teams, cities, or universities (Green Bay = football, Stanford = smart), you'd immediately access your perception of them. But you have many, many other perceptions, most of which you follow without being conscious of how they impact your decision-making.

We can have limiting perceptions about others:

- Everyone in Accounting is out to get me.
- I don't trust Marketing. They are always spending money on the wrong programs.
- They don't like the work I am doing.

We can have limiting perceptions about ourselves:

- I am not smart enough.
- This will never work.
- I believe this will fail.

While reading this chapter, dig deeper to find those limiting perceptions about your thinking and motivations that have become second-nature, such that you no longer see that you have limited your perspective.

With that smaller perspective, you reduce the choices available to you. When you reduce your choices, you reduce your freedom, your power, and your ability to lead others.

USE AWARENESS, NOT EXCUSES

It's one thing to fall into the Drama Triangle when you don't realize what you are doing, and when you don't understand the roles of drama and how those roles have become entrenched habits. But now you do know about the trap of the Drama Triangle.

As you become even more aware, you'll recognize drama when you see it, even when you participate in it. And because you recognize it, you'll see more choices available to you. By applying what you're learning, you can pull yourself out of drama when you see it—because you can now see it. And you can explore leadership and build leadership skills to create a more enjoyable life for yourself and the people you lead.

But—this is a warning—if you read on, you can no longer make an excuse that you were unaware of the potential for drama. You'll be aware when your behavior is in the Drama Triangle, and you'll know that your excuses are an abdication of your responsibility. If you are "not responsible," you no longer get to choose. If you no longer choose, you're stuck in drama and you are not going to be able to lead.

Don't forget, living and working in the Drama Triangle comes with the energy-draining potential to generate fear, anger, resignation, self-pity, and doubt. The more time you spend in this Triangle, the more you will strengthen these drama patterns and all of their associated behaviors.

Save Your Drama for Your Mama can be a map to help you navigate the sometimes rough waters of your own mind. It will also help you navigate the sometimes rough waters with your team and your organization.

PERCEPTIONS & FILTERS

Understanding how you perceive can help you understand how you engage and react in the world. Perception is the process of making meaning of sensory information. How you perceive something can actually change your brain chemistry. Your perceptions impact what information you let in and how you make meaning about that information.

High-Priced Wine

What are your perceptions about price? All of us have perceptions about what's "worth it," whether it's the cost of a car, the price of a movie ticket, or the tag on a bottle of wine.

Antonio Rangel, professor of economics at Caltech, did a study of attitude and behaviors around perceived value. He and his colleagues found that $90 wine tastes superior when compared to the same wine being offered for $10.

In this research, volunteers tasted what they were told were different red wines. In fact, two of the wines were the same, but one bottle was labeled $5 and the other was labeled $45 (the $5 value was correct). The other wines in the testing were labeled $90 and $10. The volunteers were asked to rate the wines on flavor and enjoyment.

The tasters liked the higher-priced wines better. That may seem to be an obvious conclusion, but what was unexpected was that they physiologically enjoyed the higher-priced wines better. Their medial orbit frontal cortexes (one of the locations where we experience pleasure) showed higher amounts of blood and oxygen. The changes in the wines' prices changed their perception of the wine; the perceptions changed their brain chemistry. Because the pleasure centers were activated by the expectation of quality, they literally enjoyed the higher-priced wine more than the less expensive wine, even though it was the same wine.

How you experience the world is directly influenced by your positive or negative perceptions about any experience. If you think you are going to like something, the odds go up that you will. While this is common sense, we now have a more scientific understanding about how our perceptions impact what we experience.

Filtering Our Thoughts

We process every piece of information we receive. And that's a lot of information. Some pieces of information we decide are more important than others, so we prioritize based on experience and current factors in our life. We filter information and assign each piece meaning.

Perceptual filters are made up of our underlying assumptions and beliefs, our attitudes toward ourselves and others, our experiences, our current expectations, and how we process all of this information.

- Some of this we do very consciously: I'm informed (by looking out my window) that it is raining, so I will put on my raincoat.
- Some we do on reflex: have you ever flinched when a bug hit your windshield, despite knowing it couldn't hit you?
- Some we do without clear awareness or from habit: "Dave assigned me this project and Dave's always such a jerk, so I know I won't enjoy this project."

I heard this story about how filters shift our perceptions from Kermit L. Long, an inspirational writer: two men were walking through a crowded business district when one of them remarked that he could hear the unexpected sound of a cricket. The other man was astonished that anyone could hear a tiny cricket chirp above all the city noise. Smiling, the first man pulled out a coin and dropped it on the sidewalk. It landed with a small clink—and people all around stopped and turned to see where the money had fallen. The man said to his friend, "we hear what we listen for."

Our senses register millions upon millions of pieces of information every second. We're wired to filter, sort, and organize information. At birth, as your brain is flooded with information, your neural synaptic network starts to form. Over time, you reduced the activity and pruned off those synaptic connections that you no longer used. The frequently activated connections you kept; they strengthened. You made predicative maps of meaning from what would otherwise be random representations in your head. Based on your choices, some connections were made stronger and some were diminished. This is the brain's version of "use it or lose it."

These internal representations create neurological patterns and form our personal maps of the world. These maps of the world color and guide your perceptions toward more drama or toward more leadership.

This perception process inevitably distorts and filters information; yet we act as if our individual representations are the "truth." What you perceive as the "truth" is based on your experiences and how you interpret any new sensory input. Most of what you call "thinking" is just accessing your experiences, using little new data, and sifting it through the existing filter. Our unconscious filters are based on how we have interpreted events of the past. They lead us to believe that things are more fixed than they actually are.

Each person's reality is perceived and filtered personally, individually. Have you have ever gone to a concert with a friend, and you thought it was a terrific performance while your friend thought it was terrible? You both saw the same performers and heard the same music at the same time in the same venue. But you deciphered the sensory information differently. That doesn't make one person right and the other person wrong. You just have different perspectives because you are different people. You filtered your perception of the concert based on experiences you had growing up, the values of your family, your beliefs, and the decisions you have made about the world.

Communicating Our Thoughts

It's obvious that, while perceiving such enormous amounts of data, we can only attend consciously to small portions of it all. It makes sense that we filter it in ways that fit our experiences. But then we have to communicate with others. I bring my perceptions into a conversation with you, and you bring your perceptions into a conversation with me. When perceptions come into play, it's a wonder that we can communicate and make ourselves understood.

Just consider any meeting you and your work team attended recently. You all experienced the same meeting, yet you all had individual perceptual filters that made meaning of the meeting in different ways: it was dull, it was productive, the room was cold, the room was hot, Barbara felt it gave her a chance to explain her viewpoint, Brian felt Barbara wasted time getting on her soapbox again.

Translating all of your sensory experiences into language is complex. Language and perception are fraught with issues and misunderstandings. I've known people who, despite pride in their large vocabularies, greatly distort how they convey their perceptions. Vocabulary does not equal intelligence. Often, all those words are just an arsenal of rhetoric and the ability to name something. Knowing the "right" word isn't a substitute for common sense. Too often, we assume that my definition of a word is your definition of the same word.

Richard Feynman was one of the most original physicists after World War II and a Nobel Prize laureate. But as a boy, another student ridiculed Feynman's stupidity: he had asked Feynman whether he could name a bird that they had seen in the field. Feynman's reply was "no,"—so the other boy made fun of him, mocking "hasn't your father taught you anything?" Yes, Feynman's father had taught him about that bird, but about the bird's behavior, color patterns, habitat, and sounds. Feynman remembered how his father had said, "you can know the name of a bird in all the languages of the world, but when you're finished, you'll know absolutely nothing whatever about the bird. So, let's look at the bird and see what it's doing—that's what counts." Feynman's basic education wasn't in naming things but was in nurturing an astute ability to observe sensory data and distinguish patterns.

INTENTIONS, POSITIVE OR NEGATIVE

You need to become knowledgeable at a conscious level about your filters and the "reality" these filters are developing. The more aware you are, the better you can use (or eliminate) filters, which means you can make better choices and generate better results.

Perceptual filters can drive either **negative intentions** or **positive intentions**. If you remain unaware of your perceptual filters, the intentions they create are automatic and unconscious. The result can be decisions, judgments, and behaviors which happen in drama, until you consciously examine the perception and choose how to use (or reject) it.

Indra Nooyi, Chairman and CEO of PepsiCo, was one of *Time Magazine's* "100 Most Influential People in The World" in 2007 and 2008, and rated by Fortune as the most powerful business-woman in 2009. Think about her journey to becoming a CEO in the United States. She is female, a woman of color, and from another country—not usual characteristics of most Fortune 500 CEOs in the United States. Yet throughout her career, she followed a key principle. In an interview with *Fortune Magazine*, Ms. Nooyi talked about her father: "From him I learned to always assume positive intent. Whatever anybody says or does, assume positive intent." She went on to explain, "When you assume negative intent, you're angry. If you take away that anger and assume positive intent, you will be amazed. Your emotional quotient goes up because you are no longer almost random in your response. You don't get defensive. You don't scream. You are trying to understand and listen." I try to imagine the biases that must have come her way along her career journey. I know the power of assuming positive intent, so I appreciate how that simple but powerful attitude would have allowed her to meet those biases head on. Her father provided her with a philosophy to succeed in any environment she would find herself in.

Your thinking becomes your behavior, so when you begin with positive intentions, you more often get positive results, and more often lead others to think positively, too. When we listen with positive intention to others, we stay more engaged, we become more curious and we seek to understand the world from their perspective. This is not always easy, but if we commit to this flexibility in our own behavior, it can bring out the best in others— from which magic begins to occur. Why? Because perceptual filters influence every part of our communication.

Mentally, we choose the easiest path. The brain chooses the oft-trodden, best-recognized paths on its own. The more worn the trail, the more it becomes the path of least resistance. If these paths are constructive, then we will have positive approaches to life, come up with positive solutions to problems, and positive reactions when faced with challenges. But if we follow negative paths, when we meet a challenge we are more likely to perceive it as an overwhelming barrier. We encounter difficult people, and we see them in a negative light—in fact, we're more likely to perceive all people as difficult.

Choose to enter your conversations with positive intentions. This will lead you to the behaviors associated with the Leadership Triangle. The more times you choose leadership, the easier it will become to demonstrate the pattern of leadership in the future.

The first step toward assuming positive intentions is to identify your perceptual filters, especially those that limit your choice of behaviors.

Negative intentions creep into our thinking and can completely color our perspective if we are not aware of their insidiousness. Read through these negative intentions:

- No one wants me to succeed.
- Since others are not willing to change, why should I even make the effort?
- I already know they won't agree with me.
- I can't change their minds.
- I can't seem to catch a break, despite all my efforts.
- What a waste of time to expect things to change around here!
- No one can be trusted.

- Nothing I do will make a difference.
- Things never work out, so when they don't, I am already prepared.
- I have to get them before they get me.
- Why try?

Depressing to read aren't they? Yet many such statements are "talking" to you all day long. You'll certainly never change a situation by constantly repeating to yourself such self-defeating perceptions about it.

The danger with perceptional filters is that they can turn into self-fulfilling prophecies. The mind, in its need to be "right," will do whatever it takes to justify and defend its position.

BEWARE THE SELF-FULFILLING PROPHECY

It's a self-fulfilling prophecy when an event is predicted to happen, and the assumption that it will happen propels the event to actually occur, which thus confirms the prophecy's accuracy.

- Here's a classic example of a self-fulfilling prophecy: a bank has a healthy balance sheet. For some reason, rumors begin to spread that something is wrong at the bank. Customers begin to close their accounts, spreading more rumors, which in turn create more fear and anxiety, so even more people come to the bank with increasing concern and determination to get their money. The rush of withdrawals changes the capital position of the bank. Now it's true that there is something wrong with the bank. The rumor of risk caused a sudden demand from customers, which caused the bank to lose cash, which truly increased the risk of banking there. What started out as an unsubstantiated rumor actually came true.

- If you've seen *The Empire Strikes Back*, you'll recognize this self-fulfilling prophecy. Luke Skywalker is taking Jedi lessons from Master Yoda. Yoda tells Luke to lift up his X-Wing fighter using only his mind. Luke protests, saying that it is impossible (that's his prophecy), but he tries. For a few dramatic seconds, the ship moves but then sinks back into the swamp. Yoda—using only the Force—lifts the ship and puts it on steady ground. Luke exclaims, "I can't believe it!" Yoda replies, "that is why you fail."

- Back in 1979, the media in California deluged us with warnings about our severe gasoline shortage. The irony is that there was plenty of gas. For the most part, car owners tend to keep their tanks about 25% full. Once the media had scared us into thinking there might be no gasoline for our cars, everybody started keeping their tanks closer to 75% full. This new behavior depleted all of the gasoline reserves, increased demand by 200%, and moved gas in storage into millions of people's fuel tanks. Next thing you know, we had long lines at the pumps and no gas in reserves. There wasn't, to begin with, a gasoline shortage, but the limiting perception of a gas shortage ended up creating one. The predicted worst-case scenario turned into reality.

Whether you approach a situation with a negative or positive intention directly impacts your ability to influence the outcome. This type of twisted thinking happens in drama. For example, if Bill assumes that others on the team don't trust him, he might act in an overly suspicious manner, even being hostile because, from his perspective, the team is not granting him any respect or trust. So his thinking shifts his behavior and other people see the behavior and react to it. Duncan and Leigh withhold information from Bill, because Bill seems so volatile and untrustworthy. Now Bill is entrenched in his perception that they don't trust him—because they don't. Bill's sad prophecy, "they don't trust me," has been fulfilled.

I always say that you get the team you deserve. If people are acting poorly around you, what is the one constant in that situation? You! Your perceptions have a direct impact on how others will show up around you. If you don't like how other people are responding to you, the best advice I can give you is to examine your own limiting perceptions about yourself or about others.

Are My Perceptions In My Own Way?

None of us live in a vacuum. How you react depends upon the world you're reacting to. The purpose of your perceptions is to give you a framework on which to build your response to your experiences. You then believe that your perceptions of the world are the truth about the world.

Your interpretations and perceptions are affecting your emotions, often without you consciously realizing it. Because you believe your perception to be true, you take actions to reinforce the "truth" of that perception.

Presently, in your memory banks are assigned meanings and your interpretations of past events, with your explanation or conclusion about each. You'll encounter conflict when you react to a new situation with these old interpretations. The perceptions you might have had in the past may no longer be relevant. If you once had an ogre of a boss named Kevin, how would you react to being introduced to your new boss—Kevin? You know nothing about this new guy, but just hearing the name might make your gut clench.

So, you have perceptions; you also have perceptions that are limiting. Using that limitation, you filter information you receive and finally you project these limiting perceptions onto others, modifying your intentions based on how you approach the person or situation. But the most self-defeating action is to believe limiting perceptions about yourself. These perceptions can limit what you think is possible. Are you getting in your own way?

Is your perception the same as reality?

Here's an example of the danger of a limiting perception. A team of scientists set up an experiment to observe the behavior patterns in a fish. All of the fish's needs were being met. Each day, the scientists would drop minnows into his tank, which the fish would eat. A routine was established and the fish was well-fed. Then the scientists changed the pattern.

They now put the minnows inside a clear glass tube. The tube had holes small enough for water to flow, but not for the minnows to swim out. The fish could see the minnows in the tube—they appeared to be swimming in his tank. But he could not catch them. He slammed against the tube and pushed it around. The hungrier he became, his ferocity increased. He exhausted every behavior to get inside the tube. Eventually, he realized that the minnows could not be reached. He became resigned to the situation.

The scientists altered the situation again. They took the minnows from the tube and put them in the tank to swim freely. The fish, having learned he could not catch the minnows, starved to death. He stopped trying. His perception of his inability to catch food got in his own way.

CAN YOU REWIRE YOUR BRAIN?

As you think of a thought, the feeling communicates itself to every cell in your body, through small protein molecules called neuropeptides. You generate a rich mixture of these neurotransmitters with every thought you make.

If it's an unpleasant, stressful thought, the resulting chemical stress to the body increases your blood pressure, weakens your immune system, and increases your chances for diabetes and depression. The trap of the Drama Triangle is that the more you run this pattern, the more likely you are to run this pattern in the future.

The more your thinking is positive and you are striving for leadership, the more you will use your frontal lobe, that part of the brain where you make conscious choices. The more you choose to use your brain to access leadership, the easier it becomes.

Think about how often you view a situation through a lens of truth or utility. If you think someone is a jerk, your actions will reflect that perception. How useful to you was it to label that person a jerk? Did it help you? If you think someone's behavior is open and honest, you will act consistent with that perception. The problem is that your brain wants to be right so you will have a tendency to view the world through what you perceive as true. In many cases, what you perceive as true may limit what choices you have available to you.

You have to decide which perception is most useful for you. If you perceive the world in a way that limits you in the present, you will limit your resources and opportunities. If you envision a difficult situation, you will prepare yourself to deal with adversity, conflict, and problems. In this specific way you are creating the conflicts and problems by making them a reality. You develop a variety of coping behaviors as a way to rationalize whatever happens as simply "the way it is," and become resigned to other possibilities.

Medical research used to believe that as human beings grew older, the neural network of the brain became fixed. Now we know that the brain continues to change and never stops learning. The very nature of the plasticity of the brain allows you to lay down new tracks and patterns of thinking at any point in your life.

You Can't Read Minds

Give up trying to figure out the intentions of others. You have no superpowers for mind reading.

How often do you assume to know what the other person's intentions are? Are you aware of how much time you waste trying to figure out the motivations behind other peoples' actions? If you are in a stressful situation, do you assume their intentions are negative? Don't forget: when you develop a perception, your mind will believe it to be true—and your mind will guide your behavior to react to that "truth."

Finding What You Look For

As you constantly try to figure out what people's intentions are, you will:

- Jump to conclusions.
- "See" additional behaviors that justify your conclusions.
- Hunt in your own memory for similar situations that support your conclusions.
- Compare your findings and get support for them. You'll do this by having conversations with yourself, or conversations with others. (Talking behind another's back is definitely in the Drama Triangle.)

What you are really doing is creating a set of limiting perceptions and embedding a fixed set of negative intentions in yourself, directed at the other person. Your negative intention with regards to the other person will show up in your tone of voice and in your behavior. What we are thinking will be expressed in our behaviors and, thus, our body language—the roll of an eye, the tone of voice. Unless you are a world-class actor, you constantly demonstrate what you are thinking by your behavior. When you are following a limiting set of perceptions and have negative intentions, it is too easy to attack someone or feel defensive—which, in either case, will have everyone jumping into the Drama Triangle.

The irony is that when you look for other people's negative intentions, you'll find them. Many people in the Drama Triangle habitually assume that others have negative intentions towards them. So now, who is running the negative intentions? But in drama, you'll invent reasons for your own negative intentions as a way to permit yourself to be guarded or go on the attack with an angry response.

If you are honest and have enough self-awareness to reject your old, limiting perceptions, it will become obvious that trouble brews when you judge the intentions of others.

Know That People Are Doing Their Best

In the Leadership Triangle, thinking with positive intention, your perceptions are filtered with the assumption that people are striving to do their best with the resources they possess.

- You truly see the best in others.
- Your own positive intentions encourage others toward positivity.
- By seeing positive intent in others, you can usually take a challenging situation and transform that resistance into cooperation.
- You remain resourceful, relaxed, calm, and more ready to be a Visionary, Catalyst, or a Coach.

By seeing positive intent in others, you can transform a challenging situation of resistance into cooperation.

SHIFTING OUT OF DRAMA

Want to shift out of the drama created by limiting perceptions and negative intentions? First, accept responsibility that you are in charge of your perceptions. Then, rigorously challenge your own perceptions and beliefs about the world and how it works. It seems easier to argue that your point of view is "true" and to hold that view. For instance, if your job isn't going well, you may "perceive" this is because your boss doesn't provide you sufficient training. Your brain will scramble around to find evidence to support that perception. Because of this perception you may miss other opportunities. But if you keep your intention positive, and assume your boss's intention is positive, then you'll be able to re-examine the information presented to you, adjust your perception, and you may discover other ways to provide yourself with training and develop yourself.

Drama—The Low Energy Triangle

If you drop into the Drama Triangle, you'll shift into communicating with negative intentions, and you will feel unable to have the conversations with people you need to talk with. When you are in the Drama Triangle you become unable to do your work successfully. You will notice a resignation about your organization or your team. Worse, this resignation starts to creep into other areas of your life. It affects your energy. Resignation is a slippery slope down into the Drama Triangle. When you are in the Drama Triangle you pay the price with giving up your own energy. What happens if this sort of resignation shows itself on a team? What happens if, in life, you stop trying? Resignation is a deadly trap, and it can have a profoundly negative impact on your life. (We'll talk more about resignation in Chapter 8.)

With this limited approach to your work and coworkers:

- Your energy starts to fade.
- You assume everyone else's behavior is not positive.
- You assume others have negative intentions in their relationship with you.
- You assume others don't respect you or you are behaving selfishly.

When you're in the Leadership Triangle, it is impossible for these thoughts to arise. In leadership:

- You assume people have positive intentions.
- You understand that others are doing the best they can.

- You give others the benefit of the doubt.
- You assume that others may have interests that are important to them.
- You assume that others are doing what they are doing for a positive reason.

This mindset, while it appears to be for the benefit of the other person, is really for your benefit. Being in a positive frame of mind keeps you more resourceful. With a positive frame of mind, you generate an energy that is infectious to those around you.

Fostering Positive Intentions

Assuming that others have positive motives serves as a useful filter for your perceptions. It's not always easy, because you want to be right about what your thoughts are when you perceive your colleagues acting poorly, but when you hold the assumption that others have good intentions, you're more likely to remain in the Leadership Triangle.

You may think this is naive or opens you up for attacks. Nothing is further from the truth. By following the principle of "I have positive intentions and I know others also have positive intentions,"

- You're better able to be a partner, and to coach and create a vision.
- You can still hold others accountable, but when something goes wrong, you're less likely to jump to a conclusion or assign blame. You'll first believe they acted with positive intent, so you can listen with an open mind to their accounting of the situation.

- You will become open and more receptive to those around you.
- You will find that work is easier, relationships come more quickly, and other people's defenses come down more rapidly.
- Your capacity to trust comes more easily, both professionally and personally.

You end up being the winner when you follow your positive intention out of the clutches of the Drama Triangle.

Negate Negativity

Cynics live in the Drama Triangle. In the Drama Triangle, everyone sees shadows where there aren't any. In the Drama Triangle, time and energy are spent being negative and assuming negativity, intended or otherwise.

That means that, when you and your positive intentions deal with someone who is in the Drama Triangle, you will be met with defensiveness. But you are now armed with a powerful tool that can handle that defensive Adversary. Seeing positive intent, even in those who may wish to derail you, is completely disarming. Others don't know what to do with someone who doesn't resist, who doesn't "fight back." With your positive intention, you can become a master of understanding, a practitioner of verbal aikido.

Even with someone snidely attacking you, your assumption of positive intent will keep you out of the Drama Triangle and keep you mindful and resourceful. Let's look at this in action:

Team member: I don't think you are going to succeed on this project.

You respond: I appreciate your letting me know. What do you think I am missing?

Team member: I don't like the way you are handling the analysis.

You respond: Thank you for being honest with me. I appreciate that.

Team member: Well, what I really think is—I don't think you've got what it takes to get this project done.

You respond: I really want to thank you for being direct with me and letting me know where you think I may be at risk.

Team member: Are you for real? What's your game?

You respond: I have no reason to play a game with you. You're part of the team that's going to get this project done well. I want to partner with you.

Team member: It's no game, then? Well I do plan to be part of this project.

You respond: I want to know how you think I could get this done successfully. Can we focus on getting this to work?

By assuming positive intentions, you stay flexible and adaptable. The Adversary will eventually run out of attacks (he or she is used to people backing down, not staying calm). You stay in the Leadership Triangle by being open, honest, and non-defensive.

If we are going to make up intentions about other people, we may as well make them positive because we will garner higher quality information and become more resourceful. There is power behind the mindset of assuming positive intention:

- It allows you to see the best in yourself by seeing the best in others.
- It is the best way to create cooperation.
- It is a way of genuinely listening to another person, so that whatever their intentions are, they feel safe talking about what is occurring to them.

This is not about being naïve about other people. I believe how you perceive another person has a direct and powerful influence on their behavior, and therefore this is about helping you to be more resourceful. Test it out. And no matter what you discover about your impact on others, your thinking will have a direct and powerful impact on you.

Ask for Feedback—Then Actually Listen To It

You can increase your awareness of your perceptions by asking for feedback from family, friends and colleagues. This is why you will want to receive feedback about your own levels of drama and leadership from as many people as the online survey will allow. (See the front cover for instructions.)

I've made some of my best discoveries about myself because of information supplied by someone else. The people in your life notice things about you that you either ignore or that you are oblivious to. Their input can help you. Useful feedback will reveal any limiting characteristics, speech habits, personal behaviors, non-verbal behaviors, and other blind spots. A "blind spot" is a behavior affecting your life (and often affecting others around you) that you don't even notice. A blind spot can move you into drama. If not corrected, if can obstruct relationships or even spoil a friendship.

Offering feedback is dangerous, especially to a friend or to a person in authority such as your manager or supervisor. Most team members do not attempt it or do not really deliver deep, useful feedback. But your close colleagues aren't doing you any favors by turning a blind eye to your limiting characteristics.

Here are some ways to get feedback, and use it well.

- **Ask an open-ended question**. Most people ask, "Do you have any feedback for me?" and the common response is "no." Instead ask, "What feedback do you have for me?" You're more likely to get an answer to this question. It may be positive: "I really like that you start all meetings on time." When I receive positive feedback, I then ask the person to give me feedback on what I was missing or what I may have done that was ineffective. This is an excellent way to make sure there are no concerns being left unsaid. It is also a quick way to create trust with someone.

- **Say "thank you."** Show appreciation for this gift to your personal growth. Make your thank-you short, but something you can say sincerely, such as "You've really given me something to think about. Thanks." Do not contradict the person, or tell them their feedback is wrong and inaccurate, or justify your position. That's a sure way to keep them from ever giving you feedback again.

- **Listen and consider their perspective.** You might discover behaviors and attitudes you need to correct. Make people aware that you intend to act on their feedback.

- After a blind spot is identified, then **work to change it**. When you can display a replacement behavior, you are showing your team that the feedback you receive matters to you.

- **Be accountable**. Openly discuss the habit you've decided to change, improve or develop. Ask others for their suggestions to assist you.

- If you receive feedback that calls for an apology, **apologize**. If the feedback is "you shot down Martha's idea before you gave her a chance to finish her thought," you need to apologize to Martha. A leader doesn't accept every idea that is presented, but is never rudely dismissive of any idea.

- **Be realistic.** Commit to making an effort in these areas you're developing. Make sure you are making a realistic commitment. Don't take on more than you can handle. Get help, either through training, reading, talking with others, or through support from others.

YOU CAN CHANGE NOW

It can be a challenge to be confronted with your limitations. But I've discovered that feedback, warranted or not, is a powerful catalyst for change.

You now have evidence that reveals just how powerful your brain really is. Your next step is to put these ideas into action. Examine your limiting perceptions, examine when you assume negative intentions, and capture yourself when you drop into the Drama Triangle. By consciously attending to the patterns in your life, you can start to shift these patterns to ones that will serve you better.

CHAPTER 5

Who Is Driving The Bus?

WHO IS DRIVING the bus? It's time to take the wheel and take control of your own life.

Your brain is always working. If you do nothing to help optimize its effectiveness, you will get a random result. If you refuse to drive your own bus, to take control of your own thinking, you are responding only to your environment, which means you're always going to be at the mercy of that environment—it will, in essence, control you.

I want to help you get a more positive result on a more predictable basis. You can override those unconscious, automatic patterns. You can stop being the passenger and instead drive the bus yourself.

Studies say we only use 10% of our brains for daily functions such as breathing, keeping the heart beating, and getting breakfast ready. That leaves a lot left over for purposeful application. Science is making incredible discoveries about our brains and our thought processes, and is teaching us how to produce predictable outcomes. How can we apply this knowledge?

BE INTENTIONAL

People often won't take action, waiting instead for someone, some external authority or someone in a position of power, to tell them what to do. Challenge this idea for yourself, this notion that you have to be in a certain position before you're "allowed" to change things.

Throughout history, people have stood up for what they believe to be right. Mahatma Gandhi, Susan B. Anthony, Dan West and Martin Luther King, Jr. are just a few examples of individuals who didn't wait for an "okay" from an external source before they stepped into their leadership roles. Muhammad Ali jeopardized his athletic career by refusing to be drafted during the Vietnam War, based on his principles of non-violence. He made a difficult choice and paid a significant price: being stripped of his title—but through that action, he was true to his moral values.

The actions of all of those leaders rebelled against the prevailing wisdom. However, they were Catalysts for creating new ways to view the world, and influenced everyone. They did so without support from the established institutions. They acted as individuals who decided to change a circumstance, who moved forward even in the face of adversity, and who proceeded to convince millions with their conviction. When these leaders performed brave acts, they were motivated by a profound sense of faith in their ideas. They had a willingness to take risks in order to make a difference for others. Many leaders throughout history have paid a huge price for their initiative, sometimes with their lives.

Same Market—Different Result

Lately, we have seen a number of retail stores go out of business. The heads of these businesses are blaming the economy. While I am sure that the poor economy was the final straw in their demise, the real reasons these companies have failed are comprised of a dangerous combination of poor business strategies, unsatisfactory customer service, and poor products. It is not due to a challenge coming from their external circumstances.

Circuit City tried many turnaround strategies, but they missed the boat on some fundamentals. A few years ago, Circuit City fired all of their knowledgeable employees and replaced them with cheaper labor. The result was bankruptcy, and the management blamed the economy. Circuit City then tried to reinvent their business model to get back into the competitive market, but they continued to make poor business decisions.

They chose inexpensive real estate as a business strategy. My local Circuit City was in an out-of-the-way location. The location may have meant cheap rent, but it also meant being in a spot where customers didn't naturally flow.

I never felt a visceral connection when I shopped at Circuit City: their stores felt wrong. On the few occasions that I shopped there, my experience each time was similar: the store was dark, and there was rarely anyone on the floor to give advice, just the checkout clerks. Their product mix always seemed wrong, especially after they discontinued offering household appliances. They didn't offer the brands and types of electronics available from other retailers. I never felt I was getting a deal—if I did find a product I wanted, I could usually find it somewhere else for less.

Best Buy, on the other hand, has good products at good prices, at an easy-to-reach location. When I walk in, I'm greeted by friendly staff who can help me with insightful knowledge. They have mastered the fundamentals of retail and customer support. Best Buy's Geek Squad is also helpful to customers and a billion dollar business for the company.

Circuit City took their time before providing technical support to their customers. After seeing the success of the Geek Squad, Circuit City began a support service called Firedog. It was costly for Circuit City and it never caught on.

Circuit City didn't fail because they hit a bad economy. Rather, they failed because they didn't focus on the front line of the transaction: where the customer and the product meet. On the other hand, Best Buy, in the same market, selling similar products, continued to be successful. So it's hard to justify blaming the economy as Circuit City's reason for failure, despite what their former management claims.

Best Buy, during the exact same timeframe, created success by being armed with an internally focused mindset and reliance, while Circuit City blamed the external environment for their demise. This points to a difference in the locus of control within the thinking that the leadership demonstrated in each company.

LOCUS OF CONTROL

The concept of "locus of control" was developed by Julian Ratter in the 1950s. It explores the extent to which a person believes he controls events that affect him.

- If you have an internal locus of control, you view events as coming from your own behavior and actions, and you accept the responsibility for them.
- If you have an external locus of control, you see events that effect you as being determined by others, by chance, or by "fate," and outside of your control.

Every day, in every action, you are operating from one or the other—external or internal.

To realize your full potential, you must start from an internal locus of control. You must understand that the choices you make for yourself determine the course of your life and your ability to influence others.

From childhood on, we learn about making choices. We begin as babies, completely dependent, then we grow from dependence to responsibility. As we acquire independence of thought and choice and accept responsibility for our actions, we place the locus of control internally. When oriented internally, we know that outcomes and successes (and mistakes) are dependent on our own efforts.

John Nesbit, in his 1982 best-seller *Megatrends*, predicted several trends consistent with increased self-leadership, with a pronounced shift

- from centralization to decentralization,
- from help from institutions to helping oneself,
- from a representative democracy to a participatory style of democracy,
- and from pyramid structures to network structures.

Today, in some cases, we can see that his predictions have come true. Investing, retirements, the Internet, and blogging have all become more prevalent. These trends represent a move away from external control by institutions and put greater emphasis on the person being accountable and being internally in control. Yet equally, as some institutions move toward becoming internally controlled, individuals coming of age today are feeling more and more out of control. For instance, we feel more dependent on others for our very survival: we have become so specialized we don't even know where our food comes from. Gone is the day when we could work on your own cars. More and more rules are created to limit the choices we have available, individual accountability seems to be a part of a past when we would fend for ourselves, and now we have a habit of looking to others to take care of our basic needs.

When locked into drama, a person abdicates making independent, personal choices. They give up, so to speak, the wheel that drives the bus. They get in the passenger's seat and let people, organizations, and events drive instead. But it's difficult to measure up to another's expectations (especially if they are guessing what others expect of them). There will always be external evidence that someone was better, did better, or had more than you. With an external locus of control, you're more likely to develop the Drama Triangle mindset: the major characteristic of choosing to avoid as much responsibility as possible.

The best, most sustainable personal motivation comes from having an internal locus of control. The person with the internal locus of control is aware of external influences. He takes them into account but makes his own decisions anyway, accepting responsibility for his choices. Such belief fundamentally supports the Leadership Triangle mindset.

You have an External Locus of Control When...

- You allow others to control your life. This can be anyone, dead or alive. They might know they influence you or they might never have met you. A parent, a teacher who shamed you, your current boss, the boss you had in 1995, a jerk, your ex-spouse, the Senate, your neighbor, your mortgage company, your son's Little League coach...

- You also abdicate control of your life to circumstance and events, such as the economy, where you went to school, where you did not go to school, your grandparent's nationality, your sister's successful career, your heath, your parents' health, even the weather.

- You don't take action on projects when and if you assume others have negative intentions toward you.

- You believe that success is about "being in the right place at the right time" or "knowing the right people."

- You see rewards and penalties as being outside of your control. (No reason to try for the bonus, the boss controls it and he won't give it to me anyway.)

- Results are not your fault. (It was a minor fender-bender. I wouldn't have hit the guy if he'd seen the light was green! Why didn't he move?)

- If things go wrong, you use words such as luck, fate, karma, or "it wasn't meant to be."

You have an Internal Locus of Control When....

- You see yourself as responsible for your own life, your habits, choices, and mistakes.
- You work on yourself rather than just hoping for a lucky break.
- You believe that your success depends on your own actions. You believe you can be successful.
- You take accountability for your choices. You accept consequences.
- You take into account the opinions of others but are not controlled by them.
- You design the life you want.

Name That Locus!

The following examples will provide a better understanding of where you locate your own control:

- You want to take a vacation during the Christmas holidays. On November 15th, you find a resort that you really like and you call to make reservations for December. They tell you they are completely booked up. Do you say to yourself, "What rotten luck!" or do you say, "I should have made the reservations earlier. Next time, I'll call in August"?
- You are a candidate for a promotion. You pass a series of interviews and make it to the final two. Management picks the other person, who does not have as much experience as you do. Do you say to yourself, "I have no idea what they are looking for. Anyway, getting promoted is just a popularity contest" or do you say, "I'm sure they have reasons be-

hind the decision. I will develop my skills and put myself in a position to be promoted next time"?

- You are giving a presentation when the projector suddenly stops working. You fix it and give your presentation, but it is not as good as you wanted it to be. Do you blame the projector for your failure and lament that things are always going wrong for you? Or do you admit that you didn't check the projector beforehand and that you need to develop a backup plan to perform better under pressure when things go wrong in the future?

- In your work team, when it comes to taking the initiative, are you are the one least likely to do so, and only if extremely pressured? Or are you always the first to volunteer so that you can grow and learn?

- When there is a problem in your town or neighborhood, do you assume you'll have to live with it—after all, you can't change fate? Or do you tackle the problem because you believe in your potential to be a part of the solution?

- Do you believe that your life is not going smoothly because you are never in the right place at the right time, and you don't know the right people? Or is life not going smoothly because of specific choices you made that didn't work out as you had anticipated, and for which you are patiently, persistently working to correct to learn more and affect your destiny?

A Generation of Drama

Our younger generation is "maturing" into drama. College students today feel as though their lives are controlled by outside forces. The

Internal or External Locus of Control study is one that has been given to many college students over the last 50 years. Currently, the external locus of control measurement is high among today's college students—almost double compared to previous generations. The risk is that we may be creating a generation that does not have leadership and accountability as part of their basic inherent nature.

The paradox is that today's teens and college students were raised with an emphasis on high self-esteem. But when high self-esteem is combined with a high external locus of control, the result is cynicism and a direct path to the Drama Triangle.

Combine a sense of entitlement and its delusion of self-importance with the conviction that nothing you do will make a difference— that's the mindset of many young people today. No wonder they become enmeshed in the roles of Adversary, Rescuer, and Victim. That's another reason why it's crucial that you commit to developing your own leadership ability: so you can help others develop their competencies as leaders. Potentially you will not get as many natural leaders coming into your organizations and teams. Therefore, learning how to create more leadership in organizations will be a crucial core competency now and in the future.

An external location for the control in your life isn't good for your health, either. People who let outside forces run their lives have a higher probability of becoming depressed and anxious, and they are less likely to handle stress. The result can generate a self-fulfilling but limiting prophecy: thinking things are out of control can make you sick enough so that things become even more out of control. This is a recipe for chaos.

Individuals who believe they are controlled by external forces feel obligated to gratify others and have weaker self-control. There is a higher probability that they will not work as hard and will achieve less in school because they believe that no matter how much they study or work, the end result will be the same. Never before has learning about leadership and creating an internal locus for your control been more important. We must become more self-reliant and lead by example, or the next generation might just be one filled with drama.

Opinion or Control?

Are you dependent upon others to define who you are? Do you worry about what others think about you and about decisions you make? If so, you're probably more often in the Drama Triangle than you realize. Stop to think: are you enlisting too much support from others? Or can you stand on your own?

Try this: take a break from the opinion of others. Refuse anyone's perception about you but your own. It's important that you take the time to create a foundation of independence. See if you can take a holiday from your parents' approval. Take a holiday from your spouse's approval. Take a break from your friend's opinions. I am not saying this needs to last forever, but if you have a habit to only seek out the external opinions of others, taking a break from their advice may be the best gift you ever give yourself.

It can be scary, swinging without the safety net of others' approval for a while, but if you don't cultivate this independence, you cannot develop your leadership strength. You'll find it difficult to create compelling visions and be an inspiration for change. Your ability to lead others comes from your ability to make your own choices.

With each choice you make, you learn more about yourself and you express more about who you are. Ask yourself this: "if I were passionately fearless, what would I be doing with my life?" It doesn't matter if your answer is "I'd be climbing Everest" or "I'd be stamp collecting," what matters is that it's your choice.

Learn how to develop and trust your vision—this is a feat that is nearly impossible if you're still relying on the outside world to tell you whether you're doing well or not.

Don't misinterpret these ideas as "either/or." We are interdependent and we are a social species. You do need support and advice from others, just as you need to consider their needs and opinions as you make choices. That being said, taking a break is important. If you do not become self-reliant, you will spend much of life following the judgment of others. Develop independence from the need of those opinions. I'm not saying, "be selfish." I'm saying, "rely on your own point of view first." Your insights might lead you into new territory or new goals in your life.

You can set up the safety net again after you're sure you have established a clear understanding that you make your choices without the influences of others.

Traffic Circles

Modern traffic circles not only reduce automobile accidents but also alleviate traffic jams and delays. This gives us a great metaphor for the effectiveness of following imposed rules versus making personal choices. I use this example to show the advantage to making your own choices, not to advocate breaking traffic laws. A traffic light is an external control which tells you how to behave.

You don't choose. It's up to the light to make the rules: stop now, go now. We accept stoplights as useful and safe, but we go into "automatic pilot" mode at most stoplights. We follow the command with limited awareness of the traffic around us.

Traffic circles, on the other hand, demand attention. You cannot be mindless at a roundabout. You must constantly make choices as you negotiate the flow of traffic. The only rule is "bear right." Other than that, you must make choices. You must be aware of the other cars around you and make decisions that allow you and others to safely navigate the circle.

Traffic circles improve the safety and speed of the flow of traffic. One study found a 75% decrease in injury accidents when using traffic circles compared to intersections controlled by stoplights or signs. Traffic circles also speed up traffic (up to 74%) by keeping everyone moving instead of waiting at red lights.

Sometimes following the external rule is also inefficient. Ever sat at a red light when there was not another car in sight and it was clearly safe to cross? You stay stopped because you are following an external rule. The danger, of course, is when someone else doesn't follow the rule and you are not watching out: a clear recipe for an accident. The reason traffic circles are safer is that we can't shift to "automatic pilot," and we can't let someone else (even a light) tell us how to behave—we must maintain our awareness of the immediate moment. With awareness, we are present and with presence wiser choices are made.

"It's Not My Fault"

Even behaviors that are considered bad habits, such as drinking too much, are considered to be out of our control.

In *The Codependency Conspiracy*, Dr. Stan Katz and Aimee Liu argue that when we talk about alcoholism, we mean that the person afflicted by it somehow has no direct responsibility for his behavior. If alcoholism is proven to be outside of their control, then a person can blame his reactions to alcohol on an external force—the disease. He can claim to have no personal responsibility for drinking too much.

Thinking of oneself as addicted and thus, not able to make healthier choices on their own, has people defining themselves in terms of their illness. In other words, they turn a bad habit into an "integral and permanent aspect of their identity," according to Drs. Katz and Liu. Subsequently, they do little to rectify their own behaviors. In many cases, they end up trapped in the Drama Triangle, even if they do stop drinking.

I am not saying that functional addictive tendencies aren't both neurological as well as physiological. I'm saying that abdicating your responsibility by saying it is "outside of your control" brings with it all the behaviors associated with the Drama Triangle.

It is no coincidence that addictive personalities make frequent, lengthy visits into the Drama Triangle and do their best to get their families and friends to come join them there.

Try This On In Your Mind

Here are two mental exercises I'd like you to go through. Take the time to do each one; be thorough. You should be able to see where each is headed—internally or externally—but you'll benefit from getting yourself involved in each.

Your Choices = Success

Think of your career over the next year or think of an important project you want to complete. Mentally act out the steps you need to do to make it happen.

1. Picture yourself as a very capable leader.
2. You are choosing a specific project, goal or your next step in your career.
3. See yourself approaching others and positively influencing them.
4. See yourself positively affecting others through actions and what you say.
5. Notice yourself being accountable for whatever result you get.
6. Notice what is working. Notice what adjustments you choose to make to get the best result.
7. Notice your actions as a positive expression of your core values.
8. See the outcome. Sense how you feel as you celebrate the successes that you generated.

Do As I Say

This one will be tougher. Again, mentally envision your career for the next year or the same project or goal: you don't make the decisions in your life. Others do. You're at the receiving end of what others think about you throughout your career.

1. Picture yourself as someone who does what they are told. You have to do the assignment as it was given to you:

2. Everyone has advice for you. One person tells you to go in one direction while another person tells you to take a different approach. You discount your own point of view.

3. Your ability to influence others is based on if they like you or not. You're not sure if your message is getting across. Their feedback is hard for you to read.

4. Your result is based on luck. You were in the right place at the right time or you just missed out.

5. It is easy to blame others when things go wrong. When things go right and others take credit for your work … well that's just how things go around here.

6. You slowly resign your values—they don't seem to be that valuable anyway. You have to do what you do just to survive. You tell yourself you are just being a realist, but you notice you don't have as much energy as you used to.

7. The results you generate are based on the circumstances you found yourself in.

You can see that, in this scenario, you never hold yourself accountable for any of the results. Your only feedback is from others, who tell you either their opinion of the best course of action or their opinion of you. You don't have a sense about it for yourself. If this were the life you lived, it is almost undoubtedly true that:

-   You wouldn't work as hard as you once did. After all, what difference would it make?

-   You would know what others want to do, and you would know what they want you to do.

- You would become so accustomed to relying on others' opinions that you wouldn't be sure what you wanted.
- You would feel unable to make a difference and unable to change how your life is playing out.

How was that different?

You recognized that the first scenario challenged you to think with an internal orientation, and the second scenario was externally oriented.

How did those two experiences differ for you? Did one feeling feel more familiar? Did that familiarity feel good or uncomfortable? Which experience was the easiest to imagine, and why?

You know the old adage: you get what you ask for. This is the key. You are constantly "asking" yourself for things, and your brain is listening. It will give you what you ask for.

Think internally-oriented thoughts, and you get the feeling from the first scenario. You subsequently have to move into the Leadership Triangle.

Accept externally-oriented thoughts and you will get the feelings from the second scenario. You move more towards the Drama Triangle. You'll also:

- Blame other people or situations with a much higher degree of frequency.
- Resort to more excuses for your actions.
- Be more sensitive to being blamed and react defensively.

- Not accept responsibility for your actions, even refuse to acknowledge wrongdoing (despite being faced with evidence to the contrary).

WHEN THE TEAM IS DEPENDENT

If you are in an organization where most of the employees are externally dependent on what others are thinking about them, the blame game is played often and by almost everyone. Passing blame is a common tactic in many organizations. While some on the team search for a scapegoat, everyone is trying to cover their own tracks. Once any group—work team, corporation, community, or family—starts pointing fingers, people fail to address real problems. Dangerous situations can go undetected and unreported because everyone is so busy covering their rears. In such a blaming culture, even the smallest error draws negative feedback (from a manager being an Adversary), rather than encouragement or praise for genuine achievements (from a leader being a Coach). And thus the spiral continues.

Those with external loci of control have excuses for their lack of performance:

- Having a bad sales month? It's the other sales reps—they're so pushy. And you always get assigned to customers who aren't really ready to buy.
- Going out of business? It's the bad economy—not your company's poor customer service or inefficient marketing.
- Chronically late for work? It's the traffic, it's the calendar software that failed to remind you of the meeting, or it's your old car (which means it's really your boss's fault, for paying you too little to buy a new car).

Here's an example of the blame game as it played out for two telecom companies:

For 2008, Qwest reported a net income of $681 million—a decline of 77% from the previous year. Qwest claimed that intense competition in some markets, along with the housing crisis, were the reasons for their lower revenue.

But wait. Verizon reported fourth quarter profits in 2008 were up 15%, reaching $1.2 billion. Yet, Verizon and Qwest were competing in the same markets during the same housing crisis. Verizon made a profit. Qwest didn't. Verizon invested further in itself. Qwest complained that it wasn't their fault.

MOVING TO AN INTERNAL LOCUS OF CONTROL

OK, so you want to be more internally orientated and independent. You want to drive the bus. How do you go from being externally dependent to an internal locus of control? I've got six individual steps that will help you.

These six steps begin with you first taking control by learning how to manage your own thoughts, perceptions and filters. While we can't eliminate the old patterns we've developed over a lifetime, we can provide ourselves with ways to develop new and more useful patterns. The key is discovering what you are doing well and what is serving you—and noticing what is not serving you. By learning to be more aware of your patterns, you begin to have more choices. The choice to stop doing some old behaviors, the choice to keep doing some old useful behaviors, and the choice to start doing some new behaviors.

Researchers have found that trying new things makes it easier to learn new habits. Learning something new helps you learn anything new. Unless you keep learning new things, your brain will atrophy. Although the research is incomplete as of yet, it indicates that not using your mind can predispose your brain for Alzheimer's disease, dementia, and other diseases of the brain. When I say, "use it or lose it," what I am really saying is create new tracks and pathways in your brain by learning and behaving in ways that are more productive for you.

Don't waste time eliminating your old habits. Have you ever driven by old railroad tracks? Sometimes you'll encounter a few yards of tracks that aren't used anymore. No one wasted energy digging up and removing those tracks. They put their energy, money, and time into building the new, improved roadway.

Similarly, developing new habits will create new pathways in your brain. Laying down new tracks in your neurology allows you to lay down more track. When you use the new track you are building, it becomes easier to choose that track in the future. Learning begets more learning. (The track on which the old habit runs does not go away. So beware of being derailed on it.)

Six Key Steps

I recommend these six steps to help you form new habits so you can develop independence:

1. Stop caring about what others think about you. Give it a rest.
2. Determine your most important values.
3. Become aware of the "rules" in your life.

4. Adopt principles to guide your internal choices.
5. Remember that you always have a choice.
6. Be intentional: notice what is happening around you and respond to feedback from your environment.

Let's look at each step in more depth.

1. Stop caring about what others think about you. Give it a rest.

Richard Feynman, known for his vivid and impertinent approach to physics, grew up learning to question orthodox thinking. He believed that authority and conventional thinking should be challenged. Then Arlene, his first wife, taught him more deeply to ignore what other people think. During their engagement, Arlene was diagnosed with tuberculosis. Feynman flouted convention and parental advice and married her anyway. When Feynman, a Nobel-winning physicist as bright and capable as anyone on the planet, was working on the Manhattan Project at Los Alamos, Arlene gave him some pencils for his office. She had them engraved with, "Richard Darling, I Love You! Patsy."

Feynman admitted to Arlene that he was embarrassed to use them in front of his colleagues. Feynman explained to her, "There are all these famous scientists." Arlene interrupted by saying, "aren't you proud of the fact that I love you?" She then uttered the words that Richard Feynman made one of his guiding principles: **"What do you care what other people think?"** Richard's philosophy was shaped that day. He often would say, "You have no responsibility to live up to what other people think you ought to accomplish. I have no responsibility to be like they expect me to be." Feynman crafted a career by not following conventional wisdom, and we are the richer for it.

My daughter has learned that lesson well. I was so proud of her the other day. She told me that, for the last two years, she'd been wearing clothes that would "fit in" at school—basically blue jeans and t-shirts. But she's decided that, this year, she is only going to choose outfits that make her happy. I could not have been a prouder father. She figured out, in primary school, a lesson it takes many of us years to learn.

Self-trust is one of the most powerful tools you have to move toward an internal locus of control. When you trust yourself, you generate confidence and a positive energy that eliminates fears and worries. This trust will have a profound effect on you and others. For one thing, if you don't trust yourself, you will have a hard time trusting others. And if you trust yourself, others will be drawn to trust you, too.

2. Determine your most important values.

Know your core values. So many people say that they "follow their values," but they can't name them.

Which are your core values—the five or six values on which you base your life? How did you come to value them, and how did you develop them? Why are these the values that are important to you? Are they truly your values, or more external "rules" that others told you to value?

Here are several values, with some blanks where you can jot in others that matter to you. These are all admirable, but which are yours (really yours, not just the ones your parents, clergy, or mentor lived by)?

Peace	Success	Wisdom	Innovation
Integrity	Status	Love	Freedom
Family	Independence	Friendship	Service
Fame	Growth	Fairness	Sustainability
Justice	Wealth	Influence	Elegance
Power	Happiness	Authenticity	Honesty
Truth	Joy	Quality	Accountability

Knowing your values will help you become clear about what internally motivates you and will guide the choices you make.

3. Become aware of the external rules you have adopted.

Externally dependent people accept rules simply because they are rules. This makes them susceptible to exploitation by an external authority. If a set of rules is presented over and over again, and repeated with enough emphasis and devotion, the externally dependent will readily accept and follow it. Such rules might have no basis in reality. The propaganda machine of the Nazis applied this principle to a horrendous effect.

What are the rules in your life? Do they serve you? Which need to be changed? Which need to be abandoned?

Make a list of 50 rules by which you live. (Why 50? You can think of 10-12 rules fairly quickly. But if you sit and think, you'll come up with more and more, some of them very deeply buried. It's those unconscious rules that you need to examine the most.) These external rules can be precepts you were taught by a friend, by a parent or grandparent, by your church, or by an expert in law, medicine, business, or sports. Some might be helpful, even empowering; some might be burdensome and debilitating.

Here are a few to get you started:

- Don't swim for an hour after you eat.
- Don't touch.
- Do what you are told.
- Keep your mouth shut.
- Wear your hat or you'll catch a cold.
- I am not the smart one.
- Do what the boss says.
- Put your nose to the grindstone to get ahead.
- It is hard to get ahead.
- You are not the smart one.
- You can't change history.
- Better safe than sorry.
- He is the stupid one.
- Don't yell.
- You have to be nice.
- Don't talk back.
- It's polite to be five minutes early.
- You have to bring a gift.
- You aren't very bright.
- If you don't have anything nice to say, don't say anything.

Look at each rule and ask yourself, "Is this something that I believe? Is this a rule I want in my life? Does this rule create more happiness and health in my life?"

If the answer is "no," toss it out! (Or re-write it. Maybe "don't talk back" doesn't serve you. You could change that to "speak up," or "speak politely, but with conviction.") The answer might be "yes, this is very useful to me." That makes it your rule that you have chosen to follow, not dad's rule that you must still obey.

4. Adopt principles to guide your internal choices.

What principles could you adopt, instead of external rules, to guide your internal choices? I'm asking you to think about your thinking. It's not as strange as it sounds. How can you adopt a new mindset where you choose a new principle to guide your behavior instead of following an external rule?

Internally derived principles always modify behavior more consistently and effectively than the mere following of rules. For example:

Rule: Put on your seat belt. This is an external rule, enforced by the police. It is a good rule. Many people's lives have been saved by putting on their seat belts. (Rules can be recognized because there are usually negative consequences involved with breaking them. You can get a ticket for not wearing a seat belt. I'm not saying you don't deserve the ticket, I'm just pointing out that it's a negative motivation to obey the rule.)

Principle: Keeping myself and my family safe is one of my personal principles. I follow this principle in my car by having everyone buckle up. This helps me keep my family and friends (and me) safe.

I am following the law, but my intention is completely in line with my personal principle. (Principles can be recognized because they have a positive rationale. I help my family by buckling up. There is a positive motivation in following a principle.)

Here, Feynman can also provide us with another insight: "Our responsibility is to do what we can, learn what we can, improve the solutions, and pass them on. It is our responsibility to leave the people of the future a free hand. . . If we suppress all discussion, all criticism, proclaiming, 'This is the answer, my friends; man is saved!' we will doom humanity for a long time to the chains of authority, confined to the limits of our present imagination. It has been done so many times before."

When you understand your values and principles, and trust them to guide your decision-making, you will unleash the ability to choose all the time. When you make a choice from your own internal sense of values, you end up making more elegant decisions.

One of my favorite Catalysts is futurist R. Buckminster Fuller. In 1928, Fuller, broke and unemployed, was grieving for his daughter Alexandra, who had just passed away from polio and spinal meningitis. He was so devastated and burdened by responsibility that he contemplated suicide. Then instead, he decided to start an experiment by adopting the principle "to find what a single individual could contribute to changing the world and benefiting all humanity."

In a moment of insight, Fuller decided to gamble that the universe had some use for him. He had a vision of what it would be to commit fully to creating value in the world. He decided to devote himself to the principles of "livingry" as opposed to "weaponry." He created life out of death, choosing to make a difference.

First, he withdrew from society, promising not to speak again until he understood his own thoughts. His silence lasted for nearly two years (which his wife and other daughter put up with). He examined what he believed and compared his beliefs to external beliefs and rules. He examined the physical sciences. He examined philosophies. When he knew that he could produce original thoughts, he applied these principles and went to work to benefit humanity.

His mission was to make a world that works for everyone, through sustainable, responsible technological design. The geodesic dome is one of his best-known inventions; he also wrote prolifically and gave us such terms as "Spaceship Earth" and "synergetic." He lived an incredibly rich life by defining and staying true to his internal values and principles. His only motivation was to create something that would benefit everyone. He demonstrated by example how one individual can have a positive impact.

Ask yourself, "what are the principles I want to live my life by? Is this principle effective in my situation? Are there any principles I need to reexamine?"

5. Remember that you always have a choice.

Too often we forget that we have a birthright of being able to choose what we want. The only power people have over you is the power that you give them. You are the only one who can grant or take away your choices.

We have the opportunity for choice all day long, yet most of our choices are buried in automatic behavior. For example, we each make almost 250 food decisions every day (according to Brian Wansink's article in *Environment and Behavior*). Those are just the daily choices for food. Then we make choices about how to dress, what route to drive to work, what to watch on TV…

Avoid making automatic, thoughtless choices. The best way to make a conscious choice is to think ahead of time about what choices you will be making. The more situations you can think of and plan for, the better prepared you will be when those situations arise.

If you ask yourself questions ahead of time, you give yourself more opportunity to see the opportunity for choice in the future. Ask yourself, "What do I want to create today? What are some of my automatic patterns that are not serving me? What are my responsibilities today? What situations will be best served by me being aware of my choices today? What do I want to experience today? Is this behavior helping me right now?" The act of asking a question will help stop any automatic process.

Another tool: Take a breath right before making a decision. Your brain (a mere 2% of your body weight) consumes up to 25% of your oxygen supply. Feed it so it can function to optimum effect. A conscious breath will not only oxygenate your brain, it will give you a pause to think, which will help you avoid behaving automatically.

By deciding to choose, you can learn how to choose and develop a new pattern—one that moves you from reacting to being intentional.

6. Notice what is happening around you and respond to feedback from your environment.

By heightening you sensory awareness, you will get more real-time feedback from the choices you are making, allowing you the opportunity to self-correct and adjust. Your sensory awareness in the workplace includes both you and those around you. It's essential that you know how your body reacts to certain experiences and coworkers; what you feel, where you feel it. It's also crucial to be able to see, hear, feel and otherwise sense others' physical reactions: relaxation, excitement, anxiety, anger, and energy. When you can open up your sensory ability, you will have the information, the raw data, to know how effective or ineffective your choices are.

Gregory Bateson's genius was one of close observation. A social scientist and cyberneticist, Bateson learned, as a child, to observe patterns of behavior by observing nature. He saw patterns and relationships and used nature as his guide. Bateson was fond of saying that the mind is an ecological system. He compared the introduction of ideas to the introduction of a seed: each develops based on the environment in which it finds itself. He also said, "it takes two to know one." In other words, to know something you need to be in relationship with it. To Bateson, one's ability to perceive is also one's ability to feel the difference.

Sensory information is critical. Marcia Mikulak, a cultural anthropologist specializing in the cultural understanding of childhood, has found a 20-25% reduction in sensory awareness in the technological child of modern western nations as opposed to the non-technological child growing up in a more primitive environment.

For the 21st century high-tech child, sensory input tends to be a singular event, but still these children are less able to synthesize information. They aren't anchoring a picture of an event to a feeling, nor are they cross-indexing the information, which means they then need more stimulus to feel its impact. This is why so many children need intense stimuli to engage their senses, and why they are missing subtleties in their environments.

Interestingly, the Pentagon discovered the same in a study of troops searching for IEDs (improvised explosive devices). Their tests found that soldiers who grew up in the countryside and spent time in the woods, and had thus developed more awareness of their environment, did a better job of finding IEDs than did those soldiers who grew up playing video games. The best work was done by those who grew up in environments that engaged all of their senses. They could see more, hear more, and notice more—which leads to better and higher quality decisions, whether or not your life is on the line.

Charlotte Sevelor, the author of *Sensory Awareness*, was a teacher to many brilliant people, including psychoanalysts Erich Fromm and Fritz Perls, bodyworkers Moshe Feldenkrais and Ida Rolf, and Zen philosopher Alan Watts. She lived to be 102 and taught until her death. She taught her sensory awareness principles in Germany until she had to flee the Nazis.

When I had the good fortune to meet with her, she told me, "part of our motivation back then was if we can only get the populace to inhabit more of their senses, there is no way they would be able to commit the atrocities they are committing. If we abandon the awareness of our bodies, we lose a key tool for choosing the behaviors that will lead to more health and happiness. But with more sensory awareness of our environment, we build trust in our own experiences." She made many wise choices in her life as she was constantly engaged in her senses and was able to get feedback directly from her surroundings. She helped others by directly building the capacity to sense more in their lives. She designed experiences that focused on breathing and movement, which lead to discovering more of an individual's innate awareness.

I know I make better choices when I engage all of my senses. If I have an important decision to make, I consider it from every angle: does it look good, does it sound right, does it pass the gut check, do I like the taste of it, does something smell funny about it? I have found the more senses I engage for any decision, the wiser the decision will be. I don't get information from just one sense but from as many as I can engage.

YOU CAN CHANGE NOW

When you work through these Six Key Steps, you'll understand more about your rules, values, and principles, and you'll expand the use of your senses. That's how to develop more of an internal locus of control and leave the Drama Triangle far behind. Want to move from the passenger seat of your life to the driver's seat? To move into the Leadership Triangle, you are required to drive your own bus.

CHAPTER 6

The Trap of the Drama Triangle

THE DRAMA TRIANGLE creates its own traps. The two greatest traps are:

- Being pulled into the swirl of drama by others who are already in drama.
- Abdicating your ability to choose.

Often, when we avoid choosing what to do next, we are either in a state of fear or in a state of resignation—both something we do to ourselves.

Even the strongest commitment to avoid the Drama Triangle will not prevent you from being there at one time or another. We're virtually hardwired for drama. Nobody has absolute immunity from its pull, and everyone, even the highest achievers, get stuck in a drama cycle on occasion. Yet, those who are committed to leadership development and accountability will never remain there for long.

PETTY TYRANTS WHO TEACH

When you are in the Drama Triangle, you'll see few choices available to you. There are choices, but you just can't recognize them while you are stuck in drama. You will feel that you cannot get out of it. And, in that situation of having "no choice," you will have to think differently. Let me explain one useful approach:

> Over the years, some of the people who I have coached felt like they had some individual in their lives—some coworker, manager, or business associate—who was making their life a living hell. They might have termed this person a "petty tyrant."

Carlos Castaneda, in his classic *The Fire From Within*, writes about his studies with Don Juan, the Toltec teacher or seer. Carlos had a very powerful insight when Don Juan told the story of the petty tyrant:

> "The petty tyrant is the outside element, the one we cannot control and the element that is perhaps the most important of them all. My benefactor used to say that the warrior who stumbles on a petty tyrant is a lucky one."

Don Juan goes on to say:

> "Nothing can temper the spirit of a warrior as much as the challenge of dealing with impossible people in positions of power. Only under those conditions can warriors acquire the sobriety and serenity to stand the pressure of the unknowable."

Don Juan explained that many fall prey to the petty tyrants of this world. He taught Carlos that to be defeated by a petty tyrant means a loss of one's vital energies. The warrior's duty is to gain knowledge to stand up to the petty tyrants without giving up personal energy.

But Don Juan also told Carlos that he was fortunate to have a petty tyrant in his life—because the struggle with a petty tyrant, this person who made life a living hell, would help Carlos discover where he had abdicated choice. He would discover that he had forgotten that he had the right to make a choice about what his internal state would be, no matter what the external circumstances were.

You can apply Carlos's learning to your own life. If there is someone complicating your life, that very fact gives you the clue that, "hey, this is where I need to make a choice." We all, at some point, meet someone who is living in the Drama Triangle. You can either fall prey to this situation by joining them in creating more drama or be aware of it and make another choice. It is important that you acknowledge this. Know it consciously, rather than succumb to it unconsciously, or otherwise it will rule your life.

Recognize that the people who trigger you into the Drama Triangle can teach you. This kind of thinking about them will help you to put a different label on them and provide you with breathing room so you can respond differently. By seeing these people as hooks to get you into the Drama Triangle, you can observe their behavior while retaining your sense of self. Monitor your reaction to their behavior to find the lessons you need to learn. You can stop blaming these people for their behaviors and instead discover something new about yourself. This will open up more possibilities for your own growth, and drama will not trap you so easily.

FEAR CAUSES FEAR

Fear kills the potential for leadership. Fears limit your ability to take action. Fears can be directly responsible for some aspect of your life that you did not live.

Fear can be defined as the expectation that something bad will happen. That is, the experience of fear is based on what might happen, not on a guaranteed fact. If something fearful were actually happening, you would move into terror and respond accordingly. But most fear is related to an expectation, not to an actuality.

Most often, we base fear on real or imagined failures from the past: I'm afraid I'll blush when I give my report at the regional meeting because I blushed when I gave it at the divisional meeting.

Everyone has fears; they are conditioned responses to our experiences, regulated by various parts of the brain. The amygdala again plays an important part in the acquisition as well as the expression of fear. These experiences and fears can set up a pattern that takes us into the Drama Triangle. Don't you mostly judge your fears negatively and thus try to avoid them? Our instinct is to avoid uncomfortable situations such as a direct confrontation with a co-worker, heights, airplane trips, or public speaking.

Whatever it is you fear, your thought process about it is similar. You have a disagreeable experience—it's sad or painful or embarrassing or scary—so you associate any related situation with unpleasantness that must be avoided. You might not even know why the event occurred, but you certainly understand the unpleasantness and the desire to avoid feeling the internal state (and your physical reactions, such as muscle tension, tears, even nausea). You now allow your inner voice to warn you that a similar unpleasantness might be about to happen. And we don't discriminate well: we can be as fearful of approaching a dangerous precipice as of receiving an upsetting email. So we tend to avoid the stimulus of the fear no matter the source.

Sometimes your fear is helpful: you experience that Fred drives like a maniac, so you fear getting in a car with him again. So, your fears can be a wise predictor and can help guide your behaviors. But our fears usually do not serve us. Your experience at your last meeting with a senior manager was bad, so you fear going into a meeting with her again. You get anxious. You get nervous. You meet and you again don't present as well as you would like due to your anxiety. That's not helping you or her. In this situation, fear was not your ally.

Yet the avoidance of a fear only heightens the anxiety. Avoiding the fear—the person, the event, the piano recital—might bring temporary relief, but nothing sustainable. What you resist, you intensify. Simply put, constant fear does not help us make quality choices.

To deal with your negative reactions to fear, understand that it is all an imagined situation. You are making it up. It is how you have programmed yourself to avoid negative outcomes. If you're in the Drama Triangle, you'll regularly predict bad outcomes. Your fearful state can become a habit. You need to ask yourself: do my fears limit me or do they serve me?

The #1 Fear

Have you heard the statistic that people fear public speaking more than they fear death? Let's use that fear in a simple example to show the relationship between experiences and responses.

Imagine that you are about to give your first large-scale public presentation.

Let the anxiety associated with public speaking rev up your body's "fight or flight" response, that ancient neurological mechanism designed to help us avoid hungry predators. Depending on your life experiences, some of your "favorite" fears will emerge.

Which of these fears threaten you the most as you anticipate stepping to the podium?

- Fear of failure
- Fear of humiliation
- Fear of blushing
- Fear of being judged
- Fear of exposing your ignorance
- Fear of looking vulnerable
- Fear of being laughed at
- Fear of going blank

Physiologically, the moment you perceive a threat, that fight or flight alarm in your brain triggers certain biochemical stimulants. As the threat gets closer, the fear heightens. With extreme fear, you'll find it difficult to think, even to speak (your mouth goes dry). The rational part of you understands that you're just going to give a presentation in a conference room—but the irrational part of you sees a life-and-death scenario, a self-defense situation. The body reacts instinctively in ways it considers helpful, moving blood from your brain (where you need it to think) and into your limbs (so you can use it to run).

Obviously, in the modern business world, such responses are of little use. The common factor is that these responses are based on the anticipation of assumed events. Of all the presentations you have given or witnessed, how often has a speaker died? Passed out? Lost his place and then run screaming from the room? It just doesn't happen—yet many speakers fear that it might.

Most of these threats and scenarios are created by the brain to prevent you from deliberately stepping into a stressful situation. The irony is that if, while giving a speech, you do forget what you are going to say and you do shake with fear, you end up being judged (mostly by yourself), which creates a self-fulfilling prophecy. It's not so much that you fear presenting: You fear how people might respond. When we say we fear blushing, we really mean we fear being seen blushing.

So after each stressful speech, your brain stores the evidence that public speaking is scary. You create another limiting perception, and you add to it the belief that your fear mechanism was right to protect you. Your brain sets up a little chant, "don't do that again, don't do that again, it's awful."

Recognize your fears as projections from your mind trying to protect you from a hypothetical event. This will help you to tame the projection, diffuse the fear, and stay out of drama. Assess the reality of the current situation, then act on it: that's the fear killer.

We Need To Talk

Take the example of a fear of having a challenging conversation. Whether it's at home or at work, people do not like hard conversations. They do not want to hurt another's feelings or have their own feelings hurt.

As the time approaches for the conversation, you fear the impact it might have on your relationship. That escalates your fears, which leads to an inner dialog of how wrong the conversation will go, a dialog that is not only self-defeating but also self-fulfilling. You then respond to such escalating anxiety each time you have a tough conversation with this person, letting the fear overtake you. The conversation does not go as you hope; you either forget the points you wanted to make, or you let your emotions overtake you (leading to shouting, frustration, door slamming or other unproductive outcomes).

Think of a time when you had a conversation go wrong. You may, at that moment, have created a fear of having that intense or hard conversation again. Now, every time you are in that situation—either having such a talk or considering the need to have it—the fear centers of your brain engage. I'm not saying you are either right or wrong to feel that way. Perhaps the anxiety served you at some point. But now, you would be better served if you chose an empowering response, not a fearful response. Choose a response that reflects who you are today, rather than who you were then. If you feel fearful, you impact your ability to be successful. When we are fearful, we don't operate at our best.

Anxiety or Excitement?

Most of us have experienced nervous energy and its symptoms of sweaty palms, dry mouth, and "butterflies." Usually, nervous energy is experienced as anxiety, which is nervous energy directed inward. When you are anxious, notice where you are placing your attention. Most times it will be on yourself. If you concentrate on that anxiety, on yourself, it will quickly escalate into fear. Instead, shift your attention to something external—the needs of the audience you'll be addressing, even the equipment you'll be using. The size of the room. What people look like as they enter. Place your focus outside of yourself and away from your anxieties.

Many speakers, performers and athletes are excited before their event begins, but some are downright anxious. Even famous performers get stage fright. Because fear comes from what might happen, the anticipation is usually worse than the actual event. Once they get into their speech, game, or performance, their attention shifts to the audience, to their piano, to who's got the football. This shifts their anxiety from fear to excitement.

Remember that with each repetition of shifting your anxiety to excitement, it becomes a stronger habit. Some people look forward to the excitement of nervous energy before a performance and genuinely look forward to the thrill of the event. It is because they know how to transform the energy into something positive for themselves and for their audience.

You get to choose how to direct your nervous energy. To shift your fear from anxiety to excitement, begin by identifying the specific fear. Consider the underlying assumption of the anticipated outcome. Find a more useful perception of the situation. I might lose my place. Yes, you might. Are your notes clear? Have you practiced enough? Do you have a plan for how to get back to your place? Don't most audiences wait patiently when the speaker loses her place?

By challenging the underlying assumptions behind those fears and then taking action, you are developing more choice, more freedom, and more leadership in directing your own life. Franklin D. Roosevelt was right when he said, "there is nothing to fear but fear itself."

PULLED IN TO DRAMA

It takes two to create drama. If only one person is down in the Triangle, no drama is occurring. That person is just miserable in his or her own personal hell. But that person, being in the Drama Triangle, will seek out someone who will agree with his or her point of view.

We know the roles of drama as we see them enacted over and over again. It's like watching the same play. We can see the Adversary, engaging in top dog-underdog conversations. We see the Rescuer who won't give you straight information because she knows you cannot handle it. We see people succumbing to being Victims, avoiding all responsibility for their actions—but who are quick to tell you who they see is at fault.

Find your own example from a time when you had a conflict with "Bob the coworker," but instead of addressing it directly with Bob, you took your issues to someone else. What was your thinking? Were you rescuing Bob from your feedback? Did you judge Bob as someone who could not handle your feedback? Were you out to get back at Bob in an indirect way? Were you rescuing yourself from having to deal directly with him?

It doesn't matter "who started it." In drama, at least two people are feeding off of one another, each reacting to the other's drama in turn. Imagine all this when the scale increases by a dozen people on a team, or a hundred people in a department: dozens of Adversaries and scores of Rescuers. This is how situations degenerate into soap opera-style dramas that are an enormous waste of everyone's time and resources. In these situations, you may even step back and think, "How did I end up in a situation like this, when I know better?" The answer is that drama is second nature for virtually everyone, and it's contagious.

I've heard people blame others for pulling them into the Drama Triangle. I don't accept that excuse. Nobody can take control of you unless you allow him or her to do so.

Flee the Triangle!

Now that you know what drama is and can recognize the players, watch them "on stage" as they switch roles. The person who is being Adversarial will switch and become the Victim. The Victim is now waiting to be rescued, and the Rescuer wants to be rescued by others. It's a bizarre game of musical chairs round and round the Triangle.

How do I know when I'm being part of the Drama Triangle? By my resignation, my indifference. I feel powerless. Did you know it takes 43 muscles to frown and 17 to smile, but it takes absolutely none to look indifferent? Often, people who act and feel indifferent are down in the Drama Triangle.

How do I get up into the Leadership Triangle? First, by recognizing where I am: in the Drama Triangle. Then, by returning my locus of control to an internal focus where I am creating my own reality, shifting to thoughts of being accountable, and assuming positive intent of the other person, I can make the move easily. Furthermore, I can address the question: how did I create this situation? Once I recognize that it was my choice to go into drama, I can choose something else. I can shift to continue to build my leadership competency by being more Visionary, being a Catalyst for my team, and being a Coach to others.

You probably know which people or which situations trigger you into the Drama Triangle. It might be a boss, coworker, or even a family member. It might be addressing the Board or having to drive in the snow. You automatically assume negative intentions and think negative thoughts. You give up your power to this person or situation, and they or the situation wields that power over you.

You are most likely to drop into the Drama Triangle when:

- You are not conscious of what limiting perceptions or negative intentions you have in a particular situation.
- You let resignation creep into a relationship you're in or a job you are doing.
- You feel limited in your ability to make a difference.
- You develop fear about a challenge, such as a needed conversation with a co-worker.

Sometimes you will feel that you've escaped the Drama Triangle, when in fact you just shifted your behavior. You got out of being the Rescuer, but you shifted into being the Victim without leaving the Triangle. Be on the lookout for this in yourself. Don't get trapped by seeing as change or growth what is really just movement between each of the roles. Again, check within yourself: are you being accountable for the situations you find yourself in? Have you really moved into leadership, or have you just switched drama roles?

Carl Jung taught that "anything within ourselves that we make conscious, we can transform." Here are steps you can take, when you see that you're in the Drama Triangle, to help you get out and stay out:

1. Be truthful to yourself about it. Knowledge and self-awareness are always the first steps in breaking unproductive behavioral patterns.

2. Remain non-defensive. That's the single most important thing you can do to avoid the traps of the Drama Triangle.

3. Admit it out loud (to yourself, to a friend or mentor) or, if you keep a journal, write it down. You will gain a better understanding of what (and who) hooks you and pulls you into drama.

4. Name the behavioral pattern associated with the Adversary, Victim, and Rescuer roles. This will keep you from unconsciously behaving this way in the future.

5. As you build awareness of what triggers your involvement in the Drama Triangle, you'll develop more compassion for others who are inside of the Drama Triangle—and more skills to help them out, too.

Help Others Out of Drama

I think it is important for you to consider: how can you help others in the Drama Triangle? How can you provide them with a road map out of the Drama Triangle?

Remember, when somebody is in the Drama Triangle, they aren't trying to leave—they're trying to get others to join them. They are not aware of the negative impact they are creating. Help them by not joining them. Help them by introducing them to the concept of the Drama Triangle and showing them the thinking that leads to the path out.

Often, when you are helping somebody out of the Drama Triangle, you will have to be firm with them. One of my old college professors, a cowboy at heart, told us, "Sometimes the best intervention is a poke in the snout." You'll meet individuals who need a metaphorical 2x4 upside their head to get through the fog of their limiting perceptions. When people are stuck in drama, they are trapped in this abdication of choice, this abdication of power. To help them out, you may need to hit them between the eyeballs in a very powerful way. You must lead.

You are accountable for your own growth. As a leader, you are also accountable for the growth of the people around you. It is a fundamental concept of leadership to develop other leaders. You want everyone in your organization to have the mindset of a leader. So, to fully embrace being in the Leadership Triangle, you have to first grow yourself and then help others around you to grow. They are a reflection of how you lead.

Leadership is not something you can fake: there is an authenticity that needs to go with it. It is something that you can choose at any point in time. People understand if you are genuinely speaking your compelling vision or asking others for theirs. People can grasp that you might be a Catalyst for a new idea, a new change. There is an authenticity about a leader that allows him or her to accelerate change inside of an organization. And there is a certain edge that comes from having real conversations, coaching others, and building relationships that say, "hey, I care enough about you and your growth to have the hard conversations."

Zero Tolerance

Do not tolerate the drama in others. It will lead to resentment and to more drama.

You might be vigilantly refusing to indulge in drama yourself, but if you tolerate it in others, it will start to fester and infect your life or your team. Don't let drama fester in any kind of relationship—in a marriage, a team, with a manager or a subordinate, with a colleague or friend. If you let the drama creep into those relationships, it has the chance to creep into the rest of your life.

Avoiding somebody who is in the Drama Triangle is usually not the best strategy. You either have to avoid them completely, which is impossible at work or at home, or you have to stop contributing to their growth. That would mean abdicating your relationship with them, and (if you work together) abdicating your contribution to the organization's growth. Don't give up an opportunity of freeing someone, of helping them become more valuable.

Sometimes you may decide, because of some technical compe-tence, to include someone on your team who is a habitual visitor to the Drama Triangle. The best way to manage them is to not blame them for being in the Drama Triangle, but to recognize that they are motivated by an external locus of control. You will need to manage this person closely with very clear expectations, lots of acknowledgement, and very clear consequences for not performing. This is a time when active management skills come into play.

Even as you interact with these people who are in the drama role, how do you know if you've joined them in drama? Be aware of your locus of control. Are you thinking your own thoughts and are you remaining internally independent? Or are you making decisions or jumping to conclusions based on external pressure from other people?

Can You Eradicate Drama From Your Organization?

Time in the Drama Triangle is tough on everyone's health, both physically and mentally. It's also tough on the corporate bottom line. Those negative intentions and Drama Triangle roles are contagious and detrimental.

It doesn't take too long on any job before you notice if the organization tends toward drama or leadership. You quickly see the attitudes and behaviors demonstrated by the executives, the managers, and the employees. Are those attitudes healthy? If they are not, can you shift them? Can you shift your own?

One of the great leadership tasks is to learn how to shift a culture. From the Leadership Triangle, you can learn how to create a high-performance culture, so you can work in a great place with attitudes that are consistent with your values. But change is tough. When the winds of change start whipping about, every small issue is like a grain of sand: uncomfortable at best and stingingly painful if travelling fast enough. And that's the small issues; the large issues are worse. You have to think strategically about how you would go about creating change in a culture. Awareness of the level of drama is a good first step.

While you are in an organization that doesn't understand the Drama Triangle, you'll soon notice that just a few people stuck in drama can suck the life force out of the entire team. We tend to mimic the behaviors of those around us. The Drama Triangle is an easy pattern; we see others behave as Victim, Adversary, and Rescuer, and we model ourselves on their behavior. (No one is wearing a tag that says "Victim," so we don't instantly see how detrimental their behavior is.) Little original thought is generated down in the Drama Triangle. Energy goes into covering your butt. The Adversaries, Victims, and Rescuers will pull others into the Triangle with them and quash original, creative ideas with their assumption of negative intention.

Sometimes the best solution, when people cannot be coached out of drama, is to ease them out of the company. Then, hire their replacements very, very carefully.

And here is additional hard advice we have covered before: if you continually have dissatisfying relationships at work, look at the constant in them all—you. It may be that you are the one who needs to change.

AWARENESS IS AN ANTIDOTE

The good news is that the more aware you become of the traps that snare you into the Drama Triangle—especially your own fears and the pull of others—the less likely you are to become entangled.

- Though the Adversary might come at you, you look for opportunities to elevate, or if necessary, exit the situation, rather than attack back.
- Though the Victim has yet another sob story, you avoid becoming wrapped up in the web of gossip.
- And while the Rescuer "only wants to help," or withholds feedback, you're savvy to his or her underlying motivations.

Recognizing when you go into the Drama Triangle gives you the choice to get out of it. Yes, when you're in drama, it feels all-consuming, without exit. So, take time when you are not enmeshed in the Triangle to examine your participation in drama. Where and when are you being Adversarial? Where and when are you going about rescuing others? Where and when are you being a Victim? Become conscious of your positive intentions, and make a quick exit out of the Drama Triangle.

Creating more leadership in yourself and your organization provides the best antidote for the Drama Triangle. It doesn't matter if you are an individual contributor or a manager of vast resources. You are either a leader or you are not. Leaders never stop their development. They are constantly following their vision. They are eager, almost relentless, to improve the organization and the product or to generate new ideas. They willingly take risks to bring about change in others' lives. Such are the attitudes of the Visionary, the Catalyst, and the Coach. When you fully embrace the Leadership Triangle, there is no room for creating any drama.

SECTION TWO

I N THE FIRST SECTION, I covered the reasons for drama and how our neurology virtually compels us to fall into a life of "dramatic" interaction. I introduced you to the major elements of both the Drama Triangle and the Leadership Triangle.

To recap, in the Leadership Triangle, a person's behavior and mindset is to:

- Adopt an internal locus of control
- Be accountable
- Assume positive intent

The three main roles in the Leadership Triangle are the Visionary, the Catalyst, and the Coach.

When in the Drama Triangle, a person's behavior and mindset is to:

- Adopt an external locus of control
- Avoid accountability
- Assume negative intent

The three main roles in the Drama Triangle are the Victim, the Adversary, and the Rescuer.

In this section—Chapters 7 through 11—we'll go into more depth about the major roles, and we'll look at emotional components of each.

The roles you adopt change your perception of events within your body. They provide you with an internal experience that you can label:

In drama, a person is	In leadership, a person is
▪ Resigned	▪ Engaged
▪ Angry	▪ Energetic
▪ Confused	▪ Focused

CHAPTER 7

Accountability—
Accept It or Avoid It

HARRY S. TRUMAN had a sign on this desk in the Oval Office. It said, "The Buck Stops Here."

Those in the Leadership Triangle embrace accountability. But when you are in the Drama Triangle, you do your darnedest to avoid accountability. Or, put the other way around, if you are avoiding accountability, the chances are very high that you are in the Drama Triangle.

A person is accountable when she steps up and takes responsibility for the consequences of her actions. In business, this usually means she was given a responsibility—to develop a training program, to launch a corporate web site, to get the donuts for the staff meeting—and the authority to carry it out.

The word "accountability" has been used to mean blame. Some organizations avoid discussing accountability because they see it merely as a technique to find fault or as a tool for punishment. "Who's accountable?" can mean "Who's the scapegoat?" But accountability is not about blame. The truth is that accountability cannot be avoided. In any organization, each worker is always accountable to someone: everyone has a boss. Even the CEO is accountable to the board of directors and the board of directors are accountable to the shareholders.

In the Drama Triangle, people avoid accountability because they fear it will make them more visible, and thus responsible for their decisions and actions. Avoiders don't want things to change, so they pretend everything is fine. Avoiders have a remarkable ability to not see, not hear, and not feel that things are going badly, with either their own actions or the actions of others.

At their worst, avoiders shun the truth. In recent years, we've seen an increase of avoiders in business and politics, many of whom make national headlines. They not only avoid accountability, they actively engage in deceitful practices. You cannot look at the news—TV, paper, or Internet—without running into stories of accountability shirked.

THE HALL OF SHAME

Avoidance of accountability is reaching epidemic proportions. What's at the root of these self-serving behaviors and headline-generating scandals? People are either individually avoiding personal accountability, or groups are avoiding holding others accountable for their actions. The Hall of Shame is long. Let's start with the worst offenders:

Katrina, FEMA, and Lots of Blame

Hurricane Katrina roared through New Orleans on August 29, 2005. It was the first Class 3+ hurricane to hit the Louisiana coast in 36 years.

Let's review the aftermath of Hurricane Katrina. The behavior and response of many people and agencies involved was so poor that they all came under investigation—yet there was a significant lack of accountability, even during the inquiry.

Katrina served up a murky stew of drama, missed opportunities to demonstrate leadership, and lack of accountability.

Michael Chertoff

At the time of the hurricane, Michael Chertoff was Secretary of Homeland Security, and Michael Brown was head of the Federal Emergency Management Agency (FEMA).

At least 48 hours before any hurricane makes landfall on the US, the Secretary of Homeland Security is required to appoint a Principal Federal Officer (PFO) to coordinate FEMA activities in the hurricane's wake. Chertoff appointed Brown as PFO—but he did not do so until 36 hours after Katrina reached the coast. Then, having appointed Brown, Chertoff continued with his own schedule: he went to a conference in Atlanta. By both distance and availability, he chose to avoid providing any moral or material support to the citizens of Louisiana or to his designee, Michael Brown. (This is avoider behavior, which we'll cover more fully in the next chapter.)

Secretary Chertoff did not set clear expectations for the PFO. Later, when the House and Senate launched investigations into the government's response to the hurricane, Chertoff blamed his PFO. Yet it was Chertoff who had ignored predictions from the National Hurricane Center. After the hurricane pummeled Louisiana, Chertoff agreed it was of national significance but didn't consider it a catastrophic event. These are significant distinctions, because a "catastrophic event" allows for a larger, more proactive National Response Plan (NRP).

Defending the government's response to Hurricane Katrina, Secretary Chertoff said, "I am not a hurricane expert." I find this an amazing excuse. I'm also not a hurricane expert, but all I had to do was turn on my TV to see what was happening. To me, and to millions of other TV watchers, it sure looked like a catastrophic event.

During the Senate hearing to review the government's response, Senator Susan Collins of Maine described Chertoff as "curiously disengaged." This sort of resignation is a common attribute of the Victim in drama because they feel as if nothing will make a difference, so it isn't worth doing.

Michael Brown

Michael Brown also repeatedly avoided accountability and was quick to blame others. Brown blamed Chertoff for the government's poor handling of the Katrina aftermath. Yet Brown did a miserable job as the PFO, despite being head of the federal disaster agency:

- He failed to brief Chertoff during the crisis, claiming it would have been a "waste of time."
- Brown later claimed that he didn't know there were thousands of people who had survived and were in terrible circumstances in the Convention Center after the hurricane struck. "My biggest mistake was not recognizing by Saturday that Louisiana was dysfunctional." Brown found it easy to blame others, another pattern of

someone in the Drama Triangle. Yet his team had been informing him directly, and all you had to do was turn on the television news reports.

- He seemed unable to grasp what was happening in New Orleans. When Marty Bahamonde, his public affairs officer, called him to report, Brown's press secretary didn't put him right through, explaining that Brown had just sat down in a Baton Rouge restaurant, and that "It's very important that time is allowed for Mr. Brown to eat dinner", an incredibly insensitive statement given the thousands of people in New Orleans who were deprived of both food and shelter.

Brown's comments show how he moved around each of the Drama Triangle roles. When people challenged his competency, he was the Rescuer, saying that his purpose was to save lives. Then, after he told various reporters that the government did not know that people in New Orleans needed immediate help, he played the Victim, saying his statement was being misunderstood, that he misspoke because he was so tired.

But he will be best remembered in the role of Adversary:

- He blamed a "hysteric media" for compounding the crisis.
- He targeted the American citizenry, who he felt should play a proactive role in preparing for natural disasters and not expect assistance from their government.
- He blamed budget cuts to his agency.
- He was sarcastic with senators, saying, "So I guess you want me to be the superhero, to step in there and take everyone out of New Orleans."

Sadly, whatever good ideas and relevant facts about the crisis Brown did have, they were buried under his lack of personal accountability. When someone fails to be accountable, you will usually see this as a habitual pattern. That was true about Michael Brown.

- The year before Katrina, after Hurricane Frances struck Florida, FEMA distributed millions of dollars of disaster relief to residents who hadn't been damaged by the hurricane. Brown pointed to a computer glitch that resulted in $12 million of overpayments, but placed no accountability on himself. Many were calling on him to be fired then.

- *Time Magazine* reported that Brown's biography on the FEMA web site was inaccurate. This biography said that Brown himself supervised emergency services in Edmond, Oklahoma and that Brown was serving as "an assistant city manager with emergency services oversight." However, a city spokesperson told *Time* that Brown's position was "more like an intern." The web site bio also listed Brown as an "outstanding Political Science Professor" at Central State University in Edmond, Oklahoma. According to the University, he had only been a student there.

This is an obvious case of someone stuck in the Drama Triangle: a pattern of false information, a consistent deflecting of accountability, confusion about facts, and an inability to be self-reflective. There were many times when Michael Brown could have held himself accountable, but he did not demonstrate the necessary leadership characteristics to manage this kind of event—before, during, or after it.

Marty Bahamonde

Marty Bahamonde did show real leadership. As a public affairs officer, his job was to report to the media about how FEMA was responding to the Katrina disaster. But FEMA wasn't doing much, so Bahamonde found a helicopter to take him to the devastated areas so he could give on-site situation reports to FEMA and Homeland Security. Bahamonde stayed in New Orleans (where he had to use the hallway of the Superdome as the bathroom "along with 30,000 other close friends") to get this important work accomplished. He provided eyewitness reports to Washington, letting them know about the levee breaches the day the storm hit. He advised Chertoff and Brown about what needed to get done. It wasn't his "job" to do so, but someone needed to.

Mayor Ray Nagin

Local and state officials are the primary agencies for delivering the first response to emergencies, not the federal government. New Orleans Mayor Ray Nagin failed to provide a safe and orderly evacuation of the citizens of New Orleans. His office had the power to call for evacuation, but despite the frequent dire warnings of the force of the coming hurricane, he didn't order any evacuation until too late and only after being pressured to do so.

- He had hundreds of school buses and city buses at his disposal.
- When he finally decided to move people, he could not find bus drivers.
- Later, he claimed that he needed 500 buses to evacuate the city.

He did not use the buses he had; he claimed he needed more, and then the buses he had were flooded because no one had moved them to higher ground—and later the Mayor blamed other cities for not sending their buses to New Orleans to facilitate the evacuation.

"Too many people died because of lack of action," Nagin said, but he did not accept his responsibility, instead putting the blame on Governor Blanco and the FEMA.

Setting the Bar

No one can argue that most of our government agencies failed to respond quickly or effectively to the disaster that was Katrina. Thankfully, there are stories of heroism and sacrifice among the citizens of New Orleans and the compassionate people throughout America who came to their aid. But Michael Brown isn't high on my list for public acknowledgement.

During Katrina, a lack of leadership added drama into an already disastrous situation. After Katrina, most of the major players failed to take responsibility. They blamed each other, which kept the drama alive. President Bush acknowledged Brown's leadership in public on September 2, 2005, saying, "Brownie, you're doing a heck of a job." "Heck of a job" after this became a phrase for mocking a poorly done job in and around New Orleans. In this case, former President Bush again set a precedent of placing someone's personal loyalty to him over holding them accountable for their actions.

Presidents Mislead the Country

On too many occasions, presidents of the United States have perpetrated the cruel consequences of drama onto the people who looked to them for leadership. In some cases, it was the "President's men" who developed the schemes or uttered the lies, but nonetheless, whether they were acting under the boss's orders or without his explicit approval, it's the President who is accountable for his administration.

In 1964, President **Lyndon Johnson** reported to the American people that two belligerent engagements had occurred between the United States and North Vietnam: on August 2, two American destroyers, when attacked by North Vietnamese torpedo boats, shot at and sank one of them. Then, on August 4, North Vietnamese PT boats again attacked US ships and were fired upon in response. President Johnson called for air strikes against North Vietnam in retaliation for these two attacks. This lead to the almost inescapable escalation of the Vietnam War.

Except that there had been no attack on August 4. On August 2, yes. But on August 4? Prior to the launch of the air strikes, knowledgeable officials in Washington expressed doubts that the North Vietnamese had attacked again. (The US Navy fired on something in the waters off Vietnam on August 4, but it was more likely their own wild imaginings than it was Vietnamese forces.) President Johnson "embellished" the tale and got the American public to agree with his desire to increase our military presence in Vietnam—all without having to declare war on Vietnam. Johnson later said privately about the August 4 incident, "for all I know, our Navy was shooting at whales out there." Fabricating a story from deep within drama, the President—with lack of accountability—mired the United States in the Vietnam War by misrepresenting facts to the American people and to Congress. Think of all the painful drama experienced by both the people of the United States and the people of Vietnam because of this action.

Watergate. That word alone stands for an astonishing web of lies and deceit pulled off by our country's leader. In 1972, **Richard Nixon's** people orchestrated the burglary of Democratic National Headquarters in the Watergate Hotel in Washington, D.C. Nixon was complicit in the massive cover-up of the break-in, allowing even more crimes to be committed in an attempt to conceal involvement in the first. When all was finally exposed, nineteen administration officials went to prison and Nixon resigned in ignominy. The impact on our country, particularly in terms of pessimism and eroded respect toward our own leaders, was enormous.

Ronald Reagan's administration struggled with the Iran-Contra scandal. In November 1986, Reagan, looking us "in the eye" over national television, vehemently denied that he'd countenanced the sale of weapons to Iran or the funding of the Contras. Just a week later, he retracted his statement—but insisted that the sale of weapons had not been an arms-for-hostages deal. Reagan defended the sale of arms, by virtue of its ultimate "good" intentions, but the American public doubted his honesty.

Ultimately, the Reagan-appointed Tower Commission found that Reagan was inordinately disengaged from the management of his White House. It would have been easy for staff to surreptitiously divert funds to the Contras. Although the Commission found no evidence linking the president himself to such a diversion of funds, we will never fully know about Reagan's level of involvement: many documents requested by the investigators were either lost or destroyed by administration officials. But we do know that his lack of accountability and lack of involvement in his own administration created an environment where suspect actions could take place.

In 1998, President **Bill Clinton** swore under oath that he "did not have sexual relations" with Monica Lewinsky. Later, he admitted that he had misled the American public. Ironically, Newt Gingrich, while leading the attack on Bill Clinton, was having an extramarital affair himself. These were the two most powerful leaders in America at the time, and both of their behaviors created a tumultuous storm of drama. Implicit in this story was the media feeding the public a never ending dose of drama that was consumed on a daily basis.

George W. Bush's decision to invade Iraq in 2003 gives us another example of drama from the White House. Bush and his appointees—Karl Rove, Scooter Libby, Donald Rumsfeld, Colin Powell, and George Tenant—were all implicated in embellishing the analysis of military intelligence. Although these senior officials repeatedly stated that they had evidence of Iraq's possession of weapons of mass destruction and having ties to Al Qaeda, it is now beyond dispute that Iraq did not possess weapons of mass destruction or have ties to Al Qaeda. President Bush misrepresented the nature of crucial information. He either made deliberate misstatements or created an atmosphere in which he was not well-informed by his advisors. In doing so he undermined the crucial trust upon which any decision of this magnitude needs. In short, the Bush administration led the nation to war using information that it "sold" to the world and that culminated in military action against Iraq, with an immense cost in lives and money.

Bush was wrong about the weapons of mass destruction. He was also wrong about the Al Qaeda link. He was wrong that the United States would be "greeted as liberators." A leader, on discovering his own error, acknowledges it, apologizes for it, and proceeds to act on the correct information. But when President Bush found out he was wrong, he just changed his reason for the war: "We are fighting to create peace in the Middle East." Despite all the subsequent factual evidence to the contrary and the cost in human lives (over 100,000 Iraqi non-combatant deaths and over 5,000 US Armed Forces deaths), and in the face of the massive debt the war has placed on the US, Bush still thinks he did the right thing. This is a perfect example of perceptual filters: you think you are right, you assemble evidence that shows you were right, and you ignore all the other evidence. I really believe that George W. Bush thinks what he did was right, which is one of the reasons he was such a polarizing leader: no amount of evidence to the contrary would change his point of view or make him consider an alternative point of view.

Joseph Stiglitz, Nobel Prize laureate, and his fellow economist, Linda Bilmes, wrote a book analyzing the probable short and long term costs of the war, which they titled "The Three Trillion Dollar War." That's only the cost to the United States. Think about the cost to the rest of the world and the cost to the Iraqi people. Bush has been called the United States' "first MBA President," but I'm not sure how someone with an MBA can justify this kind of return on investment. Consider the opportunity cost of what this money could have done if spent more wisely within the US economy, to create a better future for the American people.

All five of these stories of presidents in the Drama Triangle are, sadly, just a few that have come out of D.C. "Power corrupts" is the maxim. But these stories demonstrate how drama behavior perpetuates itself. Drama exists when accountability is absent. When leaders refuse to be honest and descend to discussion about breaking the law, they set low expectations for their entire team.

That means that presidents set the tone for not only their staff and our government officials, but for the entire county. No matter which president breaks our trust, he provides an example to our government officials. When the most senior ranks of our government lower their ethical standards, it's little wonder so many think, "why don't I just do the same?"

NASA and the Hubble Space Telescope

On January 28, 1986, the space shuttle Challenger burst into flames just after takeoff. You've probably heard about the O-rings: at NASA, management refused to listen when engineers warned them that cold winter temperatures could affect the O-rings that sealed the gaps between the solid rocket segments. In fact, there were written memos with unequivocal warning: "It is my honest and very real fear that if we do not take immediate action to dedicate a team to solving the problem, then we stand in jeopardy of losing a flight along with all the launch pad facilities."

But NASA had created a culture of looking the other way when it came to challenges, so NASA executives didn't listen to the warnings about the O-rings. You'd think such a horrendous tragedy would inspire the leadership to systemically change their culture, but NASA then proceeded to move forward on the same path and ignore problems with the Hubble Space Telescope.

Unfocused

The most expensive telescope in the history of astronomy, the Hubble Space Telescope, was seven years behind schedule and $700 million over budget when it was finally launched in1990. Once launched, the pictures it sent back to Earth were out of focus.

Its primary mirror had been manufactured improperly and was distorted by 1.3 millimeters.

NASA's flagship telescope project and crown jewel was cruising through space but not doing its job. How did NASA deliver a $1.5 billion project, launch it to space—where correcting the issue is just about impossible—and get it wrong? Considerable time in the Drama Triangle, for many of the participants, is the answer.

The Allen Commission, charged with investigating the situation, discovered that both the manufacturer of the mirror and NASA inspectors had used exceedingly poor quality control when building and testing the mirror.

Perkin-Elmer was the prime contractor for the defective mirror. Within their corporate culture, you did your work but you never spoke up. The Commission discovered that the Hubble's mirror had passed one of the tests but had failed another test of a less sensitive nature. The mirror aberration was recognized in the second test, but the results were ignored.

The tolerances on this project were unforgiving; there was no margin for error. Everything had to be exact for the telescope to work. Nonetheless:

- When the lens didn't position correctly by 1.3mm, the technicians assembling it decided to add three household washers to adjust it. They didn't document this change or draw the discrepancy to anyone's attention.
- When the grinding crew came in to polish the mirror, they were surprised at how much material needed to be ground off, much more than they expected. The Perkin-

Elmer manager had a possessive and controlling style and did not like others questioning his work. So the grinders asked no questions, even though every day they saw evidence that something was very wrong with the mirror.

- Formal meetings were held, but no discussion of problems was allowed.

- Optical engineers felt that things seemed strange, but they ignored the test results—even through the mirror failed the test repeatedly throughout the polishing process.

- Perkin-Elmer engineers later explained why they ignored the failed "small" tests: they decided they did not believe their results. You can't "avoid" any better than that! They had set the test, they had performed the test, and they had the test results right in front of them.

- Engineers and scientists who were qualified to analyze the test data did not do so in sufficient detail.

- Perkin-Elmer did not follow its own quality assurance plan.

- For a time, Perkin-Elmer didn't allow the NASA Quality Assurance team access to the manufacturing site.

- NASA Project Management and Perkin-Elmer Management did not have the necessary expertise to adequately monitor the optical activities.

There's More...

Sadly, there are plenty of other headline-generating stories about cheating and avoiding responsibility:

Enron: Shortly before Enron filed for bankruptcy, their senior managers received bonuses in the millions of dollars. Soon after, shareholders lost their investments and lower level employees lost their 401Ks. How did the analysts fail to notice what was happening at Enron?

WorldCom: Bernie Ebbers, once the CEO of WorldCom, was prosecuted for fraud related to securities, sedition, and filing of false documents. Ebbers ordered his CFO, Scott Sullivan, to exaggerate WorldCom's income by $11 billion dollars. Where were the auditors? How did they miss the accounting fraud? Back then, Ebbers was living a lavish lifestyle. Now, he is serving out his prison term.

Tyco: CEO L. Dennis Kozlowski and CFO Mark Swartz embezzled $600 million for their personal use. When brought to trial for committing securities fraud and conspiracy, they tried every tactic to avoid accountability for their crimes.

Bernie Madoff: And then there's Madoff, who stole $50 billion, using trusted relationships and personal introductions to find and fleece investors. The SEC, when they investigated Madoff, couldn't see the red flags even though they had specific allegations of fraudulent activity.

A good friend of mine dodged that bullet. His financial advisor, who he trusted, offered my friend the opportunity to invest in Madoff's fund. My friend said "No." He wasn't quite sure why he declined, when many of his friends invested with Madoff, but it just didn't seem right to him. For years, he had to hear from his wife about the big mistake he had made, missing such a sure thing. In the long run, both he and his wife were relieved that he hadn't made the investment.

Madoff even intimidated the SEC, supposedly objective about financial controls. The SEC received six substantive complaints, dating back to 1999, against Madoff, which lead to three investigations and two examinations. (In fact, Madoff was then able to claim truthfully that his company had passed SEC examination, which increased his marketing clout when approaching new investors.) The SEC, blinded by the financial world's perception of Madoff as a man of integrity, didn't do an objective investigation and failed to have an objective third party assess Madoff's trading practice. A simple inquiry would have immediately revealed his Ponzi scheme.

For **Qwest**, a big concern became the customers' perception of Joseph P. Nacchio, the company CEO from 1997-2002. When CEOs are not held accountable, the resulting limiting perceptions that we, the public, hold about their organizations can be difficult for a company to overcome.

In 2000, Nacchio announced that the company would pursue aggressive targets of financial growth. Internally, many of his management team said they knew these targets were impossible to meet. Once he'd announced the targets, Nacchio sold all his personal stock at a high share price. Then, when the poor network sales of Qwest were announced the following August, the stock plunged. Qwest's Board of Directors, its shareholders, and the Justice Department all saw Nacchio's actions as a pursuit of personal gain and failure to fulfill a CEO's fiduciary responsibility to shareholders. In 2005, he was indicted on 42 counts of securities fraud and insider trading. Nacchio's break in trust with Qwest shareholders lead to the perception that Qwest as a whole lacked integrity.

The common denominator? The avoider's mindset. It's classic for those mired in drama. They avoided acknowledging troubling information, which permitted discrepant data to be discounted without review. Even when team members were deeply concerned that the discrepant optical data might indicate a flaw, there were no indications that these concerns were expressed outside their division. There were many opportunities, all neglected, to catch the problem before it was sent into space.

Once a corporate culture or team becomes avoiders, that mindset can permeate—and ruin—entire projects.

"EVERYONE DOES IT"

The tendency to cheat in business begins with cheating on school tests. One particular population of students likely to cheat are those pursuing their MBAs. In a survey of over 5,000 students in 32 graduate business schools in the United States and Canada, 56% admitted they had cheated during grad school. They did so based on the "logic" that since my MBA peers cheat, I need to cheat to keep up with them.

As unethical as the actual cheating is, the bigger worry is that these cheaters are the future leaders of our financial institutions, major corporations, and even government agencies. What will happen when there is money on the line—or people's lives? Will they magically become more ethical? Or will they continue to try to compete with their peers for personal gain and prestige? **Sunbeam's** story gives us some disturbing answers to these questions:

In 2001, the SEC required Sunbeam to restate its declared income for 1996 and 1997. Sunbeam had reported $189 million in income for 1997; investigation proved that $60 million of that was from accounting fraud and misrepresentation. The SEC filed a suit against CEO Al Dunlap and other key executives, charging them with arranging a sudden, colossal increase in sales. This was not Dunlap's first time preparing creative financial records. When he'd been president of Nitec, a paper-mill company, he engineered a similar accounting trick including inflated inventory and nonexistent sales. Interestingly, Dunlap never included Nitec on his resume when shopping for new CEO jobs.

BEHAVING WITH ACCOUNTABILITY

Accountability Starts With You

Being accountable is the way to encourage others to be accountable. You must hold yourself accountable for your own actions before you can help others behave accountably. As a leader, you can be contagious in either a positive way or a negative way. Culture does not develop magically or by chance. A culture of accountability cannot develop unless the leaders, through their behaviors, demonstrate and support accountability. Being in the Leadership Triangle creates a natural state of accountability.

No one starts the day thinking, "I am not going to be accountable," but as the day wears on and things happen, and if you react to events from within the Drama Triangle, you will shirk your responsibility.

It is easy to say you are accountable when everything is going well: "I've got the project well within budget!" But is it easy when things start going poorly? Do you lay blame on outside circumstances when things go poorly? Do you blame others? Do you say, "The sub-contractors didn't deliver on time, so they put us over budget"?

I teach for an executive MBA program at the University of San Francisco. I arrived one morning and my students reminded me that I had not sent them a slide deck like I said I would. I remember asking one of my staff to send the deck to the students and I was a little annoyed that it hadn't happened. I could feel the words forming in my mind and I still wasn't able to catch myself and change the direction I was headed. In that moment of weakness and sloppy thinking on my part, these embarrassing words came out of my mouth: "I can't believe my team didn't send it to you!" You could see the puzzled look of my students in their reactions because I not only avoided any accountability, but I threw my own team under the proverbial bus. I also felt the words as I said them and I had the experience of breaking not only a commitment I had made but a more general feeling of trust with the students I was teaching. It was in that moment that I immediately apologized for not getting the deck to them and made a commitment to get it to them by the end of the day. We then talked a little bit about the concept of accountability.

I told the class that I was sorry they hadn't received the materials I had promised, that I had not checked up to be sure they'd been sent. (I could have easily asked my staff, earlier in the week, if the materials had been sent. I could have also sent the materials myself.) I apologized for not being accountable. I asked the class for their reactions to the answer I originally gave (blaming someone else) and to the answer I couldn't manifest (being accountable). They quickly answered that for a moment I did lose respect in their eyes when I avoided accountability and I quickly gained back their trust when I took responsibility. While this seems obvious, you should ask yourself, how often do you miss the opportunity to take more accountability when you are presented with an opportunity to do so?

Authenticity Matters

Accountability rests in authenticity. As a leadership characteristic, being authentic impacts your development of all other leadership characteristics. We don't tolerate duplicity from our leaders and quickly notice when someone is not authentic.

Ask yourself:

- How are my current practices and behaviors consistent with my principles and values?
- Am I being true to myself as I go about my tasks?
- Do I accept the responsibility of my actions?
- Do I seek out responsibility, and then deliver on it?

If situations take a wrong turn (as they sometimes will), there is no need to pass the buck. The best course of action is to assess the situation and take remedial action so that you can move on.

Acknowledge Mistakes

We learned this simple rule when we were kids—if you make the mess, you need to clean it up. Take responsibility when you make a mistake. Show others that you understand how you created the mistake, missed a deadline, or upset someone. Your apology can create trust while demonstrating accountability.

We all, in some way, unintentionally upset or inconvenience others. We don't keep our word, we say something rudely, our delay causes them to be delayed. If I hurt someone, however unintentionally, it's my responsibility to clean up the damage. It's not just the right thing to do, it's the wise thing to do. It's in my best interest because I value my business relationships and I want to maintain and sustain them so we can continue to achieve optimum performance.

If you make a mistake, apologize and commit yourself to better behavior in the future: you'll be on time, or you'll think before you speak, or you'll promise what you can realistically deliver and then deliver it. By acknowledging your mistakes, you accept responsibility for your behavior, which helps you to reestablish trust. After the apology, accept the consequences, whether it's having to re-build trust, work over the weekend, or forfeit your year-end bonus.

Leaders don't fear to apologize. They know it's one of the best ways to fix a mess and re-build trust.

Here's how Jeff Bezos, CEO of Amazon, took accountability after his company remotely deleted content from customers' Kindle Readers in 2009:

> This is an apology for the way we previously handled illegally sold copies of *1984* and other novels on Kindle. Our

"solution" to the problem was stupid, thoughtless, and painfully out of line with our principles. It is wholly self-inflicted, and we deserve the criticism we've received. We will use the scar tissue from this painful mistake to help make better decisions going forward, ones that match our mission. With deep apology to our customers, Jeff Bezos

In 2006, Facebook confused and frustrated customers by providing inadequate privacy controls on some new features. CEO Mark Zuckerberg apologized:

We really messed this one up. When we launched News Feed and Mini-Feed we were trying to provide you with a stream of information about your social world. Instead, we did a bad job of explaining what the new features were and an even worse job of giving you control of them. I'd like to try to correct those errors now.

People want to see you own up to your mistakes. When you do, you gain a reputation for personal accountability. You build trust as you move away from avoidance.

The Good of the Team

When the organization is team-based, the accountability applies to the team. Within the team, each member is accountable to the others; the entire team accepts responsibility for its actions.

Are you familiar with the Australian concept of mateship? I learned about and experienced mateship from my good Australian friends and business partners. Being someone's "mate" is much more than simply the Aussie slang for "pal." The concept of mateship, deeply rooted throughout Australia, speaks to the respect, trust, and loyalty between individuals or among an allied group. Mateship means each supports the other around a common challenge or purpose.

In Australia, self-reliance is critical for survival, but equally valuable is the willingness to help others. Among your mates, you know that "we are all in this together." It is individualist thinking combined with a collectivist mindset. Each individual is true to his or her values and each also values their place on the team, where no person is better than the next. This powerful combination creates strong and trusted relationships, or "mates."

When any work team in any country creates trusted relationships in such an authentic way, they are building a team accountability mindset.

Lack of execution, missed deadlines, and uninspired team members are all indicators of teams that avoid team accountability. In that sort of environment, the mindset is one of, "I'm just here to look out for my own needs." In that mindset, you will find little willingness to stretch, to adapt, or to go the extra distance, and you will also find a pattern of under-delivery of results.

But when you create a team that is accountable, the opposite happens: everyone is there for the team and for the project. They want to stretch and deliver their very best, individually and as a group.

Letting the Team Decide

At Allergan, Tom Kawata created a high level of ownership and accountability in his organization, with a culture open to change. He had a vision of creating a culture where team members at the front line of manufacturing would make more decisions in creating a more successful operation.

First, team members took ownership of their individual work projects, but then they expanded their commitment and ownership to the manufacturing plant as a whole. They implemented lean manufacturing techniques, kaizen and quality practices, from which they could look at the whole of the organization and implement solutions without regard to hierarchy. Even though their solutions involved changes in thinking, training, and policies—and we know change can be tough—everyone on the team took pride in being a contributor to the changes.

The key was that Tom held himself to the same standards he expected of everyone else. Once he had set the standard and made the expectations clear, he expected everyone to step up. He demonstrated accountability in his behavior and the result was a team that thought and acted for the good of the organization.

This team initiated a program to ensure that the operation site was clean at the end of the day, which was important for safety and quality control. Each person was assigned a day on which he or she held the accountability to have the operation site organized: room, supplies, and tools all back in their correct locations. Tom himself was part of this rotation. He modeled the behavior of accountability. I have seen other teammates speak up to hold him accountable for the standards he established. He invites this kind of feedback.

The key to creating a team-accountable culture is to have the whole team understand how to be accountable as well as how to hold others accountable.

Coach Carter

Ken Carter oversaw the basketball program at Richmond High School in California between 1997 and 2002. Coach Carter was himself a graduate of Richmond High. When he returned as head coach, the team was on a losing streak. In previous years, they'd lost 22 of their 28 games. In fact, according to Coach, "they even looked like losers."

Coach Carter had a vision for what this team could be. He wanted to turn these teen athletes into a winning team and he also wanted each of them to excel beyond high school. So he implemented a unique and shrewd strategy: he let each player choose to be on the team. He knew if each player personally decided to be on the team, he could change the direction of the team to success. But once a student chose to be on the basketball team, Coach Carter required him to sign a contract in which he agreed to maintain a 2.3 GPA. Carter wanted each student to graduate high school and qualify for college admission. Each student's parents and grandparents also had to agree to this GPA stipulation.

Once the coach made a choice to let his players make a choice, he got down to coaching, and the team started winning consistently. The school and the city were thrilled that their basketball team had a shot at the state title. Then, Coach Carter learned that most of his players had let their grade point averages go below 2.3. He took the team off the court. He held them accountable. They had to study and improve their grades before they could play any basketball.

Coach Carter made national news when he shut down a team that was 13-0, ready to advance to the state championship. He received pressure from the team and the community to just let the students play—to bend his principles. However, he knew that if he gave in on this point, he would lose everything he was working for. He knew his players' goals needed to go beyond basketball. He was right: the team members picked up their grades and were allowed back onto the basketball court. They didn't win the championship but they had a winning season, they did graduate, and several of the players attended college. Coach Carter not only helped his players make choices, he held them accountable to their choices. He positively impacted their lives far beyond the basketball court.

HOLDING OTHERS ACCOUNTABLE

You must hold others accountable if you want to create a team-accountable culture. If you let things slide to avoid uncomfortable confrontations, lack of integrity will creep into your organization. Once you let this become the norm, it affects everyone at every position. To hold others accountable requires the courage to put issues on the table.

In high-performance organizations, each team member holds himself individually accountable but all team members commit to hold each other accountable. They embrace team accountability for the greater good and larger outcome of the team. If your team has performance goals they're aiming to achieve, they are not only accountable to their individual targets, but they are also accountable to helping each person achieve their targets.

The best work and the happiest employees develop in environments that encourage and practice accountability. In 1968, the *Harvard Business Review* published "One More Time...How Do

You Motivate Employees?" which gave the fundamentals of a meaningful job as:

- Assigning work to a natural work unit.
- Increasing the accountability of individuals.
- Loosening control while increasing feedback.
- Keeping people growing by increasing the challenge of tasks while helping them become specialists in their work.

Employees respond positively to these work requirements. The HBR study found that not only did people report high personal satisfaction for the job, but they delivered:

- A high level of accuracy in their work.
- Improved decision-making.
- More cooperation with coworkers.

This study holds up for today's workforce even more. As individuals are looking to find more meaning in their work, these principles become important motivators.

Steps to Holding Others Accountable

Here are four steps you can take to help others maintain their accountability. You can use all four steps whether you're the CEO, a section leader, or a team member. These steps work regardless of the job title or project at hand.

1. Be explicit with expectations.

All expectations, each benchmark, must be clear and easy to measure. Whether it's expectations for each individual team member, or for the team as a whole, don't be ambiguous with expectations. As the football coach Vince Lombardi would say to his team, "It's hard to be aggressive when you're confused." Each member of the team should have a clear understanding of his or her individual role.

You can't assume your team members know what is supposed to be done and when it is to be delivered. Spell it out. If you clearly set the benchmarks and the expected outcomes and their measurements, you won't have to waste time debating with team members who later say they didn't understand or who thought they did what was expected.

Once the expectation is set, ask others to agree to it. This is critical: you need to create commitment. It is hard to hold someone accountable to something he or she didn't commit to. You and Denise might agree that Bob will bring donuts to the staff meeting, but you need to hear Bob say "yes."

2. Measure performance with measurements that are easy to understand and easy to measure.

Your expectations need to be measurable. If you use words such as *long, short, big, early,* or *late* when working with a team of ten, you'll soon find out that there are ten different definitions of *long, short, early…*

"Be working at your desk by 9:00," is more explicit and measurable than "you need to get to work earlier." If you want your sales force to improve performance, don't say "do better." Say "do 15% better," or "do 5% better this month, and overall 10% better by end of the year."

Setting specific measurements allows you to track progress regularly, either through reporting or staff meetings. Keep expectations realistic. Appropriate scoping of project goals and resources is critical to reaching the expected outcome.

3. Encourage feedback.

Constant and consistent feedback keeps the commitments fresh while allowing the flexibility for mutually-agreed-upon adjustments. For truly useful feedback, your culture must allow people to speak their minds without fear, and similarly feel that they are able to bring up mistakes they have committed. The emphasis must move from blame for what happened to planning how to fix it and moving on.

For team members in a blaming culture, the inclination is to hide mistakes and point fingers. In such a culture, employees look out for themselves, not for the interests of the team.

4. Don't budge on the expectation.

(It's a little like raising children: once they know you won't enforce the limit, they don't respect it.)

When something goes wrong, it is critical to hold the line. But the place to hold the line first is to look inward. A leader who approaches "holding the line" with an internal locus of control and assuming positive intent asks himself:

- What could I have done to have made this project hit its deliverable date?
- What resources could I have brought to bear on the situation?
- What communication could I have made first?
- What could I learn from this, and what could my team learn?

Nonetheless, you will occasionally work with someone who consistently fails to meet agreed-upon commitments. You might decide to add consequences—positive or negative—to ensure they are convinced that being accountable for their commitment is in their best interest.

The Conversations That Hold Others Accountable

Martin Luther King, Jr. expressed it well: "The ultimate measure of a man is not where he stands in moments of comfort and convenience, but where he stands at times of challenge and controversy."

By talking with your team members and enforcing agreements, the integrity of the entire organization will improve. Some of these conversations will be casual exchanges in the break room, or chatting in your team members' cubicles or workspaces. Other conversations will be more formal, and privately in your office or a meeting room.

Assume positive intent. Always begin with the simple assumption that people are doing their best to deliver. When you have a positive impression of the person's intention, you will be less likely to cast blame. Assume that they want to know that they have not fulfilled a commitment, and that they want the feedback (in fact, this agreement for feedback should be part of the expectations to which they agreed). If you assume negative intent, you'll see them as "guilty" before your conversation even begins, which will lead you to blaming and punishing. Your team will soon decide that, to you, the word "accountability" is just a fancy word for blame.

Avoiding the Conversation?

Are you reluctant to have a conversation to hold someone accountable? You might be operating within the Drama Triangle.

Avoiders won't have the holding-someone-accountable conversation because:

- They fear the conversation will be awkward or inconvenient. (Well, it might be. That's no reason not to talk to someone.)
- They do not like intervening, preferring to let other people grapple with difficulties without the avoider having to get involved. Avoiders often strike other people as being disengaged.
- They set low expectations. If the expectation is as low as "come to work Monday through Friday," everyone will meet that expectation, and the avoider won't have to insist that people meet it.
- They fear offending people, so they worry that a conversation to hold somebody accountable will worsen their relationship.
- They avoid the immediate need for a conversation, and then because the problem is no longer timely, they can avoid the conversation altogether.

I remember a consulting job we had with a large software company, working with a team who had just had their leader replaced. This leader deeply cared for his people and created a culture of fun and creativity. He was well liked by all. He put a tremendous amount of time and effort into making sure his people felt acknowledged and felt good. But he wasn't talented at having developmental conversations or holding his team accountable to performance standards.

While everybody liked this manager personally, the department produced only average results and no one in the group was seen as a potential leader. Other executives did not look to this department to find candidates for promotion into their departments.

This "great guy" had avoided having uncomfortable conversations with his people. He provided good feelings in the short run, but the careers of everybody who worked for him had stalled.

Contrast that with Pam Yanchick. As a former VP at Genentech, she was known for caring for her people, yet she had a reputation of being accountable herself and holding her team accountable. She was also known for developing new talent and leaders. Pam gave feedback immediately: show up unprepared and Pam would let you know. But she was fiercely supportive of her team members and fought to get her team the resources they needed to be successful. She turned around function after function and built herself a personal reputation as a successful catalyst for change in the organization. Pam's ability to provide quick and instant feedback created a culture where others could do the same. Yet it was more than what Pam accomplished: her team members were always highly considered for promotions. She created a reputation of creating other leaders and helping her team members grow. She demonstrated being accountable and held everyone to the same high standards.

Face to Face

When you have to hold someone accountable, have your conversation face to face. Let us imagine that you, as Team Leader, leave your team member Jane a voice message asking her to attend a cross-functional meeting that is critical for the team's deliverable. She sends you an email saying that she will attend. Later, Bill, the cross-function team leader, calls you to say that Jane wasn't at the meeting.

You need to discuss this with Jane directly, face-to-face.

- First, assume positive intent in Jane's reason for not attending the meeting.
- Then ask Jane (and yourself) whether you were clear about her need to attend the meeting, and about when and where it was.
- Listen to Jane. She might have a good reason; she might not. But allow her to give a full explanation. If her reasons are not good, or if she missed a step (she didn't phone you that she broke a tooth at lunch and rushed to the dentist), tell her so. She must accept responsibility and consequences.
- Let her know about Bill's reaction. Ask how you can support her in discussing this situation with Bill, in order to preserve a good working relationship with him.

This conversation will create trust between you and Jane, between Jane and Bill, and between you and Bill. By going directly to Jane and holding her accountable, you eliminate any need for drama in this situation.

Spread it Around

Changing a culture of avoiding to one of accountability starts with the way you behave with your team members.

You'll deserve the confidence of your colleagues if you:

- Deliver on your commitments.
- Own your mistakes and make any needed apologies. You'll help drive fear out of the organization when employees realize they can apologize without "getting into trouble."
- Check with team members on their progress before deadlines so you can offer support and help them to achieve their commitments.
- Focus on asking what happened and how it happened when mistakes or problems occur. Asking "why" can create defensiveness. Focus on the present and the future, not on the past.
- Have the tough conversations. If you tend to avoid conversations that hold someone accountable, find ways to motivate yourself into having the conversation. You'll build confidence as you see how productive such conversations turn out.
- Allow your team members to hold you accountable. When someone comes to you needing to have a conversation to hold you accountable, let them.

Being accountable means having authentic conversations that create trust. Addressing these issues within your team can create a sustainable culture of accountability, and along with it, the results that drive success.

A Hint of Success

We are all accountable to someone. In 2005, Kara Goldin launched Hint, a bottled water made with just a "hint" of flavor. It began when she was figuring out how to give her children something other than juice boxes or other sugar-laced beverages. She began to put bits of fresh fruit into glasses of water. From her kitchen, the idea was born. She noticed that so many children go from drinking milk out of a sippy cup to drinking juice out of a sippy cup—getting too much sugar too often. Children needed something enjoyable to drink that wasn't bad for their health.

Kara is now the CEO of a multimillion-dollar business. Her underlying principle for Hint is accountability. You might think as CEO, she can do what she wants. Yet, being focused on healthful children's drinks, her accountability is first to her customers. These customers appreciate a company that gives them beverages made without any artificial flavors, sweeteners, or preservatives. Kara is also accountable to the investors in the business. She has a responsibility to provide them with a return on their investment in Hint. Since its founding, Hint has always exceeded their quarterly goals—and Hint aims high each quarter.

Kara stresses that if Hint employees set a goal, Hint employees achieve it. She is making the company a success while raising four schoolchildren and staying active in her community. How? Kara subscribes to basic principles: she loves her family, she loves her product, and she loves her company. She keeps it simple by hiring people who share her passion and who want the business to succeed. She surrounds herself with a team that is naturally accountable.

CHAPTER 8

Your Energy is Produced
By Your Thoughts

YOU ARE EITHER generating positive energy or you are not. There is no middle ground.

And each of us, every day, generates a wide range of energies, both positive and negative. Leaders radiate energy—energy about themselves, or energy about their project or topic. In drama, people drain energy out of the environment and out of the people around them.

Our choices and the energy those choices produce create specific responses common to individuals in the Drama Triangle and to those in the Leadership Triangle.

- Being focused, energetic, and engaged comes from positive energy and generates more positive energy.
- Resignation, fear, and avoidance deplete energy. When these emotions generate any energy at all, it is negatively charged.

We're usually aware when we are generating energy or when we are pulling energy out of the environment. You recognize when you are being a jerk, or feeling resigned, or becoming angry. It is always your choice to change, to move into the Leadership Triangle, to accept accountability—or to avoid it. Every moment of every day, you choose how you respond to people and situations. Depending on your locus of control, you make those choices from internal control or from external control.

When you understand your own internal state, you'll know if you are generating energy or taking it from others. Your energy is a variable and it is under your control. The way you think, the roles you adopt and the Triangle you're in affect your energy.

Your energy affects the people around you and creates a feedback loop of either negativity or positivity. If you refuse to take responsibility for your attitude and your energy, you begin a dangerous downward spiral. If you accept responsibility, you generate energy that empowers you in your tasks and relationships, and your success in turn generates more energy.

EXPERIMENT WITH ENERGY

By energy, I don't mean just the physical energy that makes you upbeat or smiling, or able to run a marathon. Your body is more than bones, tissue, skin, and blood. It is also a complex system of interlocking electromagnetic fields of energy. For centuries, these electromagnetic energy fields have been central to traditional Chinese medical practices such as acupuncture. Today, they can be measured through MRIs. At UCLA, Dr. Michael Irwin, studying immune system response to shingles outbreak in seniors, found that those who used the Chinese energy practice of tai chi had a 50% increase in immune cells that target the shingles virus. Dr.

Irwin's study is one of many that show that our energy affects our health.

This is the energy you feel when your values are congruent with the direction you are headed, when you know your skill set is well-suited for the project and product, and when you're enthusiastic about the tasks at hand. These feelings generate a positive energy that influences you and others.

Here are two simple exercises I'd like you to do right now, so that you can feel your own energy:

Let's Be Negative

Take a few minutes and think of a negative, unpleasant situation. See it all happen in your mind's eye. It might be:

- Some circumstance out in the future that you fear.
- Having a conversation with someone who is difficult.
- Facing something you fundamentally don't want to do, or about which you don't know what to do.

Notice how your thinking has affected your energy level. Check your physical body. Often, when energy is depleted, a person's posture changes. Where else do you feel the energy drain?

Now, do the opposite: Visualize a scenario of something that you enjoy doing and that keeps you focused, or think of someone you enjoy being with, or remember a great day in your life. After a minute to two, do you feel your energy increasing? Did your posture change? Do you feel energized mentally? Physically? What happened to your breathing?

Project Energy

For this exercise, please stand up. Now, imagine that your "personal space" is only your physical body: your environment ends right at the skin level. Shut your eyes, be aware of your body, but only out to your skin. You only exist in your physical body.

After a minute or two, shake it off—open your eyes and walk around a few steps.

Now, again stand still and close your eyes and feel your physical body and your energy. Let the energy radiate off of your body, pulsing out from your skin, expand it so it radiates outwards from the top of your head all the way down to your toes, side to side, back and front. You don't stop at the physical, skin level. You are more than a visible body, you have an even bigger presence as energy.

I've taken many people through this exercise, and they all say the second "imagination" feels more like them. We are aware when our energy is high, or expansive, or fading.

RESEARCH ON ENERGY

For over 20 years, the Institute of HeartMath has been exploring the relationship between the heart and mind. IHM has generated a number of clinical studies that demonstrate how aligning your thinking changes the electromagnetic field of the heart. IHM's Director of Research, Rollin McCraty, PhD, states in his book, The Energetic Heart: Bioelectromagnetic Interactions Within and Between People, that the heart produces the largest electromagnetic field around a human. Compared to the electromagnetic field produced by the brain, the electrical component of the heart's field is 50-60 times greater in amplitude and affects every cell in the body. Furthermore, the heart produces information that measurably impacts the electromagnetic fields of other individuals in close proximity.

This research has empirically verified the concept of electromagnetic field communication and how the field generated by the heart is distributed throughout the body holistically. The heart generates the strongest magnetic field in the body, which influences all the other organs, including the brain. The IHM researchers see the heart pattern as a carrier wave of information that can be measured in other parts of the body. We're used to thinking that only the brain generates such information. In fact, each of your major organs has the same type of neurotransmitters found in your brain and central nervous system. Each organ has its own neurology, similar to the brain, though in smaller volume. We do not just think with our brains. Our heart, our liver, and our lungs each have structures that are similar to the grey matter in our heads. In many ways, we don't just have a central processing system, but we are more analogous to distributed processing or a network.

The HeartMath researchers also found that, in states of stress, anxiety, or anger, our heart rhythm becomes disordered and chaotic. When a person is in a positive emotional state, the heart rhythm is more likely to be ordered and rhythmic. This is, of course, a healthier way to operate and is directly correlated to higher test scores and improved physical performance. In one study, the results indicated that the emotional preparedness skills students learned in the Heart Math training resulted in test-taking performance improvements above and beyond those achieved through standard academic preparation alone. The high school seniors who attended the training demonstrated substantial improvements in test scores and passing rates on state-required Math and Reading tests.

Their research gets even more interesting as it applies to leadership and influencing other people. Their research shows that the electromagnetic signal produced by your heart is registered in the brain waves of people around you: the heart's magnetic component is approximately 5,000 times stronger than the brain's and can be detected by another person within five feet of you. When people are that close, one person's heartbeat signal is registered in the other person's brainwaves. So your field can impact the individuals you deal with daily.

The Institute of HeartMath is now doing research with small groups of participants who are able, intentionally, to create heart rhythm synchronization. Results suggest that a coherent energy field mediated by the heart helps improve performance and health. It seems clear, from IHM's research, that the energy field of the heart plays a crucial role in the concept of human information exchange at levels of which we are not yet aware.

SOURCES OF ENERGY

Every human being is a source of energy and every interaction involves an exchange of that energy.

Positive energy comes from having the right perspective, from knowing through experience that your energy comes from within. There are external stimuli that can add to energy in the short term, but the real source of energy is inside. It is wrapped up in your choices.

Lack of awareness about your own energy will make you susceptible to the energy drainers associated with the Drama Triangle. If you are not aware that you are in the Drama Triangle, you may not be aware of the energy you are taking from others.

Being in the Drama Triangle is an energy drain to you and to those around you. If you are being the Victim, Adversary, or Rescuer, you will—by the nature of these roles—pull on other people's energy. Even if you are not overtly in one of the drama roles, you drain energy when you ignore your own feelings or don't take care of your own needs. In this state, you will look for external approval: Instead of building energy from yourself, internally, you'll take energy from others.

Neediness can start a "tug-of-war" over energy. People might pull away from you as they sense your drain on their energy. You might wonder what you did wrong, and try harder to insinuate yourself, which will cause them to pull further away, physically or emotionally. Often, we don't do this overtly or even consciously, but as an instinctive reaction to the exchange of energy.

Ask yourself these questions to test if you are taking energy from others:

- Do I constantly ask others for favors?
- Do I need to be around others to feel good about myself?
- Do I need to remain at the center of attention?
- Will I do anything to get attention?
- Do I seek out praise?
- Do I dislike being by myself?

If you answer "yes" to most of these questions, you are biased towards drama and not operating from the internal orientation that lends itself to leadership. Your neediness might have you needing others to feel anything. When you can't, or won't produce your own energy, you'll go find it in others.

Leaders have naturally high energy levels. They produce it themselves. They do exchange it, but not from neediness. Positive energy fuels others with positive energy; it's not a drain. That is why leaders really do like hanging out with other leaders.

RESIGNATION

In drama, the three most common qualities of energy come from resignation, anger, and confusion. In some ways, they can "energize" you, but rarely toward positive actions. Mostly, they deplete your energy.

You develop resignation when you give up without getting out. You might give up on a job, a person, or a situation—but you stick around and "go through the motions." You're still at the job, with the person, or part of the situation, but you do less and less work, with less and less attention. The hidden impact of resignation is that you do not realize the toll it takes on you.

"I hate my job," is a classic statement from someone who is resigned.

Sometimes, resignation is misread as being realistic, worldly, or appropriately cynical. Thinking "Senior management will never change," is resignation when it's marked by the feeling that you can't make a change; you can't make a difference. When you're resigned, you are abdicating the ability to make your own choices.

If you believe that you have little impact on your job or in your company, you stop seeing the possibilities for your team, for your product or service, or for the company's future. That means you are in a state of resignation. If you settle for the status quo, you become resigned to no changes, and no improvement. Through such limiting perceptions, you'll decide that you cannot make a difference and you'll stop trying. You'll forget that you are in control of your responses to your environment.

Several years ago, after five years in various technology jobs, I had a change of direction in my life. I realized that I was in a career that I no longer wanted. I felt stuck because although I disliked the job, I was actually successful in it. I needed to make a career change, but I couldn't imagine such an option was really open to me.

I was in the Drama Triangle. I showed up for work completely resigned. I didn't accept my responsibility to choose another career. By not moving on, I gave up my energy every day. I withdrew and I became non-productive. Of course, my behaviors had a negative impact on my team members. I did not, then, know of the concept of resignation, so I was at the mercy of its effect. I was gone from the job—I had just not left yet.

As my energy level went down, I was no longer fun to be around. I was dissatisfied with where I was, but I did not understand that I could actually choose to do something else. Sometimes being in this cauldron of drama can help, such as when it creates the pressure that forces you to make a choice. Sometimes you have to go down into the pain associated with the Drama Triangle in order to come up and make a new choice.

Finally, my dissatisfaction with where I was propelled me to examine where I would rather be. That took me in a different direction. I finally did resign from that job, left the company, re-energized myself, and moved forward into the career that I am in today.

When you are feeling resignation, you are the person who pays the biggest price, both in the quality of your life and in the impact you have on the people around you.

One of the many executives I've coached was the president of a Fortune 100 specialty chemical company of 15,000 employees. Throughout his years with the company, he was pitted against another executive. Both men held jobs of increasing responsibility and both were considered possible successors to the CEO. But when the CEO retired, the other executive was named CEO. My client was named president: he came in "second place."

As president, he was still leading the largest team in the company and had over 9,000 people reporting to him. But when he wasn't appointed CEO, he started to resign from the job he ended up with: the role of the number two person in the company, the president. He believed that he "lost" the CEO job, so he slowly shifted his attention away from the job he had. He put his focus on outside boards, non-profits, and other activities; many of them were worthwhile, but they were not his day job. But he was like the proverbial frog who won't jump out of the warm water as it slowly heats up. Once he had, in essence, resigned his spirit over losing the CEO position, he gave up on putting his full energy into leading his team and doing his critically important job as president of the firm.

With coaching, he grasped that he had adopted this mindset of resignation. He saw the damage his resignation cost him and the team he was leading. He made a new choice: he decided to be the best president he could be. He shifted every aspect of his job. He recovered his energy and spirit and was inspired to unlock the full potential of his organization. This shift in thinking unleashed something amazing in him and he became one of the most inspiring and trusted leaders I have had the pleasure of working with.

The Dangers in Resignation

Once resigned, it's difficult for a person to be candid with their teammates, with their leadership, or with themselves. They will avoid straight conversations and making decisions. Their lack of action keeps the tension high, so problems remain unsolved, which further saps energy—and continues the drama. You'll still hear them say, "I hate this job," or "senior management will never change," but they won't say, "I'm resigned, I've given up and I'm not going to work very hard anymore."

If you have developed resignation and are no longer fully engaged in your work, you'll have difficulty leading. Worse, if you are resigned but remain unaware of it, it will control every aspect of your behavior, and it will impact your team (and your family).

It's often easier to notice resignation in others. Have you ever been in a meeting and noticed that a person sitting right there at the table was not present? (Maybe you've been that person.) If a member of your team becomes resigned, a leader needs to step up and help them out of it for everyone's sake.

Ask Yourself...

These questions will help you identify and move past resignation:

- Who is controlling this situation?
- What do I want to create?
- What is possible in this situation?
- What is outside the predictable?
- What new future can we invent?
- Given the circumstance I am in right now, what new choices can I make?

Although difficult, this insightful process is powerful and it will help you to become aware of your resignation while giving you the power to choose what you want instead.

CONFUSION

Another internal state common among those in the Drama Triangle is confusion. When confused, people have difficulty focusing their attention and cannot think with their usual speed or clarity.

This is not the confusion that comes from misunderstanding something: you're not confused about what time the meeting starts; you're confused about which reports you need to prepare for the meeting, and why.

This confusion is borne from habitual internal conflict with yourself. Once people are confused, they lose the ability to be accountable or responsible because they cannot see a clear path. Their feelings are so mixed up that they do not have a direction or clear goal. Confusion is another way of hiding.

If a person is stuck in drama, confusion can paralyze her if she's struggling with an inner conflict such as:

- She wants to resist an authority but at the same time wants to obey that authority.
- She wants to have a conversation but is afraid of having it.
- She wants to go forward but is afraid of going forward.

Being confused about which direction to take "helps" her to not do anything at all. It is a defense mechanism, keeping her safe from having to take action. This is not always a conscious, deliberate action: she may really feel confused. She may blame herself for her dilemma, or she may take the route of Victim and blame others for putting her into the situation.

If confronted to decide—by someone else needing her decision or by the calendar signaling a deadline—her brain freezes. The result is excuses such as "oh, I forgot," "I didn't understand," or "I just can't do it." When someone is consistently confused in this way, they are using confusion as a strategy, as a passive-aggressive tactic for not dealing with their internal issue.

When the issue generating the conflict is personal, it's difficult to help the confused person make a decision. It's about her personal values and choices. If her confusion was about an external event, such as how to get the project done on time, others could assist her or the deadline could be changed. But if her confusion is due to her relationship with her manager, no one else on the team can step in and fix that for her.

Confusion over the simplest decisions can lead to a struggle, which cannot be resolved until the underlying conflict is addressed and resolved. You can see how confusion saps your energy.

ANGER

When anger enters the Drama Triangle, it becomes more pronounced and more toxic.

The most helpful thing to remember about anger is that it is a secondary emotion; it is a cover for other feelings. The primary emotion is what you felt immediately before you felt angry. If you look deeper, you'll find it was fear, disrespect, disappointment, a challenge, or pressure. If any of these feelings was intense enough, your reaction to them can be anger.

You might find emotions such as anger and fear difficult to deal with, but they are not bad in and of themselves. They are simply a part of your complex wiring. It's how you respond to them that brings you to drama or leadership.

Anger can be useful. Harnessing that energy positively can motivate you in a constructive direction. Much good has been done in this world that was propelled by someone's anger at injustice, disrespect, or inequality.

But the anger we encounter in drama is dysfunctional, habitual anger when the primary emotion isn't resolved. Anger is produced when something fails to meet your expectations and you feel disappointed. You feel dissatisfied and frustrated because of some unresolved or ongoing problem or relationship. These responses and feelings are natural, yet the Drama Triangle heightens these natural emotions and twists them into something else.

Anger can fester or flare in a person in the Drama Triangle. Remember, in drama, this person is assuming negative intent, so if someone says the "wrong" thing, he will assume the worst from it. He tells himself the person meant to be that rude, be that late, be that demanding. His anger stays fixed on past issues and events; he won't let them go.

His anger becomes habitual because he doesn't ever deal with the central issues that created the anger. If a person disappoints him on Tuesday, he doesn't deal with it on Wednesday. He will instead remember all the times this person disappointed him previously. He will anticipate that all future encounters will be the same.

Instead of promptly dealing with the issue as soon as he feels the anger, he's stopped by his fear of direct action or an uncomfortable conversation. The more times that the issues are delayed, the more that the unexpressed emotion builds up, further clouding his thinking. Before too long, he's created a set of limiting perceptions about a person or a situation.

Whenever we do not deal promptly with our anger or frustration, we carry it with us into the future. It can literally sicken us, and we often bring it into conversations and conflicts with people who weren't even part of the initial incident.

My recommendation is the 48-hour rule: address conflicts, issues, and problems within forty-eight hours.

Remember, in any of your stories, there is reality and there is your perception of it. Your conclusions aren't necessarily based on the facts, but on the way you view the world. When you conclude that someone was rude, disrespectful, or did something to frustrate you, discuss it with them (assuming as much positive intent as possible) before your anger overwhelms you and you sink deeper into drama.

THE POWER OF BEING POSITIVE

Now let's get into the Leadership Triangle, where being focused, energetic, and engaged generates powerful, attractive leadership.

Leaders develop all three of these qualities and use them creatively. When all three qualities combine, you are in the flow.

Focus

When you have focus, your energy generates action, which in turn produces results.

Scott Carmer, the EVP of Commercial Operations at MedImmune, is focused. He starts each morning listing the five things he is going to get done that day. He asks all of his direct reports, and their people, to do the same.

Scott leads a team of over 500 people. Each workday, Scott knows that each of them is focused on five goals. That's 2,500 goals a day. At the end of the week, Scott himself has accomplished 25 goals, and his team has met 12,500 goals. I talked about leading by example in the last chapter: Scott leads by his example. He has focused his organization's ability to focus. He is a Catalyst, unleashing the collective energy of the people on his team.

You, too, by being focused, can harness energy and bring it to bear on your important issues and tasks.

Einstein had a useful method to keep himself focused. Whenever he sat down to read, he kept a paper and pen next to him. If some thought distracted him as he read, he would jot down the thought, repeat it to himself, then go back to his reading. In capturing and naming his distractions, he kept them from completely interrupting his focus.

Engagement

Engaged people produce positive results. You're engaged when you have clarity about where you want to go. When your work is congruent with your direction and goals, you radiate an energy that is attractive to others. You're eager to build a compelling vision of goal and purpose. People with such a compelling vision act differently than those who do not. Their approach to their goals becomes a source of energy. This energy captivates others and makes them eager to take part.

Think of people you know (or know of) who can deliver this kind of energy into their environment. You want to be aligned with them, right? Their energy is contagious. Get yourself into the Leadership Triangle, get deeply engaged with your purpose and vision, and you'll generate that sort of contagious energy. When you are engaged with your vision, doors open for you.

Keith Belling, CEO of Popchips, an all-natural snack chip company, is engaged in his vision. He's built a company on a platform of positive energy around their product—so positive that Keith coined the term "poptimists" when referring to his team. Keith really likes building businesses. He is a serial entrepreneur and is constantly finding businesses that genuinely interest him. His passion is infectious with not only the people who work with him, but also with his customers. Everyone on Keith's team shares his simple principles: put the fun back in snacking, build with an entrepreneurial spirit, and be passionate about creating a great culture.

Keith is also personally engaged with his customers. He so enjoys building a loyal following "one snacker at a time," that he personally answers emails from Popchips fans. The company's fans are fairly fanatic because they enjoy the guilt-free pleasure of healthy, good tasting snacks. When you're engaged like Keith, your energy draws in others to share your vision. It becomes infectious. Popchips has engaged customers and engaged employees. It has celebrities like Katy Perry creating her own flavor of Popchips. All of this occurs because everything the company does revolves around creating a positive energy for healthier snacking options. Customers want the full experience of both a great tasting product and a brand they feel connected to. When you perform every business task with high energy the results will follow. Popchips is now one of the fastest growing snacks in North America.

Getting Into the Flow

Have you ever been so completely absorbed in your work or project that the outside world melts away and your innate skills flow freely? Have you ever been so engrossed that you lost track of time? This type of focus and engagement is a level of energy called the flow. You can experience this at work or at play, alone or in a group.

In 1994, Jeff Bezos founded Amazon.com as an online bookstore. He developed it into the world's largest web retailer, a place where one can find anything and everything from electronics to groceries.

Jeff understands the flow state. His approach to the flow shows up in Amazon's web interfaces and product offerings. He knows that if he can create a path for you into a flow experience—so you are either lost in your shopping experience or lost in your reading experience—the energy you enjoy rebounds to the good of his company.

Steve Jobs created the same experience for Apple users. Did you ever see Steve Jobs give a presentation? He demonstrated the characteristics of flow in action. Like an athlete, he delivered his content, demonstrations, stories, and visuals in perfect synchronization. His focus was on his audience: he was engaged in his message. When he was in the flow, his energy pulsed out to not only the audience but to the marketplace as well.

Flow has been described as "a highly productive state of concentration." Your mind and body like to be in the flow because of the ease in which you get your activities done. Your energy flows where you place your attention; it flows because of your focus.

Here's a quick example of focus and energy: right now, think about your left foot. Let all of your attention go to your left foot. Focus on it. If you deeply focus on it, before long you will feel its physical presence, even feel it tingle, in a different way than you feel your right foot or left hand. Your focus on your left foot brought your energy to your left foot.

Similarly, when you are 100% committed to an activity, your energy will flow into it. If you are in a state of flow:

- You're focused on what you're doing.
- You are in harmony with your surroundings and feelings.
- You do not make a distinction between work and play.
- You have a high sense of fulfillment with the activity.
- For you, this activity is meaningful and has a purpose, whether it's performing open-heart surgery or improving your golf game.
- You are connected to your inner self and also to those around you.

Not surprisingly, such moments can be extremely rewarding, and some of your best work stems from these times of flow. You will generate a better result, in less time, and with more pleasure.

You can learn to get into the flow. We have some understanding of what causes the energy levels that move people into the flow, and more importantly, how you can get there more often.

In 1989, I had the honor to partner with Britt Ewing, a leading researcher in mind-body integration. Britt had worked with Olympic athletes, Joffrey Ballet dancers, and various performing artists to help them reach peak performance states.

During our collaboration, while developing a seminar on "Performance States Training," we investigated how others got in and out of the flow state, so that we could recreate the sequence of steps for ourselves and for others. We found that, to get into the flow, you need to:

- Create the context or the right environment. This includes the physical space, the right group of people, and the materials and equipment you'll need.

- Prepare to be in the flow, including setting a time to enter into the state and a time to exit. This includes clearing your calendar and turning off the cell phone.

- Set very clear outcomes and see them as if they have already happened. You want to build in anticipation for the activity.

- When you engage in the activity, place 100% of your attention on that activity. Your focus is outside of yourself.

- Make sure all participants are in agreement about whatever task you were going to engage in. Commit fully to success. Ask the question—and get the affirmative answer—that all agree to focus on the activity for a set amount of time with 100% focus. It might be to finish the annual report, prepare a schematic for the new building, or play a game of hoops, but you need to make an agreement with yourself.

- Britt also found that, for athletes and performers, particular postures, breathing, and movements can help them to enter the flow.

Other researchers have suggested ways to understand, and get into, a flow of energy:

- Mihaly Csikszentmihalyi, notable for "Flow: The Psychology of Optimal Experience," has spent years studying the phenomenon. He says that you must have very clear goals with your focus being keenly on the activity itself.

- In Judith Delozier and John Grinder's "Turtles All The Way Down: Prerequisites To Personal Genius," they explain what they call a "genius state." To enter this state, you must fully commit, have heightened peripheral vision, and no outside interruptions.

- Daniel Goleman, in his "The Meditative Mind," writes about a process for shifting levels of consciousness. He suggests that your action and awareness merge to increase concentration on the task, and you lose yourself in complete focus on the activity.

Each of these descriptions is describing a way to get more done and to have more energy. Leadership at its most basic description is someone who can generate more energy around themselves. That is why we describe the Drama Triangle as an energy drain and the Leadership Triangle as an energy gain.

YOU CAN CHANGE

Your personal world is defined by your energy, its type, and amount. If you spend your energy on resignation, confusion, and anger, you live in a small world. If you generate lots of strong, positive energy, yours is a world of possibilities.

Too many people sink into drama, letting their disappointments and cynicism slowly extinguish their life spark. If they become resigned, confused, or angry, they end up bitter and jaded. It saddens me to see people put time in at a job but leave their spirit at home. But they're paying a high price: if unchecked, their choices lead to apathy and cynicism, resulting in health problems, depression, and many other difficulties. At the most basic level, leadership is the generation of energy that unleashes the potential for all who come in contact with it. Drama, at its center is an energy drain to everyone who engages with it.

If you can see that you are resigned, confused and angry, then you can see that you are falling into the trap of the Drama Triangle. Get out—make a shift toward the Leadership Triangle. Your choice to be in the Leadership Triangle gives you the energy to be focused and engaged. Use that energy to create extraordinary results.

CHAPTER 9

Victim or Visionary

LEADERS AT THEIR core are Visionary.

When you discover your own deeply held values and beliefs, and then develop your vision (or visions), you'll have the capacity to generate big ideas. You'll find visions that are unique to you, the visions that matter most for you. As you envision them, (for they will develop over time, depending on your situation and circumstances) focus on them and execute the behaviors necessary to make them happen. Such focus and commitment can powerfully influence both you and the world around you. Use your heart, your mind, and your energy to dream big. Involve your organization, environment, and relationships to deliver on your visions. That's what visionaries do.

Victims? They use their jobs, circumstances, and relationships as excuses for why they can't dream big and why they can't accomplish much.

Victims whine. Things happen to them. When something goes wrong, they can tell you who caused it. It wasn't them.

Visionaries make choices. They make things happen. They invite others along.

Having a clear vision of where you want to go is one of the primary distinctions between living in the Leadership Triangle or being stuck in the Drama Triangle. The best way to stay out of the Victim role is to create and pursue compelling visions for yourself, your team, your community, your family, and your life.

FIRST: VISUALIZE THE GOAL

Let's consider a vision to be a compelling image or picture that will become a reality once the dream has been achieved.

There is great power in defining such visions for ourselves. Millions have read books about having and achieving goals, such as "Think and Grow Rich" by Napoleon Hill, "The Power of Positive Thinking" by Norman Vincent Peale and "Psycho-Cybernetics" by Malcolm Waltz. And yet few people will take the time to deploy their focus and energy, to define and pursue their vision. As motivational speaker Jim Rohn says, "I find it fascinating that most people plan their vacations with better care than they plan their lives."

Our lives and our futures are not a fixed reality, waiting for us to arrive. The future doesn't happen "out there" and it isn't in the hands of other people. Our future is molded by the way we envision it. We can imagine our future into existence.

This is especially true when we take the time to examine our values and goals and be deliberate about creating our vision. And when a person achieves his or her vision of the future, it comes about not just from their actions but includes also the collective actions of those who they inspire and bring along.

Victims also create their future, and have a vision of it, although they don't understand it to be a vision or a goal. The Victim sees his future as the inescapable consequences of other people's actions. Victims get the future they create, but in a twisted and negative way. If a Victim spends months and years thinking, "I can't get ahead because they didn't give me the scholarship to college," or "I didn't get to present my paper at the conference because the company wouldn't pay for me to attend," they are, in fact, envisioning a future that will come to pass.

Envisioning a good future (or a lousy one) begins deep in your brain, but you have considerable control over it.

Embed in Your Head

With our capacity to dream and become visionaries, visualizing the endpoint can embed that desired outcome in our conscious and subconscious helping to organize our resources to focus on making it happen.

Neural Priming

Embedded software functions automatically; it is designed to run specific applications with tremendous efficiency. That's a useful metaphor: are you running your brain as if it were efficiently programmed hardware? You can install your vision into your mind and have it continuously work for you toward creating the desired outcome.

When you embed a vision, you are priming your visual, auditory, and other senses to receive and process incoming data intentionally. This neural priming increases your focus and your readiness to identify resources in your environment, and also prepares you to deliver accurate, appropriate responses. All of us have such priming about various incidents and attitudes set up in our brains already. Janet Crawford, author of "Building Brain Friendly Organizations," says that particular neural pathways "warm up" when their particle pattern is activated: "the brain goes through its entire database of memories and information and becomes ready for the appropriate information to be interpreted…If you are a person who likes dogs then [if you encounter a dog] your emotional circuitry will direct you towards a sense of security and positivity. However, if you are afraid of dogs then a sense of fear will begin to emit from your system."

You've probably experienced neural priming, whether you know the term or not. Have you ever bought a new car, and started seeing the same make and model every time you hit the road? Those cars were on the road before, but you hadn't primed your brain to be aware of them. This is the value of neural priming to achieving your vision. When you know what you want, and prime your mind around it, you will begin to notice the people and resources available to you who will help you achieve the goal.

This act of priming can work to your benefit or your detriment. If you prime your neural pathways with the expectation of achievement, then you up the chances that achievement is likely to follow. But if you take on the Victim role, and prime yourself to expect disaster or failure…that's what you'll calibrate your mind to "achieve."

Predictive Encoding

When you can see your vision as if it were happening before your very eyes, you will be more likely to take the actions that lead to its achievement. It's about predictive encoding in which you visualize the goal and imagine the situations that will transpire on your way to achieving your goal.

Research by Colleen Seifert and her colleagues in the Department of Psychology at the University of Michigan shows that when you have predicatively encoded the outcome you desire, you will more readily and effectively find the people and resources in your environment to help you achieve your goal. You can predicatively encode the reality you want to occur into your memory, thereby creating your own potential for "luck." In fact, predictive encoding can increase the chances of your finding those resources in your environment by 50%. Think about the thin margin often found between success and failure. Why not take the time to use predictive encoding? It could tilt the scales in your favor by helping you find and focus on those resources that will help you realize your vision.

Making Your Visions More Compelling

Again, it is important to understand how the brain works to make your visions more compelling. To predicatively encode any vision takes a particular kind of thinking.

First, make sure you are asking for what you want by thinking about it in a positive manner. Your brain reacts to what you say to it, but it does not think in negatives. When someone says to you "now don't worry about the price," or "don't worry about the speed," or "don't worry about delivery," what do you do? You worry about price, speed and delivery. Your brain does the same thing, so you must tell yourself what you want to happen rather than what you want to avoid or stop. "I'll lose weight if I skip desserts,"—can you even read that sentence without thinking about dessert? Or, someone might state, "I am going to stop smoking," but their brain hears "smoking." Instead they could frame the statement positively: "I will breathe fresh air, improve my health, and enjoy my increased lung capacity." Phrasing your goal or need based on what you want might seem simplistic, but the results are real and powerful. Our brain wants to go in the direction of the internal images we make in our mind.

The second strategy is to visualize it happening right now. Just ask yourself, "If my vision were happening right now, what would I see? What would I hear? What would I feel physically? Emotionally?" Sit back and enjoy the visualization. See it! Play the movie in your mind, participate, watch others participating. Your visualization primes all of the main thinking centers in the brain—pictures, sounds and feelings, to make your vision more compelling. Do this often over the course of the steps you take to bring your vision to reality. Thinking that the result has happened already is a powerful way to prime the neurology of your own brain.

The more thoroughly and vividly you can imagine what you want, as descriptively as possible, using every one of your senses, the better chance you have for effectively priming yourself to execute in the real world.

Advertisers spend over a half a trillion dollars a year focusing on priming your brain so that when you walk down the aisle in your supermarket you will have an emotional connection to buying a specific brand of laundry detergent. Why? Because it works! Research shows that certain parts of your brain respond within milliseconds of when you see and hear an ad, well before the conscious part of your brain processes the information. Nelly Alia-Klein, a scientist at the U.S. Department of Energy's Brookhaven National Laboratory and her team were experimenting with just a single word to prime the brain. They used an MRI machine to take videos of the neural changes happening in the brains of their subjects and they would flash the word "NO" for less than one second. The result was they would see a sudden release of dozens of stress-producing hormones and neurotransmitters. People who were already stressed could be made to feel worse by just projecting a series of negative words. Results showed that No and Yes were associated with opposite brain-behavior responses; while "no" produced negative connotations and produced slower response times, the word "yes" produced positive emotions and produced faster response times.

The priming of your brain is being done to you all the time. It works. What we are suggesting is that you learn how to do it for your own benefit. When we prime our own brains by imagining the end result we are in effect doing exactly what advertisers are doing to us, except in this case we are choosing the images and thoughts we want. By cognitive priming we are making the choice of what we want and yet in this case we are doing it for ourselves. The better the image is of what we want, the better we are advertising to our own brain, increasing the probability we will focus on the right resources for making our visions a reality.

If your vision motivates you, you have a chance at motivating others. If you are not motivated and inspired, how would you ever be able to authentically influence others? Leaders realize they first have to inspire themselves before they can inspire others.

To make these visions even more compelling, ask yourself questions that bring your values into play. Ask, "How does this vision impact my life? How does this vision positively impact others? How does this vision positively impact the other visions I want to achieve?" These questions will help link your vision to your own values and will provide extra motivation to turn dreams into reality.

Integrating Behaviors

I am collaborating with Australian educator Allen Parker in research to measure specific behaviors in the culture of organizations. We've found that it takes 12 weeks to integrate new behaviors, or neurological patterns, in a large population of people. New neural patterns, and thus behaviors, take shape more thoroughly the more they are repeated. MRI scans of the brain see the electrochemical impulses and the formation of new neural patterns. Repetition strengthens these patterns; again, like exercise strengthens your cardiovascular system over time, or "reps" build muscle (that's why they're called repetitions).

On a practical level, this means if you speak, write, and talk about your visions every day, it will motivate you and embed, as neural priming, your course of action. As your visions become clearer for yourself, you can start sharing them with others.

More and more we see research results that support concepts most people know from common sense. What you think about, you become. Consider these results and put these ideas into action so you will reap the benefits.

THE VICTIM IN THE DRAMA TRIANGLE

I have consulted in many organizations over the last three decades. I have surveyed and interviewed thousands of individuals. What I come across often are people who have adopted the Victim role. They are constantly being hurt and offended, and complain as if they have no options or choices. What's truly sad is, despite their bitterness, they don't seem to want to change.

George Bernard Shaw was speaking about finding true joy in life when he said these words that describe the Victim in the Drama Triangle: "… a feverish, selfish little cloud of ailments and grievances complaining that the world will not devote itself to making you happy." That's certainly the opposite of my idea of having joy in your life.

Let's look at how people, when in the Victim role, tend to think, behave and impact their colleagues.

How Victims Think

The word "Victim" has powerful connotations. Most people, when thinking about themselves, do not use the word "Victim." But, if you've sunk into the Drama Triangle, which means you are operating from an external locus of control and assuming negative intent, you can easily fall into the Victim role.

The key to being in any role in drama is abdicating your ability to make choices. It's undeniable that at work we are given many of the tasks or the schedule for our day—but we can make choices about how we respond. We do have the choice to do a job or not. The Victim won't make choices: she reacts to the choices others make, then takes offense and blames them.

If you are stuck in the Victim role and have a bad day, you do not let it go. You will replay the bad scenarios over and over again in your mind. You then project that every day will be as bad, or that every future encounter with your team leader will be as upsetting as the encounter you had with him today. Victims pay attention to their disappointments, which then become predictably encoded.

You start to fall into the Victim role through your own destructive thinking. You let your mind focus only on what will not go well. I'm not speaking of prudent preparation for what might not go well; planning for contingencies is wise. No, the Victim consistently thinks things will go wrong and that he is powerless to change his circumstances. The Victim "knows" that he cannot influence his life or environment.

This thinking generates a self-fulfilling prophecy. The Victim's story becomes predictably encoded as a way of life. Once you take on Victim behavior or adopt the Victim role, you become more likely to organize your resources to manifest a negative outcome. Victim thinking gets embedded into your mental framework. A Victim can tell you all about how he was victimized—he has a whole canon of stories about how others have done him wrong. These wrongs can seem significant (how he was denied a college education) or petty (how he had to work through lunch). But all stories are negative, all blame someone else for the Victim's plight, and all perpetuate his self-fulfilling prophesy: the Victim's negative thoughts get him stuck in the Victim role.

If you project your positive and creative thoughts, you'll demonstrate positive and creative behavior. That's the best way to change your thinking to establish yourself as a Visionary.

How Victims Behave

When you talk with a Victim, he can—and will—tell you exactly who is responsible for his awful situation. Blaming others is his knee-jerk response, rather than looking at his own choices and mistakes.

The Victim is a master manipulator who persuades others to sympathize with his or her supposed helplessness. Victims use a variety of subtle, deceptive tactics such as playing nice, a willingness to listen, and an apparent capacity for understanding.

The Victim deals with issues indirectly, using subtle passive-aggressive communication. They are more likely to refrain from expressing themselves directly, but will talk behind everyone's backs, and express displeasure with body language such as rolling their eyes. Dishonesty and disingenuousness are fundamental traits of the Victim role.

His certainty that others are to blame makes him eager to enlist his coworkers to his point of view. He wants a team of Victims who can commiserate with each other. One Victim can create an army by encouraging "Victim think" in others, who then spread their negativity to the rest of the team.

I've conducted many corporate culture surveys and I know how prevalent this destructive mindset is. If I compared notes with my colleagues throughout the world, they would say the same. We have a business epidemic on our hands: the Victim mindset.

The biggest risk to the Victim is looking bad. The perception of who they are is more important than who they actually are. Although their insecurity is pushing them to be a Victim, they expect others to hold them in high esteem. After all, the Victim never does anything wrong: other people cause complications in her life. She turned in the reports late because Dave got the data to her late; she didn't close the important sale because the client changed his mind.

A Victim's fear of actually making a mistake can paralyze her from taking action. They generate pressure on themselves to preserve a "positive" self-image, but that restricts their ability to act effectively.

Not all Victims are whiny, mousy under-achievers. Some of them are in executive positions and have people reporting to them. They can be pleasant people and do their jobs satisfactorily most of the time. Yet the undercurrent is there. You are never quite sure how the individual in the Victim role is going to respond.

When you work with a Victim, you'll see his behavior show itself in feelings such as resentment and resignation. Often, they are subtle about expressing this, so it comes out as humor. They use sarcasm and make jokes such as "I think you're confusing me with someone who cares," or "I feel better now that I've given up all hope." You might chuckle, but these comments display the Victim's underlying apathy and cynicism.

Generally, Victims think of the world as an opponent they have to battle against. But Victims don't go into battle. (That's the behavior of the Adversary role.) The Victim will acquiesce to "the enemy" and just put up with it (while passively-aggressively working to undermine authority and enlisting others to join them).

"Benefits" of Being a Victim

To the Victim, there are good reasons to remain a Victim:

- One payoff is a perceived freedom from all accountability. You never have to take a stand for anything, nor do you have to take action. Why bother to take any action when you cannot make a difference anyway?

- You don't need a clear "map" for where you are headed. Victims have no vision of a future they can control, so it does not matter where they are going at any moment in time, anyway.

- You become very good at reacting to other people's situations. Victims aren't good at initiating action, but will react to whatever shows up on their doorstep.

- You get to let life happen to you. You do not have to generate, create, or behave intentionally—all of which are risky. So the Victim doesn't have to worry about risking anything.

- Using the Victim role is an easy way to control others. You can manipulate people into feeling anger, or turning into an Adversary toward you. You might then get people to rescue you. You can get people to embrace and wallow in your Victim story. Soon you can all be agreeing on how poorly your supervisor does her job.

Don't Be a Victim

By risking nothing and always playing it safe, those in the Victim role assume zero personal responsibility. Fundamentally, they are committed to not being committed. They can and will drain the life force of a team in no time at all if left unchecked. The only "Visionary" power a Victim possesses is to drag others down with them. Misery loves company, don't forget.

If you take on the Victim role in the Drama Triangle, you'll go through life reacting, blaming, and justifying. You'll become convinced that you have no power to effect change inside your own life and circumstance. Individuals in the Victim role really do participate in their own victimization.

Do you tend to repeat stories of how someone at work created a problem for you—and it's all about how wrong they were and how innocent you were? A person in the Victim role will tell that story to everyone, and make it larger and bigger than it ever was or needs to be. Then this exaggerated story, and all the hurt feelings that come with it, becomes the determining story of their life. Yes, you will occasionally get a raw deal, but what is the story that you tell about it, and to whom do you tell it? You can choose to glean wisdom and confidence from life's tumbles, or you can fall apart at the seams.

Bethany: Not a Victim to Her Circumstance

Sometimes, challenging things will happen to you. Flight delays, flu viruses, disasters that ruin your product or warehouse—bad stuff happens to everyone. What do you do when you've been challenged in this way? Well, first, you must recognize that you have choices; you can choose how you interpret and respond to the situation.

Leaders act with responsibility, even for things that are beyond their control. Leaders do not have the mindset of a Victim, so they take responsibility and make choices that influence the outcome.

Bethany Hamilton tells a powerful story in her book, "Soul Surfer." You cannot get into much more of an adverse situation than having a shark bite off your arm. Bethany's 13-year-old life changed in a second, off the coast of Kauai, as she lay on her surfboard, her arms trailing in the ocean. A 15-foot tiger shark lunged: her left arm was gone. Bethany lost more than half the blood in her body, her friends got her to shore and rushed her to a hospital. She recovered, but Bethany was left with the fact that she no longer had a left arm.

But Bethany Hamilton's story is about how she responded and the choices she made with the options available. Three weeks after the attack, she was back in the ocean, surfing. Through practice, she figured out how to surf with one arm—very difficult, since surfers use both arms for balance. She had a vision for what she wanted to accomplish: she decided to compete again, and she wanted to use her story to motivate others.

In 2005, Hamilton did the unimaginable: she won the Explorer Women's division of the National Scholastic Surfing Association Championship, the goal she had been working toward before the shark attack. Today, Bethany is busy with surfing competitions, her charity work, and personal appearances. Her new vision is making a difference in the lives of others.

Bethany's advice for hitting an obstacle is to get moving again as soon as you can. "Whatever your situation might be, set your mind to whatever you want to do and put a good attitude in it and I believe that you can succeed."

VISIONARIES IN LEADERSHIP

The Visionary is the opposite of the Victim. Visionaries take responsibility and initiative to bring their powerful dreams into actuality. If you create a powerful vision, it becomes impossible to enter the Victim role.

Being a Visionary means creating something with real passion behind it. For some, their vision impacts education or community improvement; others envision bold changes to health and wellness, while others focus on entertainment and leisure. For each, it's something very close to their heart about which they feel tremendous passion.

Develop your vision. Adhere to your own standards and make it meaningful for you. Make it compelling, important, and of highest priority.

In 1961, John F. Kennedy articulated one of his most famous visions: He saw America "landing a man on the moon and returning him safely to earth." JFK was not a rocket scientist: he was the Visionary. His innovative goal captured everybody's imagination, including the rocket scientists, engineers, and politicians who became engaged by this vision—which they then all achieved.

Take a lesson from JFK. He saw it. He articulated it. He enlisted others. They made it happen.

All visionaries have, or develop, the ability to:

- Speak about the future in the present.
- Commit to the vision.
- Take progressive steps with the goal in mind.
- Have optimism and passion.
- Lead others to be inspired about the vision.

Commit to the Vision

A Visionary makes decisions and commits to them. Deep and unconditional commitment to your vision is key to success. Remember, both the dreaming and the doing are essential to fulfilling your goals. If you do not possess and demonstrate the courage of your own conviction, you'll be unable to get others to join you in the Leadership Triangle.

Many people are afraid of making a change or taking a distinct path because they are afraid of failure or of being wrong. So, rather than risking being wrong, they either give up, make small choices, or take no stand at all. These people usually spend much time in the Drama Triangle.

In leadership, it does not matter whether your business is home furnishings, biologics, or entertainment: when the vision is clear, the strategy becomes clear. People naturally seek out meaning in their work and are driven to make things better. The Visionary will do things, will face adversity, and will charge ahead for causes he or she believes in.

When you have a vision, you put your stake in the ground and define the direction you are going to take. In doing so, you commit to your future in a manner that is not subordinate to the circumstances or any conventional wisdom of what is and is not possible.

Auberge de Sol: Commitment to the Best

When you stay at an Auberge de Sol resort, you'll quickly notice two special aspects of the resort: first, its timeless architecture, which allows class, elegance, and informal luxury to elevate the art of relaxation. Then, you will notice the staff's extraordinary attention to each customer.

These elements were artfully created by visionary Bob Harmon, the co-founder of the Auberge resorts. Bob's original vision was to:

- Provide a luxury hotel with a culture of exceptional customer service for every guest.
- Bring the feeling of Provence to the California wine country.
- Collaborate with other visionaries who each bring something extraordinary to the project, such as an excellent chef and an innovative architect.
- Develop properties that would only grow better with time, that guests would want to visit again and again.

Bob achieved this vision with Auberge de Sol, partly because he is a master in building a team of visionaries. Once he realized how to unleash the visions of many talented individuals, he was able to replicate this model over and over again. He since has transferred this ability into the next generation of leadership at Auberge de Sol and their properties and restaurants are able to stand out in a crowded marketplace.

Restoration Hardware: Commitment during Hard Times

Visit any Restoration Hardware store and you'll see that this organization has a point of view for home furnishings.

Gary Friedman is the Chairman Emeritus and their chief Visionary. He has the capacity to generate the "next big idea," and not only in retail. I enjoy just being around Gary; he gives me excellent insight on any business endeavor I discuss with him. He is, without a doubt, someone who knows how to see the future and speak it into existence. Gary speaks about the vision for Restoration Hardware and his new business, Hierarchy daily. He has an amazing gift of communicating his ideas to others. His ideas and enthusiasm are contagious and spread to his teammates. They, in turn, pass the vision along to Restoration Hardware's customers. This is true innovation.

In 2008, retail was one of the hardest hit sectors of the US economy. Retailers who supplied products to homes were in an unusually challenging market. Many such companies thought, "the marketplace is defining us; we need to cut back and contract to survive." Gary thought differently. He believed that during a recession, people who wanted home furnishings would spend their hard-earned money on items of quality and distinction. Gary decided to create the marketplace for that consumer—Restoration Hardware would not be defined by the marketplace; it would create a marketplace. You can see Gary's vision in the company's products, retail locations, and catalogs. The Restoration Hardware philosophy was that in the down economy, customers would spend money but they would want to spend money on exceptional goods. So Restoration Hardware engaged the best designers of exceptional products from around the world to team with them. These artesian originators created products that were distinctive, unique and were competitive with products sourced by custom interior designers. So Restoration Hardware's customer won because they got something of distinctive value, Restoration Hardware won because it created committed customers to its products and the artisans won as they had more access to more customers. Restoration Hardware's vision was clear: we are going to give an authentic experience to everyone who comes in contact with our brand. Because of this vision, Restoration Hardware is growing and getting a positive response from their loyal customers and their investors.

Create the Present for the Future

I mentioned earlier what George Bernard Shaw might call a Victim. Here is what I suggest he would say to a Visionary: "Imagination is the beginning of creation. You imagine what you desire; you will desire what you imagine; and at last, you create what you will."

Creating a vision is really about creating the possibilities you want for your future. When you imagine the possibilities for your future, you are not only creating your future but you are also impacting the present, now. You are creating in your mind the steps needed to fulfill your goal. Those steps are what you must now focus on. Just by imagining these possibilities, you expand your reality. Don't forget that the reverse is equally true: failing to exercise your imagination will contract your reality.

Most people think about the present as determined by the past, but I propose this: thinking about the future also helps to create the present.

Considering your future has as strong a pull on you as remembering your past does. Our thinking about the future is how we manifest much of our lives. Think of your hopes, your visions, and your possible futures. Look around you right now—at the room you're sitting in or out the window—at some point in the past somebody said, "let's put the house right here and let's put the window over there!" They spoke about a future that is now today.

In moments of such motivation, we use our vision to create reality. Be mindful of what direction you let the future pull you in. Create in your mind what you want that future to be. Know your purpose and your vision inside and out, backward and forward. The stronger your vision, plan, and commitment are, the more likely you are to achieve your goal—because it's easier when you're sure where you're going and you're organized for getting there.

A compelling purpose really does energize life. When the Visionary is working on a big project, happiness and joy usually come with it.

Feel It and Speak It

When you are passionate about your vision, talking about it will transform you as the speaker. You start to impact the world by giving a voice to the potential and bringing this possibility into existence. In speaking it out loud, you make a commitment to it happening and in doing so you resolve the barriers to the vision becoming reality.

You have to paint a vivid description of where you are headed. Language is the best tool to help us communicate our visions. Poets and authors understand the power of language and are masters at honing their ability to motivate and inspire. Find the right words that will articulate your compelling vision—to yourself first, then to others.

American poet Langston Hughes's work was first published during the Harlem Renaissance. Hughes infused his work with elements of blues and jazz. He was a firm believer that poetry should be read out loud, recited and sung. Say the following poem on the next page out loud. Notice your own response to his words.

Hold fast to dreams

For if dreams die

Life is a broken-winged bird

That cannot fly.

Hold fast to dreams

For when dreams go

Life is a barren field

Frozen with snow.

Your vision and leadership must become part of your daily conversations to keep your ideas and supporting behavior focused and engaged. You will inspire all parties of your organization when you express your vision in such a way that people are charged with imagination and emotion. Communicating the "big picture" on a regular basis reinforces the reasons your organization exists. The vision is a crucial component, bringing to all involved purpose and meaning in their work. Your vision determines the direction your team will follow and unites people on the right strategies.

Take Progressive Steps

Your vision is likely to be a challenge and perhaps difficult to accomplish, so you must be passionate about it. Envision the process to achieve your vision. Include in its scope all the steps you need to accomplish, in progression, to reach the final goal. Plot out challenging timeframes to keep you working diligently. With a clear, strong vision and hard work, it is possible to build a reality from a dream.

Walt Disney, Step by Step

Walt Disney was committed to his visions. Already famous for his cartoons, his movies, and his mouse, Disney conceived a new dream. He saw in his mind's eye a place where children and parents could have fun together. He planned a park on eight acres next to his Burbank studios.

Walt often walked out on those acres of raw land and imagined his park. My great uncle worked for Walt Disney as a writer and he would see him dreaming, creating in his head the world we now know as Disneyland. The more he dreamed, the smaller those eight acres looked. He realized his vision required more land. He bought 160 acres in Anaheim. In other words, his vision has already grown 20 times its original size.

Yet, once built, even Disneyland wasn't big enough to contain his imagination—his next park, Disneyworld, was 27,400 acres. Disneyworld was beyond a theme park. Walt Disney's new vision included creating a modern urban environment. He was consistently pushing the boundaries of what was possible.

But achieving his Disneyland vision required progress through other innovations. Walt Disney had a clear vision—build an amusement park that recreated a classic American small town, with a fairy-tale castle, and a mountain in the middle. But Walt's vision was so unique, investors couldn't understand it. He couldn't get funding. So he went to ABC-TV and offered to do a weekly television program with clips from Disney movies and new programs he could create for TV. He called the program Disneyland. For years, the program was one of ABC's most popular programs. Thanks to the show, Walt got the additional funding to build his park. He also found that one of the best ways to advertise the park was through the integration of shows and theme park rides. Each of his visions built upon the previous one, expanding the impact of his imagination to people all around the world.

Leaders Create Leaders

You have to believe in your vision. I mean you need to believe it as the absolute truth; you need to believe it in your bones. Your vision is worthwhile, and the depth of your belief in it will be contagious to those people you present it to. The more clear and passionate you are about your vision, the more you increase your odds of enlisting others to jump on board. Each time you engage a collaborator, you become that much stronger, that much more effective— that much more likely to achieve your goal.

- Apple founder Steve Jobs' vision was a company committed to developing "insanely great" products. Apple does make great products, but Jobs was also brilliant at communicating his vision. Apple employees and loyal customers believe right along with Jobs.

- Google had a vision to become the leading search company at a time when other platforms owned the market. The name "Google" was in many ways a part of the vision which was to organize a seemingly infinite amount of information on the web. Google not only became the dominant search engine, but we now use the word "Google" to mean "look it up on the Internet."

- Genentech was once a small biologic company when its then CEO, Art Levinson, had a vision of making cancer a manageable disease in our lifetime. This vision made

Genentech successful in the oncology marketplace and made Genentech employees passionate about their work helping people manage and survive cancer. A powerful vision can create a powerful corporate culture.

It is not enough to have a vision—you need to influence the world around you to help you create it. As you influence your team, you start to influence your marketplace with your visions. Anyone you talk with needs to be convinced that your vision will actually become a reality.

The Mission Continues

Eric Greitens, a US Navy SEAL officer, served tours in Iraq, Afghanistan, the Horn of Africa, and Southeast Asia. In 2007, he and his platoon were hit by a suicide bomber in Fallujah, Iraq. Eric suffered minor injuries but many in his team were hit worse. When Eric returned to the United States, he started to realize a vision for returning soldiers. While he was at Bethesda Naval Hospital, he visited with wounded service members and realized that veterans returning to civilian life had enormous abilities in leadership and a great hunger to lead. All of the soldiers he spoke with wanted to continue to serve, in uniform or out.

Once he, too, was a civilian, he was in a position to find opportunities of service and leadership for those veterans. Greitens, partnering with a few veteran friends and using his own pay, launched The Mission Continues to train wounded vets for leadership roles in their communities. Greitens inspires people: "I think people end up benefiting from serving as much as those they aim to serve."

Every vision is a story that will ignite passion. Also, cultivating vision is not a one-time event. However, you have to start somewhere. I guarantee you will not stop at just one vision, though, when you feel what it is like to inspire others and achieve a worthwhile goal.

When you are developing a vision, it is important to choose passion over knowledge. Knowledge can be learned. Do not wait to be an expert to dive into your dream. Curiosity and learning are all natural byproducts to desire. You need your passion in order for your vision to become compelling. Leading people to a worthwhile destination is personally and professionally satisfying. Don't wait. Start dreaming now.

Pennies for Peace

When my daughter got involved in a school project called Pennies for Peace, she learned about the educational situation in other parts of the world. Pennies for Peace was originally created by two elementary school teachers, Susy Eisele and Sandy Heikkila, of River Falls, Wisconsin, who were inspired by Greg Mortenson's book Three Cups of Tea: One Man's Mission to Promote Peace…One School At A Time.

The Pennies for Peace program works to collect money in order to build schools and provide supplies in both Pakistan and Afghanistan. The co-educational schools serve thousands of students, half of whom are female. Pennies for Peace is one way they collect funds for these schools. The pennies collected here in America buy pencils and paper for students halfway around the world. Students learn the rewards of sharing and working together to bring hope and education opportunities to the children in Pakistan and Afghanistan.

While my daughter's school was collecting Pennies for Peace, they also studied the cultures of Pakistan and Afghanistan, for whom they were raising the money. What an inspired way to incorporate current events and geography, and for American students to learn about young people their age in a different country. They certainly learned about the value of a penny in the villages of Pakistan and Afghanistan. While a penny is virtually worthless, in these countries a penny buys a pencil and opens the door to literacy. This sort of active, applicable learning made the fundraising even more rewarding.

My daughter and her schoolmates developed a vision of helping others. They wanted to contribute. They learned more than useful information about other cultures—they also learned how to be philanthropists. That's what is so inspirational about what Susy and Sandy created: it creates other visionaries. Their idea inspired my daughter to be a leader and she and her friends were able to inspire others at her school.

Have Optimism and Passion

Optimism is a key trait of a Visionary. Your enthusiasm, passion, and confidence multiply as they radiate throughout your team. When you view the world and your vision positively and confidently, you'll infuse the culture of the organization with the same perspective.

People can only be genuinely inspired when you are genuinely inspired. There is no faking being inspired. Others can tell if your "dream" is real for you or not. We are attracted to inspirational dreams and those who have them. If you are a Visionary, you can inspire vision in others.

I don't mean Pollyanna-ish confidence or cockeyed optimism. A Visionary faces the facts. They adjust their visions based on feedback and they also have the ability to stay optimistic in the face of hard realities. When the time calls for it, they are able to say, unequivocally, "we can make things better, we can achieve extraordinary results, and we will achieve this vision."

Serving others is a great way to create optimism; knowing that you are helpful and useful is tremendously rewarding. This creates an emotional connection that binds your community together. When you can create relationships based on a mutual commitment to a cause, you are connecting to the decision-making center of your brain.

Vision Rides a Bike

Gary Erickson, the CEO of CLIF Bar, loves to bike. He is an avid cyclist who would pack along some nutritional bars to keep up his energy on long rides. On one ride, he ate five energy bars and, as he said, he "just could not stomach the sixth." The infamous sixth bar is what sparked the question in his mind, "why does healthy have to taste so awful?" That was his mantra, and one that would change his world forever. That question became his impetus—the magical moment for his vision. This is how the CLIF Bar was born: from Gary's vision of creating a good-tasting energy bar using all-natural ingredients.

Launched in 1992, today the CLIF Bar is one of the leaders in its market. It is also a household name, synonymous with health and athleticism.

Vision Saves Lives

When you are a Visionary, you can create an image inside other people's minds that will guide their behaviors. In 2004, Varun Nanda was selected to be the franchise head for Avastin, Genentech's most important drug launch in the company's history.

To make sure his Genentech team was focused on the right things, he and his leaders created a vision for the future for Avastin. Its vision was summed up in three words that guided the launch of what would become Genentech's best selling drug: Every Patient Matters. This vision helped guide the team to:

- Develop Genentech's innovative payment program, which provided financial assistance to patients who needed the drug but could not afford the treatment.
- Set up a clinical trial even though it would only address a small part of the oncology market. Pondering the expense and the time required for the trial, they referred to their vision and asked, "Well, do these patients matter?" Since the answer was "yes," they conducted the trial.

This simple-to-understand vision isn't really simple. It had a rich depth of thinking to it. It allowed the leadership team to guide the behaviors not only of the individuals in the Avastin team, but also of the Genentech organization at large, keeping all focused on doing the right thing for patients. Ultimately, doing the right thing for patients led to unparalleled success for their product.

Vision Rides a Horse

Each vision has to come with people who will influence it into reality. It takes time and effort, but you will engage people with your passion for your project.

Gregg Goodman enjoyed a reputation as an executive who could turn around an underperforming organization or successfully start up a new one. Jann Goodman, Gregg's wife, was a physical therapist who had done her graduate thesis on hippotherapy: using horses as a therapy treatment for people living with disabilities.

When Gregg and Jann settled in Arizona, they wanted to create their own business, something that was personal for both of them. Their vision created Horses Help, which provides "equine adaptive therapies" for people with special needs. Horses Help helps people move beyond their limitations (cognitive, emotional, or physical) through activities and exercises involving a collaborative relationship between people and horses.

Gregg built his vision from his own experience. "When I was four years old, I had to wear a full body cast for a year. It is my first memory. I had to drag myself around on the ground to move and it left a scar on my childhood." Gregg went on to excel physically, even earning a college athletic scholarship, but he never forgot. "I know what it feels like to be trapped in a body and it helps me identify with each of the kids who come into our care."

Gregg and Jann have influenced their community to support the dream of Horses Help. They work with local universities, and with over 250 weekly volunteers, therapy interns, horse professionals, and community organizations. While they make a difference in the lives of their patients, they are equally making a difference in the lives of those who assist with the program. But Jann and Gregg both say that it's their lives that have been enriched by helping others.

A Visionary Likes to Play

Doug Penman is the CEO of Nukotoys. Doug, while facing some personal adversities that sharpened his thinking, made an assessment of what he really wanted to create in his life. His conclusion: he really wanted to be a toymaker. He had a vision of what he could contribute both as a business executive and as a member of the creative world of imagination.

His vision has inspired so many that he has been able to engage a world-class board and surround himself with creative talent to bring his dream to life. He is producing toys that allow children to create their own games and worlds.

In less than two years Doug developed a rich world of software and hardware and he released a product that combines real play, virtual play and immersive 3D environments. His vision is to give kids fun, fantastical experiences that join both online and real-world play. Once he had his vision, the relationships, connections and ideas just flowed. He has also worked extremely hard at turning this company into a reality. But it doesn't feel like work when you are following a compelling vision.

You may have already seen the Animal Planet Wildlands and Monsterology trading card game in Apple's App Store. The innovative idea is that you take the Nukotoys trading cards and press them up to the screen and the contents of the card appear right in your Apple iPhone or iPad. The physical cards are sold at most major retailers across the nation and they have also taken this business international. Not only have my own children become engaged in these worlds, I have been able to see the new adventures and the other properties he has in production. While Nukotoys is just starting out, the vision of redefining toys for today's digitally fascinated kids and engaged parents will keep it growing for a long time.

A Visionary Does the Right Thing

Often visions for companies are built because someone recognizes a gap in the marketplace or experiences a challenge in his own life. Instead of becoming a victim of the circumstance, leaders get the world to change.

Jim Conlow, CEO of Cortexion, was in the business of building buildings. I have had the pleasure of watching Jim build nearly one billion dollars' worth of office retail and manufacturing plants over the years. In 1998, he saw a troubling pattern in the construction industry. General contractors, to get business, significantly lowered the management fees they charged customers but yet they were still making a good profit on each job. Here is the murky secret: to do this, the general contractor would hold on to the money he owed to subcontractors. Subcontractors, knowing they wouldn't get paid promptly, raised their fees. Holding payment from subcontractors for a longer period of time was illegal, but the customer or owner of a building never saw this additional cost being added to the cost of their structure being built.

Jim, as a general contractor, was either going to have to use the "hold out on subcontractors" scheme in order to stay competitive and lower his management fees, or raise his management fees and be at a competitive disadvantage. In either case, he saw an opportunity to add value.

Jim's ethical dilemma led him to create the first project management software that could guarantee a lower cost of constructing a building, all the while keeping the contractor-subcontractor relationship out in the open. His answer to the secrecy scheme was to instead treat all transactions openly: transparency and security for every aspect of the payments. He was able to take a challenging situation and create a new way to do business for the benefit of all parties. Jim's vision helped lower building costs for owners, made it easier for general contractors to manage subcontractors, and helped subcontractors get their money faster.

BENEFITS OF PURSUING YOUR VISION

Developing and pursuing a clear vision has a positive effect on your health.

Dr. Patricia Boyle, who works at the Rush Alzheimer's Disease Center as a neuropsychologist, discovered "if you have a purpose in life—lofty or not—you'll live longer."

Boyle's study followed over 1,000 adults, averaging 78 years old, for about three years. At the beginning of the study, participants were asked about their purpose in life. During the three-year follow-up period, it was mostly those who felt little purpose in life who died. Those who had a strong purpose had a greater than 50% higher chance of surviving than those who didn't.

In other words, if you have discovered what has deep meaning to you, and if you can channel your energies into achieving goals based on your visions and values, you'll live longer.

Boyle believes her study is the first to connect the dots between life, the purpose of life, and longevity. But if you think about it, it just makes sense. When you have something to live for, you focus on it and become engaged with it. Focus and engagement are two main qualities of leadership. They generate the kind of energy that can have a positive impact on your health. When you have something to live for… well, you will live for it. It's as simple as that.

There are many other benefits to creating and pursuing a strong vision:

- Provides you direction in life or on the job.
- Identifies your purpose in life or work
- Promotes your commitment to achieving your goal.
- Creates laser-like focus.
- Motivates you to take action.
- Inspires others.
- Keeps you from being a Victim.

Right before my daughter was born, I was talking with Michael Norris, a consultant for Vistage, a CEO-consultant and advisory organization. He gave me one of the best pieces of advice for any new parent. He urged me to "get my skin on her skin"—during the first couple of days of my daughter's life: I should find a quiet room, let her snuggle up on my chest, and talk to her about our life together.

He was inspiring me to create a vision for my daughter and my life with her. I followed his advice to the letter. I talked to her for almost an hour, telling her about all the things we were going to do in this lifetime together. It was very powerful for me and instantly deepened my vision for my life with my daughter. It was a very emotional experience. I did the same with my son when he was born. I continue to have these vision conversations with them both as they inspire me in what I want to create for my children.

YOU CAN CHANGE

My final piece of advice on creating a vision is to dream big. If you have stopped dreaming, start again. You really can. I don't know if you left your dreams on the side of the road, but you can pick them up again. If you dream big, you'll radiate an energy that will draw people to you. Together, you can literally shoot for the stars—or achieve whatever your dream might be.

CHAPTER 10

The Adversary and the Catalyst

A CATALYST IS SOMEONE who enables a reaction to proceed at an accelerated rate and/or an agent that provokes or speeds significant change or action. In writing this book, my vision was to be a Catalyst in helping others discover their own leadership abilities. Galileo Galilei so eloquently wrote, "We cannot teach people anything; we can only help them discover it within themselves." Buckminster Fuller said, "You never change things by fighting the existing reality. To change something, you must build a new model that makes the existing model obsolete."

When you are in the Leadership Triangle, you want to be such a Catalyst that you work to develop yourself as someone who can make the right things happen. You affect people when you are a Catalyst; you nurture the leadership potential of individuals. You see the whole of a situation so you can guide the right actions to bring your vision into reality. Equally, leadership is learning when to say "no" as much as when to say "yes" to something. Taking the right actions accelerates your ability to bring your visions to life. Helping others take the right actions is a way to multiply your impact.

An Adversary is the exact opposite of a Catalyst. An Adversary is defined as one who contends with, opposes, resists or dominates others. When you're in the Adversary role of the Drama Triangle, you certainly affect people, but not for the better. Your focus is completely on what you get, not what you give. Adversaries create drama around them, attempt to control others, and lash out in attempts to control a challenging situation.

Adversaries threaten. They insist on their way and they shut down any opposition—even in the face of reality.

Catalysts inspire. They affect necessary change, even when change is difficult. They inspire others to take action along with them.

Say an issue comes up in your organization—any issue, major or minor. There will be a fundamental divide between people in the Leadership Triangle and those in the Drama Triangle:

- People in the Leadership Triangle focus on addressing the issue or fixing the problem. Leaders who are Catalysts understand that even making small changes in the corporate culture of an organization can precipitate big changes in individual and group behavior.
- People in the Drama Triangle spend their time trying to figure out who to blame. Adversaries do this blatantly. The more you try to control people, the less responsible and dependable they become.

Taking action and inspiring others to action, based on a clear vision, is the primary distinction between living in the Leadership Triangle or being stuck in the Drama Triangle. The best way to stay out of the Adversary role is to question the status quo with positive intention for yourself, your team, your community, your family and your life.

HOW THE ADVERSARY THINKS

When you are determined to prove that you are right—and prove that the other person is wrong—you are in the Adversarial role of the Drama Triangle. Adversaries also:

- Derive pleasure from finding and pointing out errors committed by others.
- Keep an eye on people, waiting for the opportunity to point out a mistake.
- Do not trust the capabilities of others. They think that most people are just plain ignorant.
- Feel they must maintain control.
- Rarely delegate, but when they do, they look for what is wrong in the delivery.
- Enjoy grandstanding and showing off.
- Demonstrate "leadership" by threats, orders, and rigidity.

Driven by Anger

Anger is a primary cause, and primary output, of the Adversary role. When in this role, you feel angry and use that anger to coerce others, to drive your own agenda and take the top-dog position in conversation. You'll ignore, discount, or minimize others, in order to "show them up" as inadequate, worthless, useless, or worse.

Adversaries can be impatient and easily frustrated. If in the role, when you see that another person lacks some ability or is ineffective, you feel resentful, irritated, "surrounded by idiots." Because you expect to find their flaws, you always do find flaws. No one's work is ever good enough, so you're never happy about it. Without you there to point out what is wrong, nothing would ever get done! You exert overt pressure in attempts to control the situation and manipulate it to meet your personal needs, or you withdraw and become unavailable as a way to punish people who actually need your input to get their work done.

Working with someone in the Adversary role is to endure a bombardment of criticism, accusations, and coercion. Adversaries are prone to dramatic displays of emotion to enforce and maintain their fragile sense of control. They use sarcasm as humor, and they have few inhibitions in putting down others. They use trickery and deceit to manipulate things to go their way.

"Benefits" of Being an Adversary

Why would someone go into such an adversarial role? To feel in control.

Whenever I have confronted someone stuck in the Adversary role and managed to get them to drop their guard, they admitted to attacking others in order to keep from being out of control or vulnerable.

The Adversary, like most bullies, needs to control others because he or she feels a lack of control. When you feel out of control, your unconscious response is to try to control all the more, thus creating a cycle. You may refuse to acknowledge the difficulty you cause others. You may mask any reaction to it, playing it cool and aloof, above the fray—or go to the opposite extreme, making a huge display of frustration or aggravation, casting blame on others.

Those frequently stuck in the Adversarial role have considerable anger just under the surface, waiting to erupt. They are a bit like two-year-olds who give themselves permission to lash out at other people. This makes them understandably unpleasant to interact with—which helps get Rescuers to come help them and keeps Victims from ever giving them any kind of feedback.

HOW THE ADVERSARY BEHAVES

Adversaries, concerned with making themselves feel better, do so by making everyone else feel worse. The Adversary's use of criticism, blame, and other antagonizing tactics pulls others into drama.

- In the Adversary role, a person uses fear and emotional attacks to control others. The unpredictability of when and where they will lash out keeps others guessing their true intentions. Everyone walks on eggshells around them.

- The Adversary's way of doing things is the only way of doing things. Do it "wrong," and they'll let you know.

- Adversaries don't have to be conspicuously mean. Some are quiet by nature and more subtle. But all are coercive, pushy, and pressuring. They exert authority through threats, orders, and rigidity, which make them unpleasant to be around.

- They take a top dog vs. underdog approach: they believe themselves to be better than you, and don't hesitate to let you know it.

- Adversaries will "show off" whenever possible. They will even boast about their team and company to outsiders.

- They are blind to the impact of their communication style. They do not understand how they are being perceived by others.

Did you recognize any of these attitudes and behaviors as common habits of yours? Let's look more closely at how people, when in the Adversary role, tend to behave and influence their colleagues. Understanding the behaviors is the best first step to stopping the behaviors.

Using Fear

When in the Adversary role, a person uses fear and intimidation to motivate team members. Fear, when used as a motivator, creates a contagious drama cycle that infects the organization. It is the opposite of inspiration, which the Catalyst uses effectively to motivate. Using fear, adversarial authoritarians create unhealthy cultures around them, robbing the organization of collegiality, speed, and flexibility. Little if any sustainable change ever happens where the "leader" is an Adversary.

They know that fear is an effective tactic, so they use it for the short-term wins. However, fear creates long-term losses: the team, even if resistant and resentful, becomes too anxious about making "wrong" decisions or giving the Adversary "bad" news. Some people will leave the company to get away from the Adversary. Others will stop making any decisions, which leads to organizational paralysis.

(In the Leadership Triangle, you don't use fear as a motivator. If you are holding someone accountable, you might point out the consequences—they might not get a promotion or a raise—which they themselves find upsetting. But it is not your purpose to cause fear. The Adversary, on the other hand, enjoys frightening people.)

Sure, fear can motivate. If you hold a gun to someone's head, that will motivate them. It's called negative motivation, because the person is "encouraged" to take action in order to avoid a bad consequence. Negative motivation has its uses but is rarely sustainable because it does not come from the person's own choice. Positive motivation comes when you want to do something because of a positive consequence, so you're naturally motivated to do it.

My Way is the Right Way

The Adversary's mindset is "I am right and you are wrong." That's why people who are in the Adversary role are so critical and use "you" accusations. They also tend to generalize in their attacks, with words such as "never" and "always." "You never get your work in on time. You always put off the important projects."

People stuck in the Adversarial role will thwart all ideas and initiatives except for their own. After all, their way is the only way that matters. When Bill attacks Joann's way of doing things, he can be doing it to mask his insecurities and weaknesses. Does it matter that Joann uses an iPhone rather than a Blackberry, or gets quality clients by networking among the book club from her alma mater, or puts soy milk in her coffee? It matters to Bill, and he will mock, ridicule, and argue with her to do it his way instead.

Joann no doubt thinks Bill is a jerk. Well, I have yet to meet someone who's considered "a jerk" who did not have deep-seated insecurities. By attacking you, the Adversary buttresses his shaky feelings of worth while keeping you off balance and on the defensive so you're less likely to discover his or her weaknesses.

Everyone Else is at Fault

Along with the Adversary's belief that their way is the right way is their conviction that all mistakes are someone else's fault. They blame with abandon, and they like to collect evidence and bring it up later. When Paula blames Dean for failing to complete the installation, if Dean reacts by blaming Roberto, then Paula will point out to everyone that Dean is "always" finding fault in people. Paula sure isn't going to take responsibility for the incomplete installation, even though she is Dean's manager. (By the way, the installation was two years ago—Paula likes bringing it up again and again, especially when she and Dean are in a group of people.)

Top Dog vs. Underdog

In the Adversary role, you want to reign supreme. You'll grandstand, show off, and exaggerate. Adversaries have no problem letting others know how wonderful they are. Some sound confident, but mostly they come across as arrogant.

Adversaries communicate in a top dog vs. underdog approach; they won't have give-and-take, peer-based dialogs. They work to control others and they often pressure others to act in a certain way.

They enjoy blaming others directly. Their favorite technique is to put others down through sarcastic remarks. Their comments can be witty, but when you find yourself laughing at someone's biting humor, stop to think: is it at someone else's expense? Is it valid? Is it helpful to the team? Or is it an attempt to undermine my trust or respect for a boss or coworker?

ADVERSARIES IN ACTION

Here are a couple of examples of Adversaries in the business world. You probably heard or read about Lehman Brothers and AIG Financial when the economy crashed in 2008. While others will look at the financial decisions these executives made, I am most interested in the culture of drama they created. Read through to see how fear, criticism, fault-finding, and abdication of responsibility demonstrate residence in the Drama Triangle.

Fearing Fuld

Lehman Brothers, the New York investment bank, collapsed in the second half of 2008. Its bankruptcy triggered a financial crisis, which was one factor that sent the global economy into a tailspin. Richard Fuld, CEO of Lehman brothers, had a nickname as he was coming up through the ranks: "the Gorilla." Fuld ruled Leman Brothers with intensity, using the Adversary role to dominate even his own team through intimidation.

Starting back in 2005, he was warned frequently (and often by many of his senior leadership team) of the sizeable risks associated with the real estate market. He was also made aware of how any devaluation in real estate growth would negatively impact the highly leveraged Lehman Brothers. Fuld, in some cases, fired the individuals who gave him these warnings. Under his leadership, Lehman entered the repackaged sub-prime business and, for a while, generated fantastic returns. Fuld bet the farm—seemingly, it paid off. The company was successful and made a significant return for stakeholders.

But Fuld also created a culture that would not tolerate dissenting points of view. This set up a pattern in which he refused to accept criticism, so people in the company felt it was unwise and unsafe to express that the company was in trouble and at risk. Somewhere along the way, Fuld ignored the warning signs to such a degree that when the US housing market became perilously overheated and mortgage brokers were handing out loans to people who could never repay them, he ignored his own leadership team's warnings of the risks.

How does creating a culture of fear impact a group's decision-making? Fuld's management style included threatening people's jobs. His favorite motivational strategy was an environment of fear: psychological fear as well as the threat of job loss. Fuld created an environment where dissenting opinions were discounted, despite (or perhaps because of) the extreme risk in which Lehman had put itself. Under Fuld's Adversarial style, some of the top talent no longer wanted to work for him because they were so traumatized by his tyrannical ways. Those who stayed on kept information from him because they worried how he would react to bad news.

His choice of words are classic for someone used to playing in the Adversarial role: "When I find a short-seller, I want to tear his heart out and eat it before his eyes while he's still alive," Fuld would tell his team. While he had a vision of what Lehman Brothers could be, his Adversarial patterns set the stage for a predictable outcome. He frightened his team to such an extent that no one dared to even share crucial information with him, since he was infamous for "killing the messenger." He created a culture where guessing his moods became more important than actually running the business.

So Lehman Brothers was being led by someone who had the financial knowledge to understand the risks the firm was taking but who couldn't tolerate opposing opinions. Fuld's "number two" man for many years was Joe Gregory, who used a similar style of fear-based management that created drama in the organization. Joe Gregory stated, "I was one of those people who didn't want to disappoint Dick." That meant you did not want to get on Joe's bad side either.

For years, Lehman's managers who advocated cautious actions or made an effort to hold back on riskier bets were removed from their positions. Former Lehman accountant Matthew Lee was immediately fired for internally raising the alarm; Lee had been corresponding with senior executives regarding his fears that the bank's financial disclosure statements were misleading. In the 2010 Senate inquiries, Lee said, "I think the public were misled as to the true leverage of Lehman Brothers." Who is going to run the risk of holding this senior team accountable when doing so meant losing his job?

At Lehman, the only strategy a staff member could take to survive in the culture was to keep his or her head down. This, combined with rampant in-house fighting, accelerated the culture of drama. Honest communication from management was stifled, and Lehman's relationship with potential partners was also strained. Fuld created an "us against the world" attitude and constantly attacked the other firms, the press, and members of government.

Then, when he needed the world, no one stepped up to help. My guess is that he had burned too many bridges over the years. In the end, the way he took responsibility for the decisions he made was by blaming others. In his own words, the reason for Lehman's collapse was due to "outside forces, including lax oversight and short sellers." When Adversaries get caught, they quickly switch to the Victim role or simply hope someone comes to their rescue. Fuld placed the blame on the government for not being able to save Lehman. Maybe he expected to be rescued, but we don't know. We do know that his behavior matches the pattern of someone stuck in the Drama Triangle.

Fuld (who was not the only one behaving like this at the time) made many public statements that exemplify the Drama Triangle. During the 2010 Senate inquiry, he was asked about an accounting principle called Repo 105, which was used to remove almost $50 billion in assets from Lehman's balance sheet, temporarily, in 2008. Fuld said, "I have absolutely no recollection whatsoever of hearing anything about Repo 105 transactions while I was CEO of Lehman." The CEO didn't know? That may be true, but Repo 105 allowed Lehman to hide its risk profile to its investors; not exactly responsible transparency for a publicly-traded firm. Whether Fuld knew about it or not, he still created the culture where Repo 105 was used, and used for the benefit of the organization and the determent of the investment community seeking transparency about Leman's business.

AIG Financial Products

Interestingly, the leadership at AIG was using a similar pattern of creating a drama culture. The insurance giant's unit that invested in credit default swaps was known as AIG Financial Products (or AIGFP). Joseph J. Cassano ran this business and, according to AIGFP employees, had an Adversarial attitude. Michael Lewis summed it up in his book *The Big Short*. He refers to Cassano as someone who did not have a good feel for financial risk but had real skill when it came to intimidating those who doubted him at any point. What Lewis heard about Cassano are classic examples of the Adversarial role:

> "Joe would bully people around. He'd humiliate them and then try to make it up to them by giving them huge amounts of money... The fear level was so high that when we had these morning meetings you presented what you did not to upset him. And if you were critical of the organization, all hell would break loose ... Joe always said, 'This is my company. You work for my company.' He'd see you with a bottle of water. He'd come over and say, 'That's my water.' Lunch was free, but Joe always made you feel he had bought it... Under Joe the debate and discussion ceased... The way you dealt with Joe was to start everything by saying, 'You're right, Joe.'"

Lewis assessed Cassano as being so insecure that he needed obedience and total control. Cassano become angry at "the faintest whiff of insurrection." AIGFP was run by a man "whose judgment was clouded by his insecurity." The people with enough guts to question AIGFP practices, and Cassano's decision were the people with enough guts to quit and get out.

The patterns of the Adversary are consistent. They bully others to mask their own insecurities. Again, I cannot comment on the financial decisions of either AIGFP or Lehman Brothers, yet the pattern of drama seems consistent: the senior executives created cultures where open, transparent conversation, in which quality information could be shared, was next to nonexistent.

YOU CAN GET YOURSELF OUT OF THE ADVERSARY ROLE

Individuals who use the Adversarial role are not necessarily always mean. They can be competent at their jobs and rise to positions of power within their organizations—which means, unfortunately, that when they sink into the role of Adversary, they lead their whole company in spinning around the Drama Triangle as people react to their behavior. Adversaries are further challenged by their own low self-awareness: they are usually the last people to be aware of this particular role and its associated behaviors.

The main challenge for you, if you're prone to the Adversary role, is to shift your critical-thinking mind away from being judgmental. Use that analytical focus to find appropriate ways to tackle obstacles, rather than attacking people. You can move instead into the Leadership Triangle, but it requires that you inventory, honestly, your own inner motivations and understand why you do things.

Can you turn your dissatisfaction with the status quo into positive, creative solutions? Can you find ways to broaden your scope beyond your limiting perceptions of others? Can you communicate your feelings and observations in ways that are inspirational rather than damaging? Yes, you can—by understanding that you have chosen a role in the Drama Triangle that is ineffective long term, and by choosing to leave it behind for a more productive role in the Leadership Triangle.

CATALYSTS MAKE THINGS HAPPEN

In the Catalyst role, a leader accelerates collective action to achieve the vision. The vision can be one that the Catalyst generated, or it can be another's vision which the Catalyst supports.

Think of the individuals who have inspired growth in your life, whether they are parents, mentors, senior executives, or friends. Who offered you a different way of thinking or pushed you in a new direction? Those people were Catalysts. You made the choice; they accelerated your change.

The Catalyst ignites the Vision. Never content with the status quo, your role as Catalyst is to act immediately, shake things up, and effectively execute. You are a creative, "outside the box" thinker. You inspire others to plug in to the vision, unleashing the power of the work force. You also put your money where your mouth is— sometimes literally, sometimes in your willingness to take risks that affect your earning potential. Action is essential. "Talk is cheap" could be the Catalyst's motto.

And you do all of this while unflinchingly facing obstacles. You are never one to shirk from the truth, and you hold a high standard for precision and integrity. Because of your no-nonsense, straightforward approach and the congruence between your words and your actions, you gain the trust of others who see you as authentic and honest.

Inside the Catalyst

Walt Disney—a man with highly-developed skills as a Catalyst— once said, "it is kind of fun to do the impossible." If you know anyone who shares these traits with Disney, you know a Catalyst:

- They constantly strive for excellence.
- They understand the details, which enables them to see larger patterns.
- They are not afraid to act. If some action doesn't work out too well, they learn from it, dust themselves off, and try again.
- They inspire innovation.
- They effect positive change in organizations. Their deep understanding of systems and people allows them to take the actions that yield the best results.
- They use thorough, open, and honest communication; everyone appreciates their trustworthiness.
- A Catalyst transforms raw information into wisdom, and out of that wisdom finds the leverage points inside of the organization to move it forward.

Let's look at how a Catalyst manifests some of these attitudes and actions.

Sincerity

Your words and actions must match. Insincerity is the roadblock for the Catalyst. It won't take long for your staff to recognize a discrepancy between your words and your actions. Have you ever worked for a boss who expected you to work late—but he always went home at 5:00? But when you have a boss who asks you to stay late and he's staying late too, you feel more motivated and appreciated.

People can't trust a leader who lacks authenticity. Low self-awareness equals low authenticity. Awareness of your strengths and limitations, in conjunction with a commitment to self-development, is the foundation for your effective actions in leadership. To be an effective Catalyst, a leader must also be sincere in his assessment of his skills and his desire to improve them.

Do It Now

Taking action accelerates change. The more you do, the more you learn. The Catalyst constantly updates and changes what needs updating and changing. She also listens to feedback, so she can know what changes are needed in herself, in her team, or in the whole organization.

You can be a Catalyst for your team's culture to lower expenses, to develop new business, to launch new products, or to improve work safety. The important thing is to find what you can improve and do it now.

It takes work. But, as Thomas Jefferson said, the harder he worked, the luckier he got.

Honesty and Trust

To be a Catalyst to any organization, you first need to have personal integrity. Once this has been established, you will have created a foundation for moving your organization forward.

Often a team or a company cannot get to the next level until a Catalyst steps up. The integrity of the person leading is critical to inspiration. Vision and passion are important, but others must trust you before they'll feel inspired. People look up to a person who tells the truth and does the right things. The qualities that people value most in their leaders are honesty and congruence between words and deeds. Effective leaders keep their promises. When people say one thing and do another, they quickly lose credibility. Without credibility, there can be no trust.

Leaders who are Catalysts inspire creativity at work. Sharing creative solutions and ideas helps build trust, which encourages others to look for creative ways to solve problems.

Confront Paradoxes

If you think about your business in the short term and then in the long term, there will be obvious paradoxes or conflicts between the two. For example, consider the opposite notions of a single big idea versus a continuous improvement plan over time. Or, being in partnership with another company versus being in competition with them. Catalysts are unafraid to grapple with these paradoxes, but they do so from a place of sincerity, of thinking through the issues strategically because they truly want to do the right thing. Furthermore, they do it all while creating a positive relationship within their team.

Prioritize

Organizations are complex entities with thousands of interconnected relationships held in equilibrium. Balance can be delicate; change can be a challenge. Team members can feel overwhelmed in the face of these challenging complexities, especially when they try to tackle them all at once.

A Catalyst knows how to prioritize and take things one at a time. Catalysts understand that small, well-focused actions can produce significant, enduring improvements if they are placed correctly. A leader needs to create an environment where everyone can make good, timely decisions, solve problems quickly and efficiently, and implement plans effectively.

In 1981, Roberto Goizueta became CEO of Coca-Cola. His main priority: to pull Coca-Cola out of a 20-year decline. One day, his senior leaders were bragging about Coca Cola's huge share of the soft drink market: 45%! Roberto asked them, "what proportion of the liquid market—not just the soft drink market—do we have?" He asked a question that changed their frame of thinking. It was 2%.

By shifting the frame of reference, Goizueta was able to expand the company's thinking to include more markets and more products. His constant questions kept the organization growing. Under his leadership, the value of the company's common shares grew by more than $148 billion—an increase of 3,500%.

Catalysts ask questions that help company leaders prioritize the business focus. It is easy to focus on things that are both urgent and strategic. What is challenging is to take time from dealing with things that are urgent and not strategic to focus on things that are strategic but not urgent. A Catalyst understands the importance of focusing on doing the right things.

Ignite the Vision

As a Catalyst, you see the overall patterns and recognize leverage points in the system. You understand that small, well-focused actions can produce significant, enduring improvements. You challenge superficial analyses and urge team members to discover the real issues before it is too late to embrace opportunities.

Identifying leverage points requires focused attention to detail. Indeed, your role as a Catalyst is to marry vision and precision. Vision without precision leads to poor decision making. Precision without passion leads to slow, plodding, and ultimately unsustainable business practices. The lack of both spells disaster for the culture of a company. The presence of both provides a solid foundation for powerful actions toward making vision reality.

CATALYSTS CAN MAKE A DIFFERENCE

Buckminster Fuller

Buckminster Fuller, light years ahead of his time, spent his life discovering, inventing, and leading others by example. He was driven by his vision "to make the world work for 100% of humanity, in the shortest possible time, through spontaneous cooperation without ecological offense or disadvantage of anyone." Best known for his geodesic dome, he was a forward thinker who worked to leverage existing and new technologies for making a better quality of life for all. He was an original thinker whose writings and lectures touched upon every aspect of the human condition. He was a Catalyst who was exploring and prototyping designs in various uncharted areas of science and humanity.

I particularly like his metaphor of a trim tab as a way to affect change in our organizations. Talking about an ocean liner at sea, he explained:

> "— the whole ship goes by and then comes the rudder. And there's a tiny thing at the edge of the rudder called a trim tab. It's a miniature rudder. Just moving the little trim tab builds a low pressure that pulls the rudder around.

Takes almost no effort at all. So I said that the little individual can be a trim tab. Society thinks it's going right by you, that it's left you altogether. But if you're doing dynamic things mentally, the fact is that you can just put your foot out like that and the whole big ship of state is going to go. So I said, call me Trim Tab."

Fuller gave us example after example of how to be a Catalyst. In fact, the Buckminster Fuller Institute is set up as an organization to carry forward the principles that Bucky created so others could be Catalysts.

- He felt that conventional institutions created barriers to progress by limiting inspiration.
- He took a worldview position that all ideas are found in nature, whether we are aware of them or not.
- He encouraged governments to pursue tools that promoted peace and prosperity for the world at large. He wanted governments to focus on "livingry" rather than "weaponry."
- He popularized the term "Spaceship Earth," reflecting his desire to work for the common good of humanity.
- He was one of the first to understand and promote that all things on Earth are in an interlocking system, and believed that actively pursuing sustainability might be the only way that we will be able to live together successfully on this planet.

What makes Buckminster Fuller an excellent example of a Catalyst is he not only created new products for the benefit of mankind but he also provided us with a system to be Catalysts ourselves. He applied his own principles to his own inventions.

One of his visions was "Make the world work, for 100% of humanity, in the shortest possible time, through spontaneous cooperation, without ecological offense or the disadvantage of anyone." To make this vision happen, he invented a game. He called it the "World Peace Game." Fuller further invented the Design Sciences as an approach to address the comprehensive problems of the world. Fuller believed that this study needed to be comprehensive in order to gain a global perspective when pursuing solutions to problems humanity is facing. He was anticipating the future's needs. He used the word "world" because we needed a systems approach that dealt with the world as a whole, and not a piecemeal approach that only addressed the needs of individual states. He called it a "game" because he wanted it to be seen as something that was accessible to everyone whereby the findings would be widely utilized. From the results of the game, he hoped to have people influence their political leaders to address the relevant issues. Fuller wanted to be a Catalyst creating a place where individuals or teams of people came and competed, or cooperated, to make profound improvements to our quality of life. His "World Peace Game" was a way to introduce the basic concepts of Design Science as a problem-solving approach which entails a rigorous, systematic study of the deliberate ordering of the components in our universe. His ideas continue to be a Catalyst for change in making our world a better place.

Gandhi

Mahatma Gandhi was a small man who overcame the British Empire, which in the early 20th century ruled almost two-thirds of the globe. Gandhi was such a powerful Catalyst for change that he brought down the centuries-old institution of colonialism in India. He did so by advocating for peace and maintaining his vision of the intrinsic dignity of man and every person's right to freedom and self-determination.

Gandhi was determined that people should see that human rights are inherent to each of us, not just granted by a controlling force, however "benevolent." Essential to his vision was the absence of all violence. His peaceful practices and the transparent authenticity of his beliefs helped millions join him in bringing about the political independence of India.

Colonialism is primarily concerned with the interests and self-promotion of the ruling country. The British Empire was built on an Adversarial relationship backed by force. The British "Raj" ruled India for generations, but when Gandhi entered the role of Catalyst, he united and unleashed the full potential of his country using nonviolence and diplomacy, not aggression. Decades later, Nelson Mandela used the same principles to promote human rights in South Africa.

Art Levinson

Art Levenson is an example of someone who is a Catalyst for unleashing the full potential of a group of people. During his first two years as CEO of Genentech, Art Levinson persuaded the board to invest 50% of revenues back into research and development. As

Catalyst for Genentech's growth, Levinson shifted the organization's thinking by concentrating on cancer research and development of cancer-fighting drugs. The reinvestment was a wise move, as Genentech went from having zero presence in treating cancer to being the single largest supplier of medicine to the oncology field. Levinson wanted to make cancer a manageable disease. An inspired Catalyst, he built a company of people who are driven to make cancer-fighting drugs that tackle unmet medical needs. He served as Catalyst for growth and change through understanding the big picture along with paying attention to the small details.

No surprise that shareholders, employees, and patients were delighted that he was leading the organization. With his insights into large organizations, people, and corporate culture—plus his ability to keep organizations focused on the right activities—he was invited to the boards of Apple and Google, both of which have also fundamentally changed how we think about technology. All three companies clearly understand every aspect of their marketplace, customer base, and employee needs. He now serves as Chairman of the Board at Apple, the most valuable company in the world.

Bob Dole and Al Gore

Catalysts take action to turn vision into reality. But Leaders cannot take those actions if they lack authenticity.

Look at both Bob Dole and Al Gore as examples. Both men ran for the presidency and both lost. What interests me is that, after they'd lost, they both revealed amazing personalities of wit and passion. Maybe during their presidential races, their political advisors told them to downplay their personalities. Maybe being out of public office freed up their thinking and communication styles. Whatever it was, their "loss" allowed both men to become articulate leaders. The authenticity in their messages comes through loud and clear.

- Bob Dole is active in efforts to end world hunger, developing (with George McGovern) school nutrition and lunch programs for which they were awarded the 2008 World Food Prize. Dole is also one of the founders of The Bipartisan Policy Center, which promotes political momentum that engages in the art of principled compromise.

- Al Gore is one of the world's leading advocates for climate change awareness. His movie, "An Inconvenient Truth" won the 2007 Academy Award for Best Documentary Feature. That same year, Gore was awarded the Nobel Prize for Peace for his work on climate change awareness.

I wonder what their political fate would have been if they had displayed more of themselves in their presidential campaigns.

Allan Parker

Allan Parker, winner of the Educator of the Year Excellence Award in Australia, is an amazing Catalyst. In the realm of organizational change initiatives, there have been few ground breaking innovations in the last two decades. And efficacy of any change initiative, no matter how well-designed or intentioned has been hard to measure. Then Allan inverted all the traditional change methods, and in doing so created an entirely new model for helping organizations change.

His process, "specific behavior modeling," allows organizations to change the culture and behaviors of their employees all at the same time. Allan reversed the assumptions of changing many behaviors and focused on changing just one single behavior at a time.

Allan, like the trim tab, has discovered this new concept of highly-leveraged universal behaviors that, when changed, shift other behaviors along with them. His innovation allows leaders to directly adjust the behaviors of their culture and bring about the full potential of an organization.

Bono

Rock singer and Catalyst, Bono has been a major force in relief efforts, peace initiatives, and is a champion of AIDS research. But he's taken a huge role, with less attention from the media, in the area of debt relief. He realized that if we can help developing nations reduce their debt, many of their other issues could be quickly resolved. His metaphor is the lever, the mechanical paradox that generates a huge force on a large object using only a minute force applied at the right location. Relieving a country's debt in one area—for example, payments on imported grain—frees up money that can be spent elsewhere, such as on processing and shipping the grain to hungry citizens.

If you find the leverage point in an organization, you can change the whole of the organization. Bono, using his star presence, is affecting great change in the world. He is knowledgeable about sophisticated financial strategies and can speak fluently with the head of the World Bank. He has become a shrewd political advocate, making sure debt relief is on the agenda for the most powerful people of the world. He is a Catalyst for change.

Archimedes, who taught the world about levers, was speaking about the physical elements when he said, "Give me a place to stand and I can move the world." Catalysts like Gandhi, Parker, and Bono would say this about their visions: "Give me a situation on which to take a stand, and I can change the world."

Gary Friedman

While Restoration Hardware's Gary Friedman is a known Visionary he has also spent his career driving himself to be a Catalyst on every team he has worked in or led. Prior to his role at Restoration Hardware, he was president at Pottery Barn during some of their most significant growth years, which means he has directly influenced how millions of Americans decorate their homes. His passion for excellence is sincere and he has mastered the art of change.

Gary challenges his teams' thinking, which creates teams people want to join. By embedding in his company the values of service, quality, and innovation, he created a culture and a business model that was able to survive and thrive in one of the worst economic downturns.

He did not sit back in 2008 as the economy unraveled, nor did he panic. He bet his business on a new strategy and made significant changes to implement it. His competitors lost $7 billion and many went out of business. Restoration Hardware had one of their best years ever. How did he do it? Significantly, he had already invested in creating leaders at all levels of the organization. When the crisis hit and Restoration Hardware had to cut back, he had strength "on the bench" and a team committed to making the organization thrive. Was it easy? No. But because Gary was a Catalyst and had created a values-based organization where everyone is considered a leader, Restoration Hardware had the foundation on which to execute its new business plan. Gary infuses into his presentations his personal business philosophy, which inspires others to be Catalysts. He is not afraid to make any change that will help his organization reach the next level. He often says that "fast is as slow as we go" at Restoration Hardware.

SPEED MATTERS

Out on the plains of Africa both predator and prey have a relationship. The fastest lions are able to catch food and eat, so they thrive and reproduce, thus faster lions make up more of the population. In the prey's case the fastest antelope are able to escape the lions, so they thrive and reproduce, and faster antelope make up more of the population. So when you wake up in the morning, if you want to survive on the plains of Africa you had better be the fastest one on the field. In no other marketplace is this more true than the Internet. In this wide-open business speed really does matter.

Marissa Mayer is the CEO of Yahoo! She understands the complex world of the Internet, having spent most of her career at Google. Upon joining Yahoo! she immediately looked at how she could be a catalyst for change in helping Yahoo! succeed. She realized that where Yahoo! could gain leverage with its 700 million users was by accelerating the speed that Yahoo! was operating at. Catalysts understand that all things being equal, going faster is better than going slower.

Under Marissa's influence Yahoo! now finds that projects which used to take months are now being completed in weeks and projects that used to take weeks are now being done in days. By focusing Yahoo! on the speed of execution today she is positioning Yahoo!'s culture to succeed in the future. Change is only accelerating with regard to the Internet and being a catalyst for speed will provide Yahoo! with a better chance for success.

CATALYSTS CONSTANTLY QUESTION

Buckminster Fuller's principles can help anyone be more of a Catalyst at work or for the world. Here are some of his questions that I think will help you find leverage points for yourself and your organization. Consider the widest possible context for your responses:

- What will happen in the future and can I anticipate it?
- Is my aim to transform the whole world or a division?
- Where is the trim tab and rudder of the system I am trying to modify?
- What is the most efficient way of exerting pressure for "moving the rudder"?
- In what way can I (or we) successfully continue through changing tides?

These questions might generate more questions. Do not hesitate to ask those questions—even the apparent and naïve questions. Make no assumptions. Buckminster Fuller never assumed. He always did his own research on a subject.

CATALYSTS TAKE ACTION

I've mentioned before that you do not need to have a certain job title, particular profession, or hold an elected office before you can take a position of authority. Don't wait for an external authority or position of power to give you "permission" to act. That's operating from an external locus of control, which means unnecessary drama.

Just look at recent history: Mahatma Gandhi, Nelson Mandela, Martin Luther King Jr., and Rosa Parks became powerful Catalysts who brought change to millions. They stood up for what they believed. They certainly did not wait for an OK from anyone else to grant them the right to lead. The actions of these leaders went against the prevailing wisdom of their time and did not have the support—more likely, direct opposition—of the established institutions. But they took the vision of new ways of viewing the world and, as Catalysts, brought it to fruition.

Let's Make Mistakes

Catalysts find new ideas, methods, and pathways for solving problems. They enjoy the brainstorming and experimenting that others often find overwhelming. Catalysts allow team members to innovate, take responsibility, and be creative.

They also allow mistakes. This is a big one. Catalysts expect mistakes. Unlike the Adversary, they don't lie in the bushes waiting to pounce on you when you make one. The Catalyst knows that progress doesn't tread a well-lit path; things go wrong. Learn from it but learn from it fast.

Coca-Cola's Roberto Goizueta expressed it well: "The moment avoiding failure becomes your motivation, you're down the path of inactivity. You stumble only if you're moving."

This trust and confidence is enhanced by a leader being a Catalyst for the organization. A leader can accelerate trust by the quality of his decisions. To make quality decisions, a leader must have quality information. Thorough and trustworthy information is available to those who have built trusting relationships within the organization.

In essence, a leader who is a Catalyst must:

- Question the status quo. Identify processes that need to be revamped so they will impact the organization or team positively.
- Model the right behaviors. Show people what to do by doing it yourself first.
- Help inspire others to take action. Understand the underlying need for the change and communicate it in a compelling way that is comprehendible to your entire team.
- Provide the necessary resources to be successful. Give others the means to get the job done themselves.
- Be collaborative (yet decisive), flexible, steady, swift, and mindful.
- See both the details and the big picture, the forest and the trees.
- Provide direction clearly, while remaining humble and authentic.
- Be fair to the community, maintaining a team focus while respecting individuality.

CATALYSTS CONSIDER THREE PERSPECTIVES

Being a Catalyst is, as is navigating the high seas, a delicate art. If you move too far in any one direction, you can be thrown off course.

During World War II, my father was a lieutenant in the US Navy serving as a navigator on the aircraft carrier USS Langley. He took bearings on the stars to chart the course of the ship through the Pacific. His job was to give pilots the correct coordinates, so they could find the ship and land their planes. Their very lives depended on his expertise.

My dad passed on a love for astronomy, and he taught me how to use a sextant. (Later in life, he marveled at GPS units. To him, they were borderline magic.) The sextant that navigators use today has changed little in 250 years. With it, you need to take a measurement of at least three celestial bodies in order to know where you are in the world. You need **three distinct perspectives.**

I find this three-distinct-perspective principle essential for those developing the skills of being a Catalyst. For someone to make a wise decision, they need to orient themselves against three essential states of awareness: self-awareness, other awareness, and objective awareness. Let's examine each:

- **Self-awareness**. This is the perspective of emotional honesty, healthy and authentic actions, setting reasonable boundaries, and self-control. Before making a decision, you need to know what you want from your own personal perspective.

- **Other awareness** centers around empathy and creating a culture of understanding, teamwork, and emotional intelligence. Other awareness is a crucial element in the Catalyst's ability to develop relationships. In making decisions, you need this important skill of being able to find what other people want and how they feel about issues.

- **Objective awareness**. This involves big picture, strategic thinking, and fully understanding your environment. It is the ability to look at an issue from all perspectives and see patterns in the relationships. It is the planning perspective and entails both political and organizational understanding.

These three perspective skills will assist you in the subtle and sophisticated art of gaining insight into complex issues. Then you can navigate your way through any scenario regardless of its difficultly or complexity.

Your ability to shift perspectives is critical to making decisions that set a course of action or involve a group of people. When you, as a leader, are confronting a tough issue, shift though the Self, the Other, and the Objective perspectives. They will allow you to examine the issue from all three points of view, giving you insights toward making the appropriate decision.

Shifting your thinking between these three perspectives is powerful. By assessing the situation this way, you first arm yourself with information and then show others your grasp of the data and your willingness to discuss. People will see that you are looking for an elegant solution; this will be inspiring and motivating to them. Through your open-mindedness, you'll create an atmosphere of trust, not of antagonism.

Working in the Group

Tackling an issue with a group can be like tackling a wide receiver in the mud: messy. Not everyone is comfortable sharing their opinions in public, even among co-workers, and not everyone will instantly grasp different viewpoints. But as participants keep plugging away, insights appear. Over time, people gain wisdom and see how to move forward. By helping your team, you become more adept at framing issues in proper context, and this will help a group of people think.

(In group work, I always suggest that you capture people's comments in notes, graphs or other visual means, so everyone can remember them, easily review them, and map the path to key issues.)

Let me tell you how I facilitated a group of individuals who discovered the value of framing issues and seeing issues from other points of view.

Back in early 1990, a Northern Ontario mining operation was stuck in a difficult negotiation between managers and steelworker leadership. A previous collective bargaining agreement produced both a strike and lockout that impacted everyone in this small town, where the mine was the largest employer. I was invited to come into the discussions because of my work in negotiating, mutual gains bargaining, and reestablishing environments of trust.

First, to better frame the issues, we needed to change the style of communication. The company had been using an adversarial approach toward the union. That style had split the town apart during the six-month strike. The mining operation leaders now took a new approach—mutual gains bargaining—and both sides were learning the new way to negotiate. It was slow going because both sides found it difficult to let go of the underlying suspicion born from years of adversarial bargaining.

Trust was also a big problem. A month before I arrived, the mine manager had made a unilateral decision on a particular issue which the union felt was a slap in the face to the workers. The union continued to fight this decision, and the mine manager resented the union for pursuing the issue. Both thought the other was grandstanding for political purposes. Looking through a filter of "politics," neither individual trusted the other. Finally, these two men were able to see that at the heart of the issue was a value that they shared: respect for people.

On the fourth day of my training session with them, we had a major breakthrough in building trust and creating an alliance. The key union representative and the mine manager, having resolved their issue for themselves, demonstrated their insight to the rest of the group. In a communication exercise, I had the two men switch places. The union's health and safety representative "became" the mine manager, literally putting on his mine manager jacket. The mine manager donned a steelworker hat and took on the role of the union's safety rep.

Both men role-played each other's perspective in front of their peers. The mine manager argued the point of view of the union, and the union rep articulated the point of view of the mining company. The group saw that management truly understood the union's perspective and vice versa. This role-reversal exercise went a long way toward creating a cooperative spirit for the negotiation between the two organizations—which, in the years since, has had five successful mutual gains bargaining sessions.

YOU CAN CHANGE

Buckminster Fuller said, "you never change things by fighting the existing reality. To change something, you must build a new model that makes the existing model obsolete." As a Catalyst, you can make things happen by thinking in ways that unlock your potential and the potential of others around you.

CHAPTER 11

Rescuer or Coach

DURING MY COLLEGE DAYS, I was an Emergency Medical Technician providing first-responder care to people in need. I was also on the National Ski Patrol, helping people injured on the ski slope. I was rescuing people; helping those in need or in danger.

Rescuing seems such an admirable action that its role in the Drama Triangle confuses people. Why would you not want to rescue? But rescuing within the context of the Drama Triangle is not the same as being an EMT at the scene of a car accident.

The difference lies in your reasons for doing the rescuing. In drama, the Rescuer is not helping someone who is in genuine need or who cannot help himself or herself. The Rescuer instead habitually "rescues" people who can take care of themselves, because the Rescuer is convinced the person is incapable and must be rescued, whether they ask for help or not.

In leadership, you take on a different role: the Coach. The Coach has faith in other people's abilities, so invests time and energy helping others develop his or her innate abilities. The Coach does this with the other person's knowledge and cooperation. As a

Coach, you guide rather than rescue and give assistance only in the sense that you help the other person develop his or her own skills.

A Rescuer's message to the rescued is, "you are not doing well. It's a good thing that I'm here to save you."

A Coach's message to the coached is, "I'm here to assist you to further develop your own innate potential."

THE RESCUER

The role of Rescuer is the most subtle of the three roles within the Drama Triangle, because rescuing is easily confused with helping. When you are helpful in an appropriate, balanced way, you're a leader. If it gets out of balance, you're deep in the Drama Triangle (and vice versa: if you're in drama, your intentions to help will turn into rescuing.)

There are many styles of the Rescuer: Mr. Nice Guy, Ms. Helpful, and Everyone's Best Friend. Rescuers can be, in fact, pleasant and even popular. They don't start disagreements, they are apt to go along with the other person's agenda or the majority opinion, they are often agreeable, and are always ready to pitch in and take on work.

But they are deep in the Drama Triangle. They operate from an external locus of control—desperately needing the good opinion of others. The reason they don't start disagreements is because they avoid conflict at any cost, which means they won't offer any direct, honest feedback. They go along with the majority even if it means discarding their own judgment or values. They're agreeable because of their overwhelming need to be liked, a need that keeps them from being honest and sincere. They will take on your work—while secretly assuming that someday you will repay them for doing so.

Do you sometimes help out a bit too much? Maybe you're spending time in the Rescuer role. Here are some additional distinctions to help you determine if you're being helpful or a Rescuer:

- Are you doing other team members' work?
- Are you behaving passively in relationship to others?
- Do you avoid giving others feedback out of fear of how they will take the news?
- Have you ever taken over a task because you thought the other person was not capable, but you did not offer feedback to that person?
- Do you find it difficult to ask for what you want?
- Do you frequently think that other people should just know what you want?
- Do you continually say "yes" to requests when you really mean to say "no" or renegotiate the task?
- Do you worry that, if you refuse to do a task, people will not like you?

If you've answered "yes" to more than one question, you need to take a serious look at the role of Rescuer—so you can get out of it.

Why Rescuers Rescue

The role of Rescuer emerges in a person with an extreme need for approval and recognition. They want others to like them. This leads them to develop:

- An overwhelming desire to do things for people, so people will be grateful, approve of them and like them.
- An avoidance of confrontation. They are unable to speak frankly and give feedback. By not giving feedback, they don't give others the opportunity to learn and improve.
- A desire to be rescued. In repayment for "everything I've done for you," Rescuers secretly expect others to save them.

As a Rescuer, you see yourself as a savior. Like the cavalry, you gallop up at the last moment and save the day. There are several problems with this. Let's look at them in detail:

The Incompetence of Others

In the workplace, most folks are awake, alert, and have the competence to get their jobs done. They might need your help, but they don't need your rescuing. However, in the role of Rescuer, you truly believe that others require rescuing. You have no belief in your co-workers' capabilities. You don't even have faith that they can handle hearing feedback. You take on work that's not yours rather than hold the appropriate person accountable and give them help so they can do the job themselves.

The Rescuer's style is to ignore, discount, and minimize team members by assuming they are hopeless, helpless, and unable to solve problems. Assuming that others are flawed supports the Rescuer's notion that it is incumbent upon him to be the "savior."

Rescuers commonly take on more than their fair share of work and responsibility. In the role of Rescuer, you can go so far as to martyr yourself by taking on more and more—all the while blaming the other person for not doing their share, even though you won't tell them so.

Withholding Feedback

It's difficult for the Rescuer to say such things as "you made a mistake," or "here's how you can improve," because that conversation seems too confrontational. You won't hold coworkers accountable. You believe that people cannot handle the feedback—they'll become upset at hearing it, or they'll be unable to improve their performance—so you withhold the feedback or water it down. Then, you step in and do the work yourself.

Yes, giving feedback can be uncomfortable at times, even for an experienced leader. But if you withhold feedback, you'll be unable to build quality, trusting relationships.

If you have feedback but decide not to share it, you miss three opportunities:

- To give the other person information they need to learn and grow.
- To have a conversation from which you'll also learn.
- To create a greater level of trust in your relationship.

Because Rescuers won't give feedback, they can't be sure whether or not their feedback is valid. Without giving the feedback—"Hey, Lena, you did this presentation using the wrong template"—the Rescuer doesn't engage coworkers in a useful dialog—"No, Duncan told me he wanted me to use this template." The Rescuer instead jumps in and re-creates Lena's presentation in the "correct" template. That's a waste of time and energy. And suppose Lena really had used the wrong template? She might thank you sincerely for pointing it out to her; she might moan. But she can sit back down and redo her presentation herself. After all, getting the presentation ready is her job.

The absence of honest feedback ultimately becomes a roadblock. How can a team member learn about his job or develop new skills and competencies if no one tells him what he is doing right and doing wrong? How would you discover if your feedback has any validity if you don't have the conversation?

Please Like Me

You'll be prone to go into the Rescuer role if you have a deep need to be liked. Of course, we all want others to like us. But the Rescuer's need for approval isn't healthy: in this role, you will sacrifice your own needs and even your principles just to get others to like you. When you abandon your own needs in order to assist others, you'll end up depleted and in need of rescue yourself.

Remember, feeling good about yourself based on the outside approval of others is a clear sign of life in the Drama Triangle. Rescuers (as well as Victims and Adversaries) abdicate their ability to generate genuine self-confidence. In the role of the classic Rescuer, you will be unaware of how you feel, but desperately aware of how others feel. When other people struggle with difficulties, you take the conflict personally. You focus your attention on pleasing others. You want to eradicate all conflict rather than leave others to solve their own problems. With your fear of hurting others' feelings (what if they stop liking you?), you baby them, which limits their opportunities for the growth and wisdom that comes from the healthy resolution of their own issues. This makes you feel better, but you're ultimately selling the other person short.

My Fault!

Guilt eats at the person in the Rescuer role. You blame yourself for things that go wrong whether or not you had a hand in it. If someone is angry, you are to blame. If someone is upset with you personally, you will go the extra mile to fix the issue. If someone's harried or frustrated, you feel it must be your fault—and it's your job to make the other person feel better.

Avoid All Conflict

The Rescuer works hard to avoid uncomfortable situations. Coping mechanisms include:

- Saying "yes" to a request when you really want to say "no."
- Avoiding a person with whom you need to have a conversation.
- The compulsion to control and rescue people by fixing their problems for them.

If you are deep in the Rescuer role, you may have a challenge establishing boundaries with people. I used to work with someone who habitually said "yes" to any request. To manage his inability to give an honest "no," he avoided phone calls and face-to-face meetings, instead asking for all requests to be emailed to him. This gave him time to reflect before replying. This person knows his tendencies, and has established a system where he uses distance as a way to say "no."

Rescuer? Or Rescued?

The Rescuer feels good about helping. Yet the Rescuer assumes that when she's in need, the people she has helped will come to her aid. Rescuing in this case is a conditional gift: if I help you out, you will help me out in the future.

If you are letting a Rescuer help you in your work, you might sense that they have a covert agenda. They do: they are expecting your explicit approval of them.

But because of the Rescuer's avoidance of honest, frank conversation, they never mention this "promise." They assume it is understood. They expect to be rescued and are usually disappointed if the rescuing never arrives. This disappointment can either distress the Rescuer into acting the Victim, or annoy him enough to become an Adversary.

And, having not been rescued, the Rescuer will try all the harder to get people to like him, thinking they'll be more likely to come to his rescue next time.

Rescuers Within the Triangle

If you are in the Rescuer role, you'll be pulled into the orbit of others in the Drama Triangle. As a Rescuer, you will attempt to solve other people's problems because you assume they can't fix things themselves. You'll want them to like you, so you'll avoid holding others accountable for their commitments, which means:

- You'll make excuses for the person in the Adversarial role. You see that the Adversary is flawed in some way, but you won't ever confront the issue to get to its source and resolve it. Adversaries recognize this, and know they can bully or manipulate the Rescuer to do their work for them.

- The Rescuer feels that the Victim needs help more than honesty. A cagey Victim is well aware that a Rescuer can be helpful, so the Victim will engineer his or her problems to become the Rescuer's problems. You, the Rescuer, will listen and you will care—and you will do the Victim's work.

- Rescuers, in fact, respect neither Victim nor Adversary. You think they are incapable and in need of rescue because they cannot do their jobs satisfactorily without help—your help.

Rescuers have little faith in anyone's capabilities (including their own) and this compels them to help others. But at a deeper level, they find rescue exhausting. They continue to do so out of guilt and fear of conflict. Fear of rejection guides the Rescuer's behavior. It determines everything you say or do. If you enter into conflict, people won't like you anymore. Giving to others is the Rescuer's way of feeling as though she makes a difference in the world. That might provide some short-term help for others but it is not a sustainable strategy if you and your organization want to grow.

GREAT COACHES, GREAT COACHING

The opposite of the role of Rescuer is, of course, in the Leadership Triangle: the role of the Coach. Coaches work to create real growth for themselves and others. They enjoy developing the leadership capabilities of those on their team. Leaders create leaders.

You have to unleash the full potential of your own leadership in order to unleash the potential in others. The Coach brings out the best in himself or herself and in other people. John Wooden (who was much more than a basketball coach) said it well: "A coach is someone who can give correction without causing resentment."

In George Bernard Shaw's classic "Pygmalion," Eliza Doolittle began as a lower class shop worker and developed into a charming and sophisticated lady. One of the most striking lines from the play is a statement about human nature: "treat a man as he appears to be and you make him worse. But treat a man as if he already were what he potentially could be, and you make him what he should be." That's something great coaches would agree with.

Do you believe in your people? Do you believe in their ability to grow? Do you anticipate the best from the people you work with? If you do, you're a Leader and a Coach.

Coaches Can Make a Difference

Think about times when others have believed in you. When you had someone "in your corner" who believed in your full capabilities, you probably noticed it was easier, faster, and more pleasurable for you to learn and grow. You can grow alone, but it's immensely easier with the support of someone who believes in you. I know that I am made up of a large portion of the beliefs my parents held for me. They saw what I was capable of and set the stage for me to lead and contribute to a life that mattered in the world.

In addition to my parents, I look back at the many individuals in my life who helped me to grow more than I thought was possible. I had a teacher, Bay Butler, who saw my potential as an educator and hired me to be his teaching assistant. Beyond that, he challenged my worldview and got me to expand my thinking toward what he saw was possible for me. Another such mentor was Eugene Albright, who was able to open doorways of perception and intuition that I had no idea even existed. My experience with Lansing Barrett Grisham allowed me to see where I could create more choices in my life. Each of these coaches spent a lifetime growing, learning and mastering their craft and then they were able to turn these gifts to the benefit of many others, including me. In each case, someone saw my potential and showed me the possibility of that potential. I was able to grow in part because of their belief in me. You never know when you will have the opportunity to give the gift of growth to someone else. It is one of the most valuable gifts you can give.

Bill Walsh, Great Coach

Bill Walsh thought of himself principally as a teacher. His son Craig and I have known each other since our college days. Craig coauthored an exceptional book on his father, Bill Walsh; The Score Takes Care of Itself, in which Bill talks about the four most powerful words a leader can deliver: "I believe in you."

In the 1960s and 70s, the 49ers were a second-tier football team—I know, I was growing up in San Francisco back then. All of that changed when Bill Walsh took over as head coach. In the 1979 NFL draft, Walsh picked the talented young man he needed to run his offense: Joe Montana. Walsh knew what he wanted Joe to learn during his rookie year: a new way to run the offense and counter the different defenses then practiced in the NFL. Walsh taught this in such a way that Joe became the superbly successful quarterback of a legendary football team. Montana has said of Walsh, "Outside of my dad, he was probably the most influential person in my life."

With Walsh as head coach, the 49ers won 13 League Championships, five Conference Championships, and five Super Bowl titles, most of them with Montana at quarterback.

Walsh worked with people he believed in. (If he did not believe in you, he would move you out of the organization.) And he always let his players and his coaching staff know he believed in them. Walsh invested in his people and brought out the best in them, both on and off the field. Yet, he was relentless in his ambition to get the best out of his people and his team. He treated both players and coaches with great respect, and this care and support transcended the fierce rivalry of the NFL because it was rooted in faith and trust.

Bill Walsh created and fostered an environment that created other leaders. Many sports fans know how Walsh developed his players. What is less known about him is how well he developed his coaches. He understood that, in order to create a winning organization, he needed to create a winning system. His system was clear and explicable, and he taught it to his coaching staff. Thanks to Walsh, his staff was so well trained and so competent that other NFL teams hired them to be their head coaches. At one point, over half of all NFL coaches had either worked directly for Walsh or were part of a "second generation," trained by coaches who had learned from Walsh. The list includes Mike Holmgren, Dennis Green, Ray Rhodes, Herm Edwards, Lovie Smith, Sam Wyche, George Siefert, Jim Fassel, Paul Hackett, Andy Reid, Tony Dungy, Steve Mariucci, Mike McCarthy, Mike Tice, Jon Gruden, Marv Lewis, Jeff Fischer, and Brian Billick.

One Conversation Can Make a Difference

As the director of NLP Comprehensive, Tom Dotz creates learning communities. But even when he's not at work in his training business, he helps people learn. He relayed to me this great story of how a quiet, simple moment of coaching can help to shift a person's thinking—and change their life.

One evening, at a restaurant in Santa Cruz where he often dined, Tom was greeted by a hostess he always enjoyed speaking with. The pace was slow that evening, so he had the chance to chat with her. To his casual query, "how are things with you?" she responded seriously: "I've just turned twenty-nine, and I really don't know what to do with my life."

Surprised by her frank response, Tom asked, "Well, if you could do what you really wanted, what would that be?"

"I'd go to the Parsons School of Design and get my art degree."

"Well, what stops you?"

"It would take five years, and I'd be 34," she sighed.

"So, let me get this straight," Tom said. "You really want to go to art school, but you're 29 now, and you'd be 34 when you finished. Right? And in five years you will be 34. Your choice is simply that you'll either be 34 with your art degree, or you'll be 34 without it."

While she looked surprised, Tom's waiter came up to lead him to his table. Tom then forgot about the conversation. The hostess did not. The next time he visited the restaurant, Tom saw a marked difference in her demeanor; she was vibrant. She told Tom excitedly, "you've changed my life. I applied to Parsons, I've been accepted, and I start school this fall. I've only got three more weeks here and I'll be moving back east."

Huge impact! But Tom's casual question really was not an idle comment.

Tom's purpose was to get her to shift her thinking. Through coaching questions, he showed her a new way to contrast her choices and to view them as choices in the first place. He didn't simply commiserate and he didn't tell her what to do. He got her to think, which helped her to change her mind—by which she changed her life.

If we expect great things of people, great things have a chance of happening. If we expect average performances from people—or from ourselves—we've got an excellent chance of getting average.

Values in Every Conversation

DeMonty Price is the Senior VP of Restoration Hardware and their Chief Values Officer. In all of his coaching conversations, he focuses on core corporate values. These values are not just in print, on a sign on the wall. DeMonty delivers motivational speeches that let his teams know they have his genuine support, while they also hear how determined and explicit he is about the values of the organization. In the years that I have watched him give speeches or coach his executives in group settings, I have never once heard a speech that did not include the company's values. DeMonty says "if you can get a team who can live your core values, you can achieve anything," and he works hard to find such people and bring them into the organization.

Expectation of Greatness

DeMonty as a Coach inspires his team every day, but he also expects greatness from them. DeMonty asks his people a lot of questions, so he can find out what is important to his team and what they value. He makes sure their deepest values can be expressed in the organization. DeMonty has seen "managers miss linking their values to the values of the organization. They see motivation as just giving pep talks," so he avoids that trap. He creates natural motivation because he models the behavior he expects in others. His encouragement and support of their work is not fake or "rah rah," but comes from the core of who he is and what he does.

DeMonty's passion is so authentic that it creates an environment of excitement, and the enjoyment of being genuinely passionate about your job. If anyone he coaches does not have a passionate attitude, DeMonty says, "They will not make it in our environment."

DeMonty leads his team with what he calls "impossibly high standards." He says, "I know my standards are hard to reach, but that lets me sit down and have the coaching conversation we need to take the organization to the next level. It's not punitive. If we don't meet the standards, it is just as much about me as the next person. When I coach I do it from the perspective of how do I need to get better also."

How can you, like DeMonty, learn about the employees in your workplace? You take an interest in them. Ask them questions—first during their hiring interviews, then one-on-one while they're on the job, then in performance reviews. Get to know them through questions of genuine inquiry and conversations in which you share viewpoints. Focus on learning what the person believes and values, and what ignites his or her passion. A Coach is an expert at asking questions that help the person being coached reach new insights and perspectives.

DeMonty's authenticity as a Coach stems from his principle of "you lead from being incredibly vulnerable." He talks about his past: he grew up in a rough part of town. His dad was a blue-collar worker who held down three jobs and who sacrificed a lot to help DeMonty achieve his success—DeMonty was the first member of his family to go to college. Now, he honors his dad's commitment to him, by himself helping others around him.

Because DeMonty never had a senior leader guide him as he was coming up through the ranks, he's determined to be that guide to others. "I work really hard to give all my people what I didn't have when I was just starting out." Everyone has his phone number; they know they can call him. When his people call, or drop by, each conversation provides DeMonty with knowledge of the personal values of the people he works with. He believes that having the constant conversations raises everyone to their best game.

Coaching Performance

Steve Reid, COO of Goldcorp, has one of the best strategic minds I know of. He demands a high standard of performance and expresses his expectations so that goals are clearly understood. He wants to grow every aspect of Goldcorp: reserves, margins, production, safety, partnerships and people—and he makes sure each of his leaders is engaged in activities that foster such growth, all at the same time.

Steve's organization wants to perform well for him because he created high-quality relationships with each member of his team as he created high standards. His approach was, when first on the job, to work with the team to create a simplified way of measuring success. He realized if he could get the organization to focus on the things that were most important, he could unleash the full potential of Goldcorp. He also realized that this principle applied to himself. When Steve began, Goldcorp produced over 250 reports on safety each month. Safety is an important value in the mining industry and no one takes it more seriously than Steve. But while a huge amount of effort went into generating these safety reports, over 95% of the information was not being used. He coached his people into making sure the reports had value and relevance. Soon Goldcorp had reduced the 250 reports down to two. Two meaningful reports. The statistics they provided were useful to everyone and helped create a higher standard for safety in the organization while eliminating work that added no value. Through Steve's coaching, he was able to move the organization to focus on what was important and eliminate busy work. By coaching others, he also increased the level of trust the team had in his leadership.

Coaches Coaching Others

Todd Piece is an excellent Coach. While he has run large Information Technology organizations for both Genentech and Salesforce.com, his educational background is in social services and health policy. It is a powerful combination when someone has both great people skills and expertise in data processing. Part of the reason for Todd's success is that he consistently pushes the envelope to get his teams to rise to the next level of performance. Todd uses his background, his understanding of people and his coaching expertise in strategizing about how he can influence large groups of people in ways that are sustainable. Like many great coaches he has put together a philosophy for unleashing the full potential in others. In his Personal Excellence Program (PEP) deployed at Genentech he outlined a series of principles:

- Training and development is often approached as an event, rather than a process. But sustained development requires engagement over time.

- A lot of training and development is about transferring content, models, ideas, and information. It focuses on people only from the neck up. But lasting growth and change requires focusing on the whole person—head, heart, and body.

- Attending a class, reading a book, or getting online training is useful, but limited. People grow best in community. There's an exponential impact when people have an opportunity to grow and learn with and from one another.

He used these principles to create the PEP development process that included three large group workshops, individual coaching sessions and monthly peer coaching. The heart of the program centered around facilitated small group discussions where participants shared honestly with one another. The quality of the relationships developed in the group allowed them to support one another in sticking with the key goals they went into the program to develop. When the small groups received coaching from their peers each person in the group grew from those insights.

Understanding the value of data, Todd measured the results of the program. The success was evident in the numbers, with the results showing a 50% percent improvement in employee communication, collaboration, conflict management and coaching; and a 77% reported "significant measurable business impact" as a result of not only being coached but being coached while in a learning community of peers. Todd was not only able to have his team grow, he also had them supporting each other in growing - in essence he created a sustainable coaching culture.

COACHING TECHNIQUE: STORYTELLING

Those who you lead need to hear from you directly, consistently, and often. They need to know what it takes to succeed. They need to hear about the organization's history and values. You can communicate all this to them through stories. Storytelling is one of the most powerful coaching tools in your leadership toolkit.

Smart leaders periodically gather their "tribe" around the corporate campfire to recall the legends and share new tales. By touching the hearts as well as the minds of their employees, they create a legacy of experience that inspires others to generate certain behaviors.

Your values reside in such stories. Stories, of course, are more memorable than facts and figures because stories reach the heart as well as the mind. Stories have long been the glue connecting people with their cultures and with one another, to the point that some social scientists say that humans are hardwired for storytelling.

DeMonty Price, at Restoration Hardware, again wisely advises, "tell stories all the time." In DeMonty's own stories, he talks more about his failures than his successes. He has two reasons for this: to teach people, so they don't make the same mistakes he made, and because stories about mistakes "humanize you. You don't get trust and respect by being the boss. You get it by earning it, and you get it by being open, honest, and transparent."

As a leader, the best stories you can tell are stories that:

- Strengthen your culture.
- Get to the point fast. They are easy for people to remember.
- Are relevant to the listener, have a point and make an emotional impact.
- Teach by showing how to behave or solve a problem, or by explaining why something happened the way it did.

Stories are about people, their relationships, their challenges, and their values.

The Learn-from-My-Mistake Story

DeMonty Price uses this story to convey his approach to work-life balance: "Once in my career I opened an athletic shoe store. I didn't spend time with my twin baby girls and my wife worked to support us and I ended up reversing the order where work came first. The business failed. I didn't have enough experience or money and the location was wrong. What I learned from that is I always treat the business people and assets as if they were my own. I also learned if my home life is not solid, it translates into poor business decisions." Through the telling of stories, DeMonty can coach his team. He can share his life experiences in the growth of others.

The Allegory

Steve Jobs felt that Apple's success at integrating different technologies is the result of deep collaboration between all relevant departments. He made his point in a *Time Magazine* article through an allegory. "In a car show you see the concept car, and it's really cool, and then four years later you see the production car, and it sucks. And you go, 'what happened? They had it! They had it in the palm of their hands! They grabbed defeat from the jaws of victory!' What happened was, the designers came up with this really great idea. Then they take it to the engineers, and the engineers go, 'nah, we can't do that. That's impossible.' And so it gets a lot worse. Then they take it to the manufacturing people, and they go, 'We can't build that!' And it gets a lot worse." He was contrasting the concept car building process to how they build products at Apple through deep collaboration and partnering. Notice how quickly he conveyed his idea through this story.

The Corporate History Tale

Nike was founded more than 40 years ago, but their executives still enjoy telling this story about the late co-founder, Bill Bowerman. Bowerman, then the track coach at University of Oregon, was eating waffles one morning when he was inspired to pour latex on his wife's waffle iron. That impulsive act led to the development of Nike's famed waffle-soled running shoes. This story still ensures that Nike employees understand the company's heritage and philosophy.

The Formal Presentation—It's Still a Story

Southwest Airlines has a structured forum to introduce new employees to its corporate culture. It's called "LUV at First Bite," because it's a luncheon at which new employees are invited to sit down with senior leaders. The new people hear stories about the culture of Southwest Airlines. The senior executives at Southwest know that employees need more than lofty mission statements and industry buzzwords. To understand and appreciate what their organization stands for, workers need to hear about its people, its values, and its history through stories.

The Advocacy Story

Restoration Hardware systematically tells stories about employee "heroes" who fulfill the company's promise of outstanding service. Current Restoration Hardware COO Ken Dunaj tells a story about the shipping department manager at their main distribution center. There came a time when he was not happy with how the trucks were being unloaded and loaded. He decided to move his desk, phone, and computer out to the actual loading ramp. With every truck that came in or went out, he was right there moving the product around with his team until his standards for quality were established. He stayed out on the loading dock, both loading and unloading the product with care and precision. He was both showing the way and teaching others until he saw that the new behaviors were successfully implemented by the team.

Advocacy stories help you celebrate your corporate heroes while also motivating others to emulate them. You see at least one advocacy story every year during the State of the Union address, when the President tells a story of a challenge a particular American met or exemplifies, and then introduces the "hero," who is sitting in the gallery. These stories are designed to capture the heart, to be easy to remember, and to be close enough to our everyday lives that we can put the moral into practice.

Have Ten Core Stories

Do you have ten core coaching stories ready to go? For instance, what is the core story of your organization? Of your team? Of your leadership? Have at least ten.

Do you have a story that reflects your attitude toward leadership? About being Visionary? Around being a Catalyst? About being a Coach? How about stories about the pitfalls of drama?

If you aren't prepared to tell these stories, now is the time to get prepared.

If you have these stories, how frequently and how effectively are you telling them? Are you choosing them or modifying them appropriately for your audience? People born in the 1940s and people born in the 1980s will react differently to your "I remember JFK" story and your Vince Lombardi quotes. Make your stories relevant for your audience. Think about the impact you are looking to create. What results are you seeing from the stories you tell? What results do you want? Use your stories to create a culture of leadership around you.

TURN COMPLAINTS INTO COMMITMENTS

Great coaches turn a complainer into someone ready to take action. Complaining seems to be always in style. People spend vast amounts of time complaining. This includes gossip, covert conversations, and casting blame without taking responsibility. Some corporate cultures—the ones with lots of drama—are biased to allow complaining. Unaddressed, such complaints breed and fester without being addressed and solved.

Even in great organizations, you'll hear complaining. As Coach, you need to get the complainer to make a commitment to change. When anyone comes to you with a complaint, listen for the commitment inside of the complaint. Identifying the problem beneath griping takes real talent. It takes lemons-into-lemonade thinking. If you develop the ability to examine the complaint, you can open up the capacity to discover new opportunities and create change. It is a core skill of all great coaches.

Dig into the Complaint

Every complaint is about an issue or value that is being stepped on. At its core, the complaint speaks about something a person wants to have. Their complaints camouflage a deeper underlying need. They are clumsily expressing what they want to see changed.

- Someone complains about his adversarial manager. He might want a more open, flexible relationship with his boss, in which they can discuss issues freely.

- Someone complains about the antiquated equipment with which she's expected to work—maybe it's her computer, maybe it's her delivery truck. She might be committed to doing her very best, and want the right tools to achieve this goal. She might want her manager to recognize this and either give her the tools, or assure her that the results she's achieving with poor equipment are understood and accepted.

When you are the one hearing the complaint, it's easy to become defensive or reactive. But then you might fail to grasp the real opportunity and miss the chance to respond as a Leader.

For you to help the other person, you need to first shift how you are listening and hearing them. This is known as reframing. The first frame of the complaint is in the way the person presents it. You can "reframe" by giving your understanding of the complaint and then by asking questions that get to the underlying issues. Your first reframing can be to tell the person with the complaint, "I appreciate, Donna, that you care enough to bring this up and to invest time, energy, and effort in getting something fixed."

When team members bring up complaints, they are investing themselves in identifying flaws with processes, products, or communication. Their very willingness to complain stems from their belief that you want to know about the problem and fix it. (In fact, beware of the team members who never complain and never suggest improvements. They may be stuck in the Drama Triangle and suffering from resignation, as we covered in chapter 8. When such people do complain, it's the covert, gossiping, disruptive form of complaining.)

You can coach the team members who are committed enough to give you feedback, even if their comments feel negative. Perhaps the person is frustrated and does not have an elegant way of asking for something. Make sure she knows you understand the problem and how the situation is not up to her expectations. Learn to listen for her unspoken requests or needs so you can bring them into the open and discuss them.

When this team member has her issues addressed, she will not only learn to solve her own problems, she'll learn to bring suggestions and opportunities to you for your assistance. She'll also become one of your strongest advocates.

Handling the Compliant

When your team member comes to you with a complaint:

- Listen beyond the words for the request.
- Look for underlying commitment.
- Determine what the person is asking for and what you can provide.

1. Listen beyond the words.

Listen to the concern and empathize with the emotion behind the concern. Verify your understanding of the issue by asking, "How is this a concern?"

Peel the issue a layer at a time, continuing to ask questions like: "...and how is that an issue?" or "hmmm...so the problem there is...?" (Be sure your tone of voice is one of genuine inquiry, not challenging or defensive.) Each time you ask a question about the complaint, you are getting to the core value or issue that is at the root of the complaint.

Listening to the person helps him as well. Many people don't know what their real complaint is, so you can help them move and get to the root issue by asking questions.

2. Look for commitment.

Once you both agree that you have the real complaint identified, ask "what would you rather have?"

While it is a simple question, it shifts the other person's thinking. As you continue your discussion, find out what she is committed to having. You could ask: "what would having that do for you?" or "what would that allow you to accomplish?"

As you can see, these questions move the discussion from complaint to commitment, from issue to outcome, from the present situation to a desired future. Once someone is thinking about what she wants, she'll move forward, leaving the complaint behind.

3. Determine what the person is asking for and what you can provide.

As your conversation proceeds, you'll find the point where you're ready to get some realistic options on how to make the change. Asking such questions as, "can we take a look at this together to find out what we can do to solve it?" or, "do you have a request for me about helping to resolve this?" will help you get to the decision-making point.

Remember, you can always say "no" or negotiate their request. You'll find, though, that when you coach the person to change perspective and view themselves as problem-solvers, not complainers, they can find solutions to their own problems.

We can use complaining as a coaching opportunity for positive change and positive action in our own lives, at work, and in the world. The key is to turn complaints into commitments.

USE WORDS WISELY

Language matters when you are coaching someone. The words you choose when asking your questions are as important as the questions themselves. So is tone of voice. When expressing your ideas, choose your words wisely.

Why You Shouldn't Say "Why"

When you are coaching someone, avoid the query "why." It sounds judgmental. Consider your boss asking you:

- Why did you do it that way?
- Why did you think that was a good strategy?
- Why did you send that email?

Did you feel a visceral reaction just reading those questions? Very few people can pose such questions in a tone of voice that sounds curious and inquiring rather than accusatory.

Nine times out of ten, when asked "why", a person starts to defend himself. Think back: the first person to ask you "why did you…?" was mostly likely a parent, and you'd just drawn a Crayola mural on the wall or kicked your sister. Even as adults, when most people hear "why"—especially from authority—their inner two-year-old emerges, ready to proclaim innocence or at least extenuating circumstances.

Two quick caveats: 1. You can ask yourself the question: "why did I…?" Sometimes that's helpful. 2. In scientific endeavors, "why" is a critical part of the process. Asking why an experiment failed is, however, different than asking why someone did something.

Use instead "what" and "how" questions, such as:

- What happened?
- What was your thinking behind this strategy?
- How did that help? How did that change things?
- How would you approach it next time?
- What can you learn from this?

- What do you really want in this situation?
- How did this impact you?

The questions feel different, don't they? They are looking for a different quality of information. They invite discussion, not justification.

People are more likely to answer "what" and "how" questions, so you get information rather than power struggles. With higher quality information, you can build a better solution for how to take action and move forward.

You might not be aware of how frequently you use "why" when speaking with others. Listen for it in yourself. Give trusted colleagues permission to point it out to you. If you catch yourself about to ask "why", make a different choice. If you hear "why" come out of your mouth, briefly apologize and ask a better question. Also, notice the reactions you get if you ask "why".

You are much more likely to ask "why" when you are in the Drama Triangle (because there, you are more likely to be judgmental). Asking "what" and "how" questions is a good indicator that you're asking from within the Leadership Triangle.

Good Advice but...

"But" is another word that gets in the way of good coaching. Imagine you are coaching a team member and he or she says to you:

- "I really appreciate your coaching, but… "
- "That's a great idea you have, but…"
- "You did a fantastic job with this, but…"

What happens when you hear the word "but"? Most of us decide that everything that went before the "but" is irrelevant—the real opinion is what is said after "but."

Imagine what "but" does when you say it to someone you are coaching. Because it negates whatever precedes it, the person you're talking with will give more attention and more value to what you say after you say "but."

Often we'll say "but" at the end of a compliment. No matter how sincere your compliment, once you stick "but" on the end of it, the hearer forgets the compliment—or, worse, thinks you didn't really mean it.

"However" is nothing more than a dressed-up "but." "However" and "but" are essentially the same word when you're coaching someone.

If you are using "but" at the office, I guarantee you're using it with friends and family. I've heard people try to compliment friends, spouses, and children, then sabotage the effect by adding "but." As I mentioned with the overuse of "why," you might be unaware of how frequently you use "but." Listen for it in yourself and give a trusted colleague permission to point it out to you.

Two Strategies to Rid Your Speech of "But"

1. **Replace "but " with "and".**

   The word "and" creates an inclusion of both parts of the sentence.

   So, instead of saying: "I like your strategy, but it would put us over budget for this year."

Say instead: "I like your strategy and it would put us over budget for this year."

2. **Start a new sentence.**

    You don't need to insert either the conjunction "but" or "and." Insert a period. Give the compliment as an independent sentence. Give the concern as a second, independent sentence.

    "I like your strategy. It would put us over budget for this year."

The use of "and" or separate sentences will make your coaching sound more elegant. Your hearer will be less likely to resist what you are saying, as they will not feel judged and defensive.

You might need practice to change your speech habits. The more you practice, the more you will be aware of your language and the more effective you will be. Put it into action. As you shift your thinking, you'll shift your behavior, which will make you a more effective Coach. One of the easiest behaviors to be aware of is the choice of language you are using. It will give you a direct insight into how you are thinking.

YOU CAN CHANGE

Of course, the word "Coach" brings to mind sports. You can find a wealth of excellent advice from great team coaches, and their words are often applicable to our professional lives:

> "I think what coaching is all about, is taking players and analyzing their ability, and putting them in a position where they can excel within the framework of the team winning."
> —Don Shula, Football Coach

"Most people get excited about games, but I've got to be excited about practice, because that's my classroom."
—Pat Summitt, Basketball Coach

"Coaches who can outline plays on a black board are a dime a dozen. The coaches who win are the ones who can motivate their players."—Vince Lombardi, Football Coach

"A coach is someone who can give correction without causing resentment." —John Wooden, Basketball Coach

Practicing to be a great Coach will only make you understand yourself more. A great Coach must first have great self-awareness. Listen to what you say and how you communicate, and you will grow in your ability to help others. These valuable tools will serve you well: you'll develop a foundation from which you share your point of view, and your team and colleagues will know you listen and work hard to understand their points of view. Coaching is about growing yourself first and from the insights you gain from your own growth you will be able to share your wisdom with others.

CHAPTER 12

Leadership is a Choice

YOU ARE RESPONSIBLE for everything that happens to you. You may be challenged by this concept yet the essence of leadership is to act as if you are responsible. You may not generate everything that happens to you—say, for example, the earthquake that shakes your house and breaks the windows—but you do have to live with the outcome. You can't accurately determine what percentage of life is your responsibility, but since you are affected by everything that happens to you, the best strategy is to live as though you are responsible for everything. By taking personal ownership, you gain the leverage and the energy to create what you want in your life.

Leadership requires you to make choices and take an active role in events. If you want things to turn out in a particular way, you will want to be taking responsibility to make sure they do turn out that way. In doing so, you are saying, "I am capable and willing to address this situation." When you take responsibility, you gain the tremendous influence that comes with actively shaping the future.

Conversely, when you avoid responsibility and place the blame on other parties, you are effectively stating, "Others created this situation. Clearly others are the ones with the ability to effect change, and I'm waiting for someone else to get it done." Then you wait. Maybe nothing gets done. Maybe it gets done in ways that displease or inconvenience you. But you're in no position to complain. You made the choice to let others choose for you.

IT'S ALL ABOUT CHOICES

How much of what you do is your own choice, and how much comes from your acceptance of the "choices" dictated by society's norms or the current culture?

Think about your own life and how much of it you are actually choosing. If we look at society's values today, how many of those values did you choose and how many were installed? How much of what each of us actually believes is nothing less than the socialization of behaviors from our particular existing external environment?

For instance—

- Where do you live?
- How close, or far, is it from where your parents lived when they were your age?
- What college, if any, did you attend? What colleges did your parents go to?
- Is your career in the same field as your parents?
- Is your political party different from your parents?
- Are your religious beliefs different from those of your family?

It's one thing to have attended the same alma mater as your dad. It's something else to have attended it because your dad went there.

It's one thing to vote either Democrat or Republican or whatever—it's another thing to vote that ticket because you always have, or because everyone else you know does. Who's making your choices for you? The answer should be, "you are."

We adopt the norms of the culture we are in. Looking at those norms to discover if you want them or not is a useful exercise in assessing your personal choices.

When you think of society as a whole, how do you know that people born and raised in the suburbs of Dallas have similar habits, attitudes, and viewpoints compared to the habits and attitudes of, say, the Mayoruna tribe along the Amazon in Brazil? Consider how those Mayoruna would define "well dressed," and how the folks in Dallas would define it. Yet, even though you might spend time thinking about what clothes to wear, if you grew up in Dallas, you don't really think about whether to wear clothes or not, as they do in the Amazon jungle.

Examine the beliefs you hold to discover if they are truly yours or if they are beliefs you adopted based on someone else's example, guidance, or even insistence. Some of your beliefs are values and attitudes you actively, personally chose, but some were embedded from your environment. As you notice them, decide if they are truly yours. If they aren't, make the conscious choice to either keep your belief or actively set out to change your belief.

Examine what you believe about your religion, your political stance, about family, about education, about relationships. You can examine what you believe about global warming or climate change. What do you believe about raising children, leading others, or health care? What do you believe about foreign aid or welfare support? Make sure what you believe is representative of your choices today based on what you have experienced and examined in life. Then you will be able to understand the opinions of others, because you have thoroughly examined your own.

Experience Choice

Lansing Barrett Grisham is the creator of *Integrated Awareness*®, a discipline that incorporates a number of different modalities of healing, wellness, and personal growth. At one of Lansing's workshops, he gave us the best description on choice I've ever heard: "the soul's primary reason to incarnate is to experience choice."

Further, he explained that all the great religious traditions of the world have some "concept of unity." For some, that's heaven or being with the divine, or being one with all. Lansing says, "The idea behind unity is that there is no separation or difference between beings since we are all connected." He went on to explain "right now, we are all obviously separate. I am over here and you are over there, and we experience ourselves as different and separate." And then he asked the question, "What do you get with separation?" The answer is that you get the ability to choose. He brings this logic to its obvious conclusion by saying, "Our specific function here on this planet is to choose and therefore not choosing is in direct opposition to your spirit, your growth and your learning."

Lansing teaches that the act of choosing is a personal growth path. By avoiding choosing, a person makes sure to not learn what he or she needs to learn.

I hope you will discover, as I have, that when you make a conscious effort to examine the choices you are currently making, you will begin to lead a much more productive and happy life.

Read All About It

Books abound about decision making or making a choice—they fill shelves at bookstores and libraries. Many of my favorites present the latest neurological research on choice and decision-making, such as:

How We Decide by Jonah Lehrer

Proust Was a Neuroscientist by Jonah Lehrer

Blink: The Power of Thinking Without Thinking by Malcolm Gladwell

Think!: Why Crucial Decisions Can't Be Made in the Blink of an Eye by Michael R. LeGault

Buyology: Truth and Lies About Why We Buy by Martin Lindstrom

Neuromarketing: Understanding the Buy Buttons in Your Customer's Brain by Patrick Renvoise and Christophe Morin

Why Choose This Book?: How We Make Decisions by Read Montague

These authors have all done excellent jobs at explaining brain function and behavior, to give us a fresh understanding of the latest research behind choice and making decisions. Books that give you that sort information are well worth reading.

But after reading them, you might find yourself asking, "So now what…? How do I go about making more choices in my life?" I wrote *Save Your Drama for Your Mama* for that purpose, to help motivate you to activate your own ability to choose.

Should Do, Must Do, Have To?

Leadership at its most basic level is found in your ability to choose, to be clear about your intentions and actions. Leadership is a choice and must emanate from within you—whether you are the leader of a nation, a company, a softball team, or no one but yourself. When you lead, you free yourself from being a slave of circumstances. The subsequent power you receive from your choices enhances your ability to create, actively join with others, develop new ideas, and generate value for society and yourself.

Think about the rules you follow. Ever notice how having to do something feels much different than getting to choose to do something?

If you examine all of your should do's, must do's, and have to's, you will discover rules that may or may not be either accurate or useful to your current life. Many of us follow rules that came out of our experience or were dictated to us by people in authority. You might still be following a rule that was valid for you two decades ago, but isn't any longer. You may be following a rule you adopted in childhood that is no longer relevant. Choose today to choose again!

Rules can trap us in our own thoughts and keep us from exercising the ability to choose. If you speak as if you were a slave to your job, if you feel burdened by your life's responsibilities, if you feel as if you cannot create something meaningful because you do not have the time or resources, you will feel trapped. You will believe that, unless you are operating under a perfect set of circumstances, you will not be able to create the life you want. That kind of thinking will limit your choices. Leadership at its most basic level is found in your ability to intentionally choose. This is the practiced discipline of leading yourself to conscious choice. Leadership is a choice and must emanate from within, and in doing so, you free yourself from being a slave of the environment or your situation.

On my wedding day, I said "I do" to my wife, and with that vow I made a commitment. If I have to be married today because I once said "yes" during my marriage vows, I will feel resigned and my behaviors will invariably be worse than if I were to make the choice, today, to be married. When I wake up and choose to be married to my wife each day, it is a very different experience for me than having to be married because of a choice I made years ago. When you choose to do something today, you will find yourself more engaged and energetic. Leadership at its most fundamental level is about generating more energy. You get more energy when you make a choice.

Think about your work. If you were to use the phrase, "I have to go to work in the morning," I would challenge your thinking and ask, "do you?" Sure, there would be consequences if you failed to report to work, but you really do not *have* to go to work. When you have to do something, you give up your power. Even using the statement out loud or to yourself, "I have to" will drain your energy. The function of external rules is to restrict the number of conscious choices you make. Beware dictating to yourself an arbitrary list of rules. By following them, you abdicate choice, which means you abdicate potentially your power and your freedom. You will not be able to lead.

When you do not make a choice, it is usually because you are not clear about what you want to create. For example, you may not have a vision for your next career move. If you have not developed a vision for yourself, or if you are not sure what impact you want to create, it will be harder for you to make informed choices. Do you think about your life as a series of events that happen to you or a series of events that are generated by you? If you have not planned where you want to go, then you might end up somewhere you would not want to be.

Sometimes you may get stuck deciding which action you should choose in moving forward. Should I stay in my current job or do something new? Should I change my team or not? Should I have a conversation or avoid it? These are some of the traps of inaction.

Fear is another major trap to inaction. When you are conflicted about what choice to make, consider whether you are making a decision based on a fear. If your decision is based on an irrational fear, you risk taking an action that is not the best. When you can't make a choice, it's time to look at what you are afraid of. Are you afraid of looking bad, of someone else being sad or disappointed? Are you afraid of failure? Discover which fear is stalling you. Try this tactic: name the fear and step into the feeling of it. See if it is serving you or not. Stepping into the fear allows you to "get to know it," rather than hiding from it. You might overcome it entirely, or you might change your relationship with the fear, but embracing it will help you make better decisions. Moving into the fear is the quickest way to mitigate its negative effects.

I had a fear of heights. I have no idea where this fear came from. As a child I was afraid to climb up in a tree. I could watch a television show of a mountain climber and quickly have sweaty palms even though I was sitting comfortably in my living room. In personally challenging that fear I had to move into it. I started out visiting climbing walls until I felt comfortable enough with being high off the ground. After a little rock climbing to test myself I moved into more extreme sports that pushed me way beyond my fear of heights. A useful saying for me was "if I can't do something then I must do it". I used this phrase as a way to build more and more capabilities, stepping in and exploring any of my fears. By examining my fears I was able to see if they were helping or hindering me. Most were not helpful and with each one that I eliminated it helped me in moving past others. Each fear I have examined and worked through has allowed me a lot more choices in my life.

The Power of Choice

Making choices from an internal locus of control and based on your personal values doesn't guarantee a trouble-free, easy path in life. Yet it can mean…

- Better health and a longer life.
- Better parenting style, so you will bring up the next generation to be values-driven and equipped to make their own quality choices.
- The ability to motivate yourself and increase your ability to motivate others.

More Choice = More Life

Having more choice in your life allows you to live longer. Ellen Langer, Harvard's first tenured female professor of psychology, is an innovate thinker in the field of understanding the way our thoughts directly impact our physiology.

Dr. Langer designed research to determine the power that choice has on health and well-being. One of her studies showed that residents in nursing homes lived longer if they were given more control over their lives. Participants at the Arden House nursing home, all of similar physical and psychological health and from similar backgrounds, were divided into two groups. One group had more authority to make decisions about their own lives. The other group was encouraged to rely on others to make decisions for them.

The "choosers" had the responsibility of caring for themselves and choosing how they should spend their time:

- They could decide how they wanted their rooms arranged.
- They could select and schedule a movie to watch.
- They could schedule when they wanted visitors.
- They were given a plant and expected to tend it.
- They were asked to give feedback on what they liked and did not like about the facility.

The "rely-ers" were given the message that they could rely on others, who would make all of their decisions for them. They were never denied a choice, if they expressed one. They were not encouraged to make choices. The message was, "we will do it all for you."

- They were told Arden House would take full responsibility to provide a place for them to be happy. (And Arden House did give them thoughtful, appropriate care.)
- The staff chose and scheduled movies for them to enjoy.
- The nurses took care of them based on the staff's perceptions of their needs.
- They were given a plant which a staff member tended.

After one and a half years, the researchers discovered that residents with more freedom were happier, active, and more alert as compared to the other group. The most impressive metric was that many more of them were still alive.

Langer showed when people are given a greater sense of choice and personal accountability, their lives and attitudes improve. We live longer when we have the power to choose. When people give up their ability to choose, their quality of life deteriorates. With choosing, they became more mindful, which kept them engaged with the world and living their lives more fully. Loss of personal responsibility for our lives leaves us less happy and less healthy.

A part of Langer's conclusion was, "whenever you're making a choice, you have to notice things, and that makes us engage."

Many studies since this original 1976 experiment support the need for personal choice as we get older. As a result of this study, many care facilities provide more choice for people in their care.

Rule-Based vs. Choice-Based Parenting

Active involvement in making choices in your life isn't to be restricted to older individuals. My wife and I know that allowing our children to make their own choices now takes more effort as parents. Sometimes I just want to set the rule and force them to do things, but in doing so I remove their ability to learn from their own decisions. The more practice they have making decisions, now, in a safe environment, will allow them to make better decisions later in life. If I shield them from the consequences of their choices, I remove their ability to learn. Then I am doing them a disservice as a parent.

Parents who realize providing the power of choice in how they raise their children will create a better environment for their children to discover their own values. Learning how to choose is a skill set that will help them through adolescence and into adulthood.

Parenting by the Rules

A rule-based parent says, "do it or else," or "be quiet or I am going to punish you" or "if you don't clean your room, you won't get any dessert."

When the child breaks the rule, you dish out the punishment to the child.

A rule-based parent is rewarding the child for complying with external controls. The child learns to be a rule-follower. He'll continue, as a teen and adult, to look to external controls to guide his behaviors and tell him what's the "right" thing to do. He'll either follow the rules or break them (and maybe feel guilty for doing so). He doesn't know how to choose for himself, because he's never learned how. He was taught to listen to Mom and Dad and to adhere to their values, so he has no idea how to listen to himself or determine his own values. He will need the external environment to tell him the right thing to do. When you teach your children to only listen to you, then that is all they will have later in life. They will not know to listen to themselves or to their own values. This kind of thinking makes it much harder for any kind of leadership capability to develop.

You've got a Choice

Choice-oriented parents coach their child to help her discover her own reasons for doing something. Rather than pronounce a rule, they explain the pros and cons of both sides of a decision. They assist the child in developing her own barometer of right and wrong.

The child's abilities, and safety, are always factors. When crossing the street, I removed my children's choice—they had to hold my hand. Most children don't choose to get a flu shot or visit the dentist. The parents are responsible for those choices. But even very young children can make good personal choices in many situations.

Choice-oriented parents acknowledge their children for what they have done well. They help the child explore her feelings and discover the reasons for the choices she is making. These parents are comfortable having their child discover what happens when she makes poor choices. Spent your allowance already? No, you cannot have another $10 for a computer game. There is enormous lifelong value in encouraging the child to learn how to choose for herself. They learn to trust themselves, to understand their values, and to accept responsibility even if things go wrong.

It requires more time and more effort between the parenting partners to raise a child this way. Parents who use a choice-oriented approach to raising children are preparing them to be our future leaders.

If Things Were Better, I Could ...

Have you ever said to yourself, "if only I had a promotion, then I could really make a difference," or "if I could save twice as much money, then I could really do what I want to do?" Don't wait for outside conditions to change. It's a long, long wait.

A true Leader is not dependent on outside conditions. In fact, requiring a perfect set of circumstances is not a hallmark of leadership. True leadership lies within. Until you tap into your own leadership potential, until you move your locus of control internally, you will be at the mercy of your external environment.

There has been no more challenging a place to practice personal choice than in a Nazi concentration camp. Viktor Frankl, Austrian neurologist and psychiatrist, was interred in various concentration camps from 1942-1945. He experienced unimaginable terrors and hardships, including the loss of his wife. In the most harrowing of circumstances, Frankel was able to exercise choice in his own mind. It was this ability that allowed him to structure experiences in his mind so that he could keep his humanness and his humanity. In "Man's Search for Meaning," he talks about the understanding that came to him in Auschwitz:

> Then I grasped the meaning of the greatest secret that human poetry and human thought and belief have to impart: The salvation of man is through love and in love. I understood how a man who has nothing left in this world still may know bliss, be it only for a brief moment, in the con-

templation of his beloved. In a position of utter desolation, when man cannot express himself in positive action, when his only achievement may consist in enduring his sufferings in the right way—an honorable way—in such a position man can, through loving contemplation of the image he carries of his beloved, achieve fulfillment.

You, like Frankl, are always free to choose your perspective at any moment in time and some moments will impact your life in fundamental ways.

How To Bring More Choice Into Your Life

1. **Acknowledge that you can.** Easier said than done, I know. But the more often you acknowledge to yourself that you have ideas, opinions and goals, the more conviction you will develop about them, and the more choices you will make to bring them to fruition in your life.

2. **Decide which "rules" you choose to follow**. Make a list of the rules you follow—and see which ones are really a choice, not a "have to." Which are unhelpful or someone else's idea of how you should behave? Guide yourself by choices, as opposed to following a rule, and you'll bring more power and flexibility to your life.

3. **When you face a problem, examine it before acting.** Look at the issue from your perspective, the other person's perspective, and from the perspective of an outside observer. Think about the issue from the past (its evolution), the present (its current impact), and in the future (as if it were resolved). As you do this examination, you will shift your thinking through multiple areas of the brain, cognitively

integrating the information, allowing you to choose a solution in congruence with your values.

4. **If you are stuck, reach out for help.** Find someone who can coach you through the impasse. Others may see your blind spot and be able to provide you with the action steps to move forward. Often, talking over a choice with a trusted friend or colleague brings clarity you can't find when thinking about it alone. Two heads can be better than one. It's a little like parallel processing for creating a clear direction for what you need to choose.

5. **Be accountable.** Taking responsibility for a situation helps create a deeper understanding of that situation and its ramification. When you understand—and embrace—your accountability, the correct choice becomes more obvious.

6. **Ask, "What would making this choice do for me?"** Ask this question over and over, to each answer that emerges, to get to the underlying values driving your choice. The expression of values will help motivate you to action.

7. **Spend time considering your vision.** Write it down. Keep a journal. Do it daily. The more clarity you have about where you want to go, the easier it will be for you to make choices that take you in the direction of that vision.

8. **Notice the energy you get when you make a choice.** Every leader has an energy about him or her. It is how he or she influences others. Eliminate "I have to" from your vocabulary. Replace it with "I choose to." If you practice making more choices you will increase your personal energy. Build yours so your impact will be greater.

Genuine Leadership Comes From Within

You must be true to yourself by exploring your own motivations, gathering feedback on your personal behavior, and ensuring that your actions are consistent with your stated values and principles. This can be done by carefully examining the choices that you make. For example, take the time to pause and ask yourself, "am I on automatic pilot here, or did I choose this path?"

It is our choice to participate or not. If we assume others are responsible and we are just spectators not choosing to be responsible, then these others might just lead us into a future that we do not want. It is always a choice to not be responsible, but we lose the power to make a difference when we give up our birthright to choose. You get to choose your response at any moment in time. Positive intentions take you up into the Leadership Triangle. Negative intentions drag you down. Boldness and choosing to act create results. Shifting from drama to leadership pays off with big dividends.

The true definition of leadership is in its ability to generate more energy both for you the leader and the people you lead. The more you choose, the more energy you will generate. It is a practice, and practice requires self-discipline. My advice to you is to become a student of leadership. Study it, learn it, and master it. The world needs more leaders now more than ever.

Seeds to Plant

The concepts here in *Save Your Drama for Your Mama* are seeds for you to plant in your life, your team, and your community. Stored within these ideas is vast potential.

But—as Morpheus tells Neo in *The Matrix*—"There is a difference between knowing the path and walking the path." What good are seeds unless you prepare the soil, sow and tend the seeds, and feed the plants healthy food and water? Great concepts often lead to impassioned starts that fizzle in the middle. Become a student of leadership and keep learning, perpetually.

You will need to both learn and teach what you know as you continue to discover all the facets of leadership. The concepts in this book are good, solid ideas, but understanding the concepts is not enough. You must put them into action to realize the results. You have to put them into practice in your own life to create your full potential.

Make the Commitment

Football coach Vince Lombardi said, "The difference between a successful person and others is not a lack of strength, not a lack of knowledge, but rather in a lack of will."

Powerful concepts with consistent follow-through are a potent combination. Following through on this material will transform your leadership potential and change any organization you're part of. The catalyst of this synergistic combination is honoring a contract with yourself. The contract holds you to your word to see it through.

To become and remain a leader, make the commitment—a contract with yourself—to learn more about leadership. Be determined and exercise your willpower to bring the skills of Visionary, Catalyst, and Coach forward in your life.

- The world engages with determined people, with people who have a clear vision and commitment to accomplishing their goals.
- Following through has great power embedded in itself.
- Determination imparts to you a level of influence and personal power.

When you contract to create your vision, guided by your personal values, you take charge of running your own mind and your own life. You no longer are buffeted by the winds of fate. You realize that personal determination can move mountains, but luck and chance do not. The difference between "impossible" and "we did it!" lies in the ability to commit to it and to stay determined.

Determined people do not give up. They achieve what they want because they insist on doing rather than just trying. In "The Seven Habits of Highly Effective People," Stephen Covey states that making and keeping commitments is the foundation for attaining growth and effectiveness. He says that through "making promises, setting goals, and being true to them—we build the strength of character, the being, that makes possible every other positive thing in our lives."

Really Follow Through

There's a difference between making a choice and following through on it. Too often, choices and commitments are made in an offhanded manner, with no determination driving them.

- I've heard people say, enthusiastically, "I might put these ideas into action!" Might?

- I've known people to set a goal, but not a plan to execute steps to achieve the goal.
- And we've all heard—or said—"I'll try to get this done."

You cannot con yourself. Whenever you hedge your bet with language like this, your mind knows it. You send yourself the message that you do not believe you'll follow through. Your effectiveness decreases each time you make a fake commitment to yourself.

When you hedge your bets, you are telling yourself you probably won't achieve your goal, almost as permission to not try too hard, to not worry about the work it will take—because the work won't ever happen. But when you "go all in" on a commitment, you send yourself the message that this choice is important and this commitment matters.

There is a magic in being thoughtful about the commitments you make to both yourself and others. Become a student of leadership, live in the Leadership Triangle, and make a pact to grow your own leadership competency and those of the people around you.

Make a contract with yourself as it will help you to hold yourself accountable. And if you publicly declare it in conversation with others, you'll enlist their support also. When you commit yourself to any project, cause, or even a relationship, you become more of a leader. Leaders have vision. Leaders are Catalysts and leaders Coach others to be leaders.

YOU CAN CHANGE THE WORLD

Being a leader is the best way to keep yourself and your team out of the Drama Triangle. Just knowing the various roles and patterns associated with drama will help you stay out of the Drama Triangle, because you'll see it for what it is. And if you ever slip into the Drama Triangle, you'll recognize what's happened, the traps it brings with it, the energy it drains from you—and you will have the power to choose a path out.

By being determined, by being a leader, you stay out of the world of the Drama Triangle. When you are out of drama, so is the world around you. When you are in the Leadership Triangle, you can be a leader, and create more leaders, directly impacting the world around you. By remaining determined, you can make your choices count in ways that can change the world.

Acknowledgements

The concepts in this book are built upon the ideas of many great thinkers. The original idea for a Drama Triangle was pioneered by Stephen Karpman in his groundbreaking article, *Fairy Tales and Script Drama Analysis*. This book wouldn't have happened without his pioneering work. Julian B. Rotter developed the concept of Locus of Control, which refers to a person's belief about whether internal control or external control causes the results in their lives. The control theory of motivation was originally developed by William Glasser, and according to him, behavior exhibited by a person is not a response to external stimuli. Instead, he has proposed that all behavior is inspired for the most immediate and pressing needs and wants of an individual. Also considered is Robert Dilts' work on identity and the impact it has on someone's values and beliefs. I have undertaken to simplify and make accessible these concepts for a business audience, though families and other organizations have also found them useful.

My own thinking for this book has been expanded by many colleagues and the work they have done in researching human excellence: Allan Parker, Judith Deloizier, Lara Ewing Ember, Genie Laborde, John Grinder, Loretta Malandro, Jim Conlow,

Jennifer Buchanan, Victoria Blackstone, Michael Blackstone and Britt Ewing. The initial research into Leadership was done in partnership with Kelly Gerling in our work on the Deep Structure of Leadership taught at Rockhurst University. It has also been heavily influenced by my teachers: Bay Butler, Gene Albright, Brooke Kaye Albright, Lansing Barrett Grisham, and many others. The MCS consultants Zemo Travathan, Simon Lovegrove, Trish Barron, Judy Francolini, Simon D'Arcy, Renee Shea, and Art Giser have contributed greatly to the development of this book. Additionally, a team of MCS consultants and dear friends were in a consortium and they pioneered many of the concepts found in Chapter 7 addressing how to build the behaviors of Leaders, and so a special acknowledgement goes to Mary Boren, Mark Fourman and Charlotte Milliner for their insights and their support. Along the way both the research and the writing was enhanced by Felecia Chavez, Tom Hyma, Glenn Sullivan, Caitlin Ewing, and Kirsten Curtis. Lindsey Gower spent many hours editing these concepts, making them more accessible. An important acknowledgement goes to Jim Peal, whose collaboration helped influence this model in many fundamental ways. His work on having the real conversations is a critical component for demonstrating the behaviors of leadership. Additionally, each and every participant who has attended the Leadership is a Choice® seminar has directly influenced and refined this material. The book is also far more valuable because of the fantastic leaders who contributed their wisdom in interviews. Finally, I would like to acknowledge my wife Renee and children, Ethan and Nicole, who gave me the support through the long hours it took to capture these concepts in words and story.

Drama or Leadership
Multi Rater

Our Drama or Leadership Multi Rater tool makes it easy for you to complete a self-evaluation of your own levels of drama or leadership. This insight will further your learning of the Save Your Drama for Your Mama and Leadership is a Choice® material. You will discover what role you are most likely to go into if you enter the Drama Triangle. You will also discover what your strength is with regards to the Leadership Triangle. This tool will also show you the area where you could most improve your own capabilities inside of the Leadership Triangle. If you choose, you can then use this information to compare your self-perception of leadership and drama with the perceptions of others. A multi-rater assessment enables you to collect feedback from yourself *and* from those who work around you—such as managers, peers, direct reports, team-members, professors, clients, or even family members. The results are then rolled into personalized reports that enable you to see where you excel, and where you have room for improvement based on not only your own view but the perceptions of others. All of this is done confidentially and under your control. You will be the only individual that will have access to the results of this survey.

You can find your "single use" code on the front cover inside flap of this book. This code enables you to one usage of our Drama or Leadership Multi Rater tool. You will enter the code at www.achoice.com to complete the survey. The instructions are simple to follow and there is a Frequently Asked Questions section to further guide you if needed. Because this tool is provided as a free service with a copy of this book it does not come with live technical support. Please follow the instructions carefully as the code is only good for one application for you to receive your multi-perspective feedback of your level of drama and your level of leadership.

If you choose to invite other individuals to rate you, the system provides up to 20 invitations. You will need a minimum of three responses to see the results from the individuals you invited. Using these aggregated responses, the system creates a report that will only be shared with you. In this report, the response rates are provided, indicating the percentage of raters who have responded to the questionnaire. However, the identity of individual respondents is protected. No written comments will be allowed. After 30 days, if you do not receive a minimum of 3 responses, you will only have access to the self-rated report. The report will come to you via an email with an attached PDF file of your results. You will also have a year to access the report online. Please enter the individuals you are choosing to rate you carefully. If you enter an email address incorrectly and hit the submit button, you will not be able to be correct the submission. Part of the security of this system is neither the publisher or you will be able to modify or access this program outside of the parameters presented. We want to protect all participants in the confidentiality of their responses.

If you are invited to be a rater, please provide honest and constructive feedback to aid in your colleague's leadership development. Embrace this tool. Invites others to rate you. It is the fastest way for you to gain additional insights about your own leadership capabilities and how to take them to the next level.

Leadership is a Choice® Seminars

Learn how to raise your leadership competency
Become more intentional about your choices
Drive drama out of your team and organization

Our Leadership is a Choice® seminar will provide you with a high level of Dramamunity™ in your life, your team and your organization. Creating a leadership development approach that eliminates drama while it encourages learning is the primary task of our leadership model, and is perhaps the only way that a leader can genuinely influence or inspire others to achieve their own high level of leadership. The rate at which a team learns to lead together may be the only thing that will give them a sustainable, competitive advantage in the future.

When speaking of leadership, it is easiest to refer to those in obvious positions of authority. However, leadership is first about leading yourself. In truly successful organizations, all participants are leaders, regardless of their official title or role. Leadership, however, begins with a choice. Making the choice to be a leader—whether you're the CEO or just starting out —is what the Leadership is a Choice® model is all about.

Great teams occur where there is a team of leaders. A good team structure is one in which the elements "hang together" because they continually affect each other over time and operate toward a common purpose. We provide the Leadership is a Choice® seminar for individual contributors, for front line sales professionals and for all levels of management in an organization. When a leadership culture is adopted by every level of an organization the level of drama will drop rapidly and you will naturally get a higher level of engagement directly impacting performance.

To learn leadership, you need to learn its opposite. There are hundreds of courses out in the marketplace on leadership and most of them cover the basics well. Most leadership training, in telling you what it is, contrasts the concept of leadership with management. The question we researched was "how come these programs are so ineffective in creating new leaders or inspiring a shift in thinking?" What we discovered is, at the behavioral level, management is complementary to leadership, so contrasting the two makes learning about leadership more difficult to understand. As an organization that has researched leadership and its associated behaviors for 25 years, we have discovered you cannot learn leadership without first understanding its opposite: drama. Management is not the opposite of leadership, but drama is. Our team can directly aid you in helping your organization to become a drama-free zone. We will also help you unleash the full leadership potential of your team. The multi-rater Drama or Leadership survey will help your examine where you still have drama in your life. If you want help in changing yourself, your team, your organization we have a depth of experience in creating drama-free zones in all walks of life. We plant the seeds of leadership in your organization with a number of specific outcomes so drama won't have a place to propagate and fester in the minds of team members. We also will rapidly build your leadership competency at all levels of your organization.

This seminar is offered in half-day, full-day and two-day sessions. We also have a Leadership is a Choice® Mastery program which is 3 two day classes and a year long curriculum. It is also offered as a keynote. Either one of our highly trained and certified consultants can deliver these programs in-house or you can inquire about certification for your own trainers. We also offer the training using the KnoNow social e-learning platform. Contact us at 415-482-1100 for more information.

KnoNow Learning Platform

The Leadership is a Choice® seminar is a way to eliminate drama and create what we call Dramamunity™ in your life your team and your organization. This seminar is supported through online learning with the KnoNow social learning community platform. The reason we built Leadership is a Choice® on KnoNow is to replicate the classroom learning experience online. Think of any seminar you have attended. While the stories and lectures may have been interesting, it was through the experiential learning that you gained new insights. These insights were expanded and enhanced by the discussions you had with your team members after the learning event. KnoNow takes all the best aspects of experiential training and combines it with a learning community to create real knowledge transfer. This approach replicates what is best about attending a seminar and putting it into an online experience. The KnoNow approach is a cloud-based secure environment for delivering The Leadership is a Choice® seminar to your organization as you build an engaging learning community around these concepts.

What is different about KnoNow?

The other learning management system vendors focus on three things:

- Re-creating classroom presentations online. *(It was boring in college, and it's going to be even more boring online.)*

- Testing and evaluation in an outdated quiz and marking system. *(This may be appropriate for things like compliance training but it's ineffective for changing behaviors in real life, and even less effective online.)*

- Administering classes.

The other private social networks focus on:

- Recreating Facebook-like interaction in private intranets.

- Micro blogging.

That's fine for unstructured sharing and discussion where you have a bunch of peers who want to share information and you're willing to rely on someone in the network to have information that others in the network need. But to make it work, you need a combination of luck, high-quality searching and system filtering of the conversation to show the most relevant info to each user. However, that model is totally irrelevant when you want to teach someone a curriculum, or change specific behaviors in an organization. Unstructured conversation is more than inefficient when it comes to changing behavior; unmoderated and undirected, it can actually become an obstacle to reaching your goals.

Some companies have combined both features above but really you are getting two separate systems. They are the same two platforms:

private social networks and learning management systems that you would get if you purchased them yourself. But simply bundling these two platforms doesn't provide you with the integrated capability we have created with the KnoNow system. We are innovating a new method while others have copied and refined what has already existed. We took our experience in high-impact face-to-face training and re-created it online. Our methods work well in real life, and we've blazed a trail by replicating that experience in a virtual environment.

KnoNow provides Leadership is a Choice® with the most advanced online pull-through experience for the seminar or can even replace the seminar experience. This program allows someone to take the seminar or the keynote and have 48 weeks of learning delivered to their inbox throughout the year. The Leadership is a Choice® KnoNow Platform allows the learning to happen over time and is based on solid research on how real learning occurs in any environment. Repetition of any skill will improve learning retention. When you repeat the key insights from the learning event, you stimulate recall and improve the likelihood that the participants will apply the information in the future. With KnoNow, your insights are kept alive in your learning community. And, because participants can practice and receive timely feedback though this platform, they can refine their understanding of the Leadership is a Choice® material and share those insights with their colleagues. You can learn more about the KnoNow social learning platform at www.knonow.com.

Index